THE BIRD ERA

THE BIRD ERA

A History of the Boston Celtics
1978-1988

Bob Schron and Kevin Stevens

QUINLAN PRESS
BOSTON

Published by Quinlan Press 131 Beverly Street, Boston, MA 02114

Library of Congress Cataloging-in-Publication Data

Schron, Bob.
    The Bird era.

    1. Boston Celtics (Basketball team)—History.
2. Bird, Larry, 1956-   . 3. Basketball players—
United States—Biography.   I. Stevens, Kevin.
II. Title.
GV885.52.B67S37   1988   796.32'3'0924   [B]   88-42931
ISBN 1-55770-070-2

For my wife, Edna Talbot Schron, our daughter, Laura Ruth, and in memory
of my mother, Ann Schron

R.H.S.

For Janice and Christian

K.S.

We would like to thank Henry Quinlan for his belief in us and in this project. The staff at Quinlan Press were very helpful, and we would like to thank Lisa Lazarek, Elizabeth Pond and Larry Curcio in particular. Typesetter *extraordinaire* Peter Gottlieb (FIN/CO Typography) worked well under pressure to make this book look good. Thanks to Marilyn Schron Likosky and Dr. William Likosky for their support and encouragement. And special thanks to the Boston Celtics organization, a family that deals so well with the complexities of a family business, especially Mary Faherty, Mildred Duggan and other members of the staff.

Over the years, many people contributed to the making of this book, directly and indirectly, but we would like to express our gratitude especially to Tod Rosensweig, Red Auerbach, K. C. Jones, M. L. Carr, Jimmy Rodgers, Cedric Maxwell, Robert Parish, Chris Ford, Dennis Johnson, Danny Ainge, Kevin McHale, Tiny Archibald, Bob Berry, Porter McKinnon and Bill Fitch. Finally, our thanks to Larry Bird, who, in Cedric's Maxwell's words, carries a unique public burden on his very human back and remains himself so well.

CONTENTS

1

THE ROOTS OF A TRADITION • 1

2

CELTICS JOURNEY • 17

3

ROOKIE YEAR • 33

4

THE FIRST CHAMPIONSHIP • 65

5

TRYING TO REPEAT • 101

6

CHANGING OF THE GUARD • 127

7

THE RETURN OF BIG BILL • 153

8

THE END OF AN ERA • 177

EPILOGUE • 197

An insert of color photographs follows page 100.

THE BIRD ERA

Assistant general manager Jeff Cohen said in 1980: "Red Auerbach will tell you that Larry is just about what he expected. But the deep truth is that Larry is even more than Red expected."

1

THE ROOTS OF A NEW TRADITION

There are some early summer days in Boston when the air is so clear and the sky is so deep that the whole city seems to expand upwards and outwards into the crystalline blue, and the precise, urban edges of office block and elevated train and billboard seem stitched surrealistically onto the taut fabric of the firmament. On such a day you may find yourself traveling down I-93 from Manchester, New Hampshire; or rolling into the city on the trolley or commuter rail from any of a hundred Massachusetts communities; or cruising up Route 3 from the Cape, a crisp breeze blowing in off the Atlantic, the sun glazing the trim geometry of the city's glassy tributes to eighties prosperity. On a day like this you feel the promise of a long and welcome summer trilling through your spirit like a song you haven't heard in years, like a glimpse of a girl you've been looking for all night. Content, relaxed, at one with what you know the day will bring, you tune into the latest oldies station and think about the long beach day ahead, or the friends you'll meet later, or the Red Sox' latest run at first place. Then, as if giving perfect expression to your happiness, the expressway rises, the city collects around you, and from out of the rusted depths of North Station pigeons wheel across the sky, revealing beneath their fan of motion the familiar twin brown flagpoles, the durable yellow-brick facade, the long, thin windows and the simple, elegant letters that have, for as long as you can remember, spelled basketball nirvana: BOSTON GARDEN.

If you are a true Boston Celtics fan, the sight of those letters sends a shiver through your viscera and calls forth a parade of memories. You may think back to your first visit to that hallowed

1

building: the first time you inspected the cramped balconies, the rough-and-tumble seats and the championship banners hanging majestically from the rafters; the first time you wandered down to court level at halftime and saw for yourself just how big and smooth and gifted those professional basketball players actually were, loping with seven-foot grace and jamming the ball through the hoop with enough force to shake the building; the first time you took your seat in section 112 and, hot dog and beer in hand, held your breath and shouted your support as the latest version of the Celtics dynasty wove its magic on the parquet floor. It is a pilgrimage every real Celtics fan has made or will make, the voice of Johnny Most ringing in his ear, the images of a thousand telecasts or radio reports finally coming to life with all the color and immediacy and thrill of being in that little bandbox of an arena with everything wrong about it and everything absolutely right.

Ah yes. But right now it is summer and the season is over, so you cruise by, thinking only briefly of that last championship, savoring for just a second the memory of a key steal or miracle comeback or 40-point performance by the greatest player ever to lace up sneakers. The sun is bright, the summer is young, and you are headed for the beach with your radio blaring and your cooler stocked, so perhaps you take a little bit for granted those wonderful games that helped you get through yet another long New England winter. Yes, you admit, the Celtics can spoil even the most dedicated fan.

But at the end of the day, after the Sox have lost another close one, or the breeze off the water has gotten a little too tart, or the thought of work the next day has descended like a long rebound as you pack

the car or shuffle off to the train, you think again of that glimpse of the Garden, its memories and meanings, its place in your heart, and the imprint of the pale, maligned structure deepens in your mind like an evening shadow. Thank God for the Celtics, you think. Thank God for Larry Bird.

It was on just such a day in June 1978 that the Celtics' brain trust, members of the media and assorted basketball junkies assembled in the Boards and Blades Club of the Boston Garden to participate in the NBA's annual college draft. But though the world outside may have been spangled and sunny, inside the labyrinthine depths of the Garden the atmosphere was stygian: hot television lights shone on the shag carpet and old-fashioned decor; cigar smoke mushroomed into the warm air; the rustle of rumor and press release floated above the packed room like a sirocco. An exciting event at the most ordinary of times, today the draft had a surge of electricity running through it that everyone there could sense. Today, the hot lights seemed to beam, was a day when history would be made.

The Boards and Blades Club was the perfect setting for such an event. Gracing the dark walls were reminders of everything the Celtics dynasty had been: mementoes, awards, photographs of previous champions. Celtics history seemed to come alive in this room, an inner sanctum for the real acolytes of the game. One photo seemed particularly meaningful—Larry O'Brien, commissioner of the NBA, posed with Red Auerbach, Tommy Heinsohn and John Havlicek, three men who had been

The Boston Garden floor, circa 1948. The floor was built in 1946 with wood from a forest in Tennessee. There are 264 pieces, each five feet by five feet and one and a half inches thick. Its original cost was $10,000.

responsible for so much of the Celtics' success through the years, three men who, as general manager, coach and star, had the led the Green to its most recent championship, in 1976.

Only two years had passed since the 13th banner had been lifted to the rafters, a banner made especially sweet by the memory of the Greatest Game Ever Played—the triple-overtime classic against Phoenix on another early day in June— but to Celtics fans those years had been more like a decade. The 1977-78 season had been a debacle, a season of sadness, hurt feelings and defeat. Far and away the worst season of Auerbach's legendary association with the club, it had seen a total collapse of the team, highlighted by the midseason departure of coach Tommy Heinsohn and the bartering of guard Charley Scott, a key player on the '76 champs. Dave Cowens, destined for Celtics heaven and the Hall of Fame, had finished the season fatigued, leaking to the press that if the team could not acquire a backup center his career might be through. Satch Sanders, taking over the helm after Heinsohn's exit, had never really gotten the team together. Worst of all, the team had bricked its way to a

32-50 record, good for a dismal third place in the NBA's Atlantic Division, 23 games out of first, and a disappointed place in the hearts of its fans, who were now whispering that the team was dead, that Celtics Pride was a thing of the past. Never in the Auerbach era had the team compiled a worse record. Adding to the disappointment, for the first time in seven years Boston fans had no postseason to enjoy, no possibility of vindication, no customary playoff action to usher in the summer. For once, Arnold Auerbach looked almost human.

But today there was a feeling in the air that transcended disappointment, a sense that the wizard with his magic wand of a cigar had merely taken a break from the rigors of genius and was back with grander, more mysterious tricks up his sleeve. People who had been around the Celtics for a long time were saying that they had never seen Red looking so dapper. Dressed in a light blue sports jacket, light pants and white shoes, his ubiquitous Bances resting easily between his fingers, he radiated confidence. It was if he knew something that no one else did, as if he had made a pact with the hoop god that would end the team's troubles once and for all. Today, he seemed to be saying, things start changing. Today is the day the dynasty returns.

There was certainly some reason to be confident, in spite of the terrible season. Rookie forward Cedric Maxwell had played with promise. Though fatigued, Dave Cowens had given his usual 110 percent to the team. In the Scott trade Auerbach had acquired power forward Kermit Washington, an intimidating player in the Paul Silas mold who had turned suddenly expendable to the Los Angeles Lakers after an infamous incident in which he had punched Rudy Tomjanovich, hospitalizing Tomjanovich (for a time there were fears that he would lose his eyesight). Washington was an enforcer, a man who could dominate the boards while allowing Cowens to roam the perimeter as an outside scorer, and in his 32 games with the Celtics in the second half of the 1977-78 season, he had played to his potential, retrieving over ten rebounds a game and overcoming a gun-shy attitude bred by the regrettable fight and the consequent 60-day suspension. And with today's two early first-round picks (the sixth, due to the team's record; the eighth, part of the Laker deal that brought Washington), the Celtics did seem to be in a position to do some significant rebuilding that could put that dreadful year to rest once and for all. But Red's confidence was so obvious, so distinct, that it made the atmosphere in the room even more tense.

As noon approached, tap-off time for the draft, the room's buzz thickened. The conversation was fevered and knowledgeable, insiders' conversation.

"Can he run the floor?"

"Can he handle it?"

"No way he's gonna go in the first."

Thumbing through booklets distributed by the team, culling notes kept through hundreds of college games, the reporters and junkies squinted in the smoke, chugged on morning beers and evaluated the talent as if they were at the track. The consensus was that three players were the cream: Minnesota's Mychal Thompson, a machinelike scorer with the flexibility to play three positions and an ability to run the floor; North Carolina's Phil Ford, one of college basketball's greatest point guards ever; and Rick Robey, the solid power forward who had helped lead

Kentucky to the national championship. Auerbach, who had spent weeks on the phone trying to determine how the five teams ahead of the Celtics would pick (and who had his own preferred choice in the draft), knew better than anyone in the room that these three players were likely to go one-two-three to Portland, Kansas City and Indiana.

At twelve sharp the speakers that linked the Boards and Blades Club to Commissioner O'Brien and the NBA offices in New York crackled to life. The rustle died down.

"To all those participating in the National Basketball Association's 1978 college draft, welcome. As commissioner, I deem the draft officially opened."

O'Brien detailed procedure and the time allotted each pick as the rustle of anticipation returned. The first three choices went quickly and as expected. Connected by conference telephone to New York, part of the circle of NBA cities radiating out from the epicenter in New York, those in the room could feel the drama develop. After the big three, though the talent level was still high, the role of chance in the draft increased. Teams were less likely to pick the best available player, going instead for the key position or talent that would best fit their needs. But who could say what college star among the many seniors and eligible juniors remaining would last until the Celtics could lay claim to him? Who was to know how the New York Knicks and Golden State Warriors, owners of the fourth and fifth picks respectively, would choose? Everyone had an opinion, a prediction. But everyone kept an eye on Red.

Red looked at the speakers with a glint in his eye. Chance had never played a big role in his career. He was a man who created basketball history instead of allowing it simply to happen, and the way he tapped his cigar and rubbed his chin and studied the ceiling now, you would swear that he was willing those intervening picks into existence, telegraphing through some exotic medium the message that the Knicks should pick Montana star Micheal Ray Richardson. And so they did, raising the tension level in the room another notch and turning even more heads in the spotlit direction of Red. What was he thinking?

The Golden State Warriors considered their choice, the final hurdle between the Celtics and the destiny of a decade. Al Attles's club, NBA champions in 1975, had also fallen on hard times. Superstar Rick Barry, whose career had been plagued by contractual and stability problems, seemed ready to leave the club. Butch Beard, a key to their championship chemistry, was also gone. The fans in the Bay Area were restless, and the club wanted some offensive punch, a star who could come onto the team and score some points. There was an eligible junior who could bring that kind of help, and everyone in the room knew that, but the Warriors decided on a more certain commodity, a senior they could count on to produce right away. The name Purvis Short came over the speakers, and a puff of smoke rose to the ceiling.

Anyone who bothered to look at Red at that moment saw a man who knew what fans and hoop junkies and media would discover to their intense enjoyment over the next ten years. No one should have doubted the man's vision. No one should have suspected for a millisecond that Celtics Pride was dead, not as long as Red Auerbach had any say in the running of the club. Wasn't this the man who had

Ed Macauley, then coach of the St. Louis Hawks, presents a tea service to Red Auerbach in honor of Auerbach's 1000th game as an NBA coach. Asked to describe the Celtics once, Red simply stated: "A way of life."

always been able to see the future, the man who had the foresight to recognize and the ability to develop the championship potential of a Bill Russell or K. C. Jones or Bill Sharman or Dave Cowens or the player whose name he now whispered into Jeff Cohen's ear as the rustle rose to its highest pitch of the day and the venerable photographs and paneled walls fairly quivered in anticipation? He was doing it again. He was recreating history. He was creating the future. He sat back and puffed on his victory cigar as Cohen announced the Boston Celtics' first 1978 draft pick.

The Bird Era had begun.

Y ou leave Boston at dawn, stopping just long enough to fill your gas tank and coffee mug, keeping that distinctive, gaptoothed skyline fixed in your rear view mirror for as much of the Mass Pike as possible. The Bay State passes quickly, and by midmorning you are angling down through upstate New York on I-88, the Dutch and Indian placenames filling the roadsigns like messages from the past, the clear waters of the Susquehanna paralleling your journey like an ancient guide. The wide arc of Highway 81 brings you down through eastern Pennsylvania, joining 80 just where the contoured, striated beauty of the Appalachians begins, and the long hours and longer miles of the afternoon are spent crossing wooded hollows and lazy rivers as you travel with the sun. By the time you reach Ohio the mountains have long since flattened out, and the nasal edges of Eastern speech are only an echo in the rush of air at your window. The woman who serves you coffee in the roadside diner has freckles, a wide smile and a honeycolored twang that calls you *hon'* and asks you where you're headed with such languid friendliness that you want to stay here forever, here with the tired truckers and Kent-smoking salesmen and people like yourself who are out to see a different America.

By now you are making it on caffeine and anticipation, and as you pass the twilit towns of Akron and Youngstown, and Mansfield you realize with the full breadth of the Ohio horizon that you are in very different territory, everything so sprawling and recent, so distant from New England's tended, ordered maturity. You grip the wheel and blink hard as the road threads the landscape with steady monotony and the red-rimmed evening circles you like a giant saucer. Far from the brownstones and steeples of Boston, you are beginning to learn that the

Midwest has its own rhythms and view-points; the roadsigns now direct you to Knockemstiff and Businessburg, Newcomerstown and Coolville, but you stifle any latent East Coast condescension and concentrate on staying awake. You do not have far to go.

Frazzled and roadweary, you reach Columbus after twenty hours on the road, knowing you should check into the Edgewater Inn or Amity Motel and finish your journey in the morning. But something inside pushes you, and you drive on into the second day, past Springfield, Fairborn and Dayton, closer and closer to America's heartland and the state you've told yourself you have to see. The first time your headlights catch the signs for Richmond and Indianapolis, the surrounding darkness seems sliced by lightning, and your heart does a little dance. When you cross the state line around four in the morning, dawn is already frosting the sky behind you and the Atlantic seems a distant dream. If it were daytime you might shoot up Route 227 to Bethel and check out the highest point in Indiana (all of 1,257 feet) or drive south to beautiful Brookville Lake. But right now it is the hour of the wolf, and you pull into a rest stop, stretch your legs beneath the stars and consider where you've arrived while the car engine clicks in the moonlight and the lonely trucks roar by. You are now in the state where basketball is a religion and down-home values run deep. You are now on Larry Joe Bird's true turf, breathing the air he breathed and hearing the sounds he heard as he honed his craft and learned his moves over thousands of lonely practice hours in the gyms of French Lick and Terre Haute. And though you may never really know what it's like to be a Hoosier

(any more than someone who has not been raised in New England can fully understand your distinctive character, your Yankee soul), your pilgrimage has brought you a little bit closer to knowing what it is that makes this great player tick. And if nothing else, your round-the-clock drive has taught you one thing: it is a long way from Boston to the Hoosier State.

When Red Auerbach whispered the name of Larry Bird to Jeff Cohen on Draft Day 1978, he was doing more than securing the best college player in the country. He was also doing more than effecting a renaissance of the dormant Celtics dynasty, though that in itself was enough to make it the draft pick of the decade. No, Red's foresight had a symbolic importance that raised this pick to a level transcending sports and placed it in almost mythical context. By bringing the best basketball player in the history of the country's premier basketball state to the most dominating dynasty in professional sports, Red was doing no less than merging the two greatest basketball traditions in the nation. No one knew it at the time—no one, perhaps, except Red himself—but that draft pick was to forge a link in basketball history that was permanent and significant. It may be a long way from French Lick to the Boston Garden, but as of that sparkling June day a lifeline was established between those two very different places that will never be severed as long as there is a hoop god.

No one can argue that at the amateur level Indiana has a basketball tradition unrivaled in intensity, quality and cultural importance. The long, frigid winters of America's central lowland can make

Bird with agent Bob Woolf at the press conference after he signed his first Celtics contract in 1979. Although they were happily resolved, the negotiations took nearly three months. Bob Ryan wrote: "Insiders say that the list of demands would rival Woody Allen's New Yorker *stories as humorous bedtime reading...I admire Bird's ballplaying as much as anybody you'll meet but don't want him* that *badly. Do you?"*

Indiana a forbidding state, and one of the ways its natives have learned to banish the winter blues is by celebrating the exploits of the local high school or college hoop team. But "celebrating" is not a strong enough word for the participation of the usual Indiana fan. In any other state a ballgame is a ballgame; in the Hoosier State it is a rite, a communion, a proclamation of one's individual and social identity.

Anyone who has walked through the shackled air of a subzero, wind-whipped high school parking lot on an early February night, cheeks stinging, eyes watering from the pure, dense, unremitting cold, knows how welcome the sight of a suddenly opened gym door can be.

As steam billows out, buoyed by a cacophony of cheers and music, the promise of light, companionship and healthy competition streams from that warm rectangle, and the impersonal infinity of the cold night condenses into a statement of all you value. Stepping inside, you see through befogged glasses the earnest faces of the cheerleaders, the down jackets and truckers' caps of neighbors and friends, the glittering school colors and bright signs, the Cokes and licorice shoelaces and popcorn, and most importantly, the ten young men on that 94-by-50 piece of hardwood who play out the drama that keeps the night and cold at bay. What better way to warm your spirit on an evening in deep winter? What better forum for friendly gossip and down-home camaraderie?

But you won't go far towards understanding the Hoosier spirit if you think that basketball is simply entertainment or an excuse to meet other folks in town. The social function is certainly important, but that pulsing little building in the middle of the broad plains has a far more profound cultural message. At its best, Hoosier basketball is a metaphor for all the people of this state value, all they have come to hold dear in their harsh, distinctive history. It is not that long since Indiana was a completely rural territory at the edge of America, infused by the seemingly contradictory pioneer values of self-sufficiency and cooperation. To make it on the frontier you had to be both a team player and an individual. You had to be hardy and competent, but you also had to realize that no man or woman could tackle nature alone. You had to learn how to get along with your neighbor, how to combine individual talents to master the lonely landscape and tough weather of the Great Plains. These are the values that defined the culture, that continue to inform the Hoosier spirit today, and one of the places they find expression is on the basketball court, where individual talent and team play merge to strive towards winning the ballgame. It is no accident that Indiana basketball has always been marked by sacrifice and teamwork, by doing whatever is necessary to achieve the collective goal of victory. Creativity and elegance are not frowned upon as long as they are contained within the team concept, but there is no room for the hot dog on the quintessential Indiana basketball team.

This is the milieu from which Larry Bird emerged, the same milieu that pro-duced Bobby Knight, Piggie Lambert and the greatest college coach in history, John Wooden. Unless you know that background you will never understand the paradox that is Larry Bird—the greatest individual player in the history of the game who also makes everyone on his team look better; the scrappy, blue-collar forward who is also the definition of basketball elegance; the man with an infinite arsenal of moves who nevertheless does only what is appropriate, what is necessary, on any given play. And yet the rhetoric of this description, like the superlatives that are heaped upon him daily by fans and media and fellow players, is nothing compared to the simple, inspirational sight of him taking a classic left-handed runner, or making a deft touch pass to a streaking teammate, or launching one of his high, parabolic three-pointers that riffles the net to a chorus of Garden cheers and the dejected face of a burned defender. This splendid assemblage of basketball talent and refined skill is the logical conclusion of the emphases of Indiana basketball, the man who brings all the virtues of the pioneer ethic together in pursuit of basketball excellence. He is the definition of the American heartland. He is the Great American Hero.

But Larry Bird did not spring fully formed from the thigh of Zeus. He would be the first to tell you that the transformation of a slow white man who cannot run or jump into the greatest player in the game came about first and foremost through constant practice, intense self-scrutiny and persistent attention to detail. Not that Larry isn't a great athlete: he is one of the greatest in the game, with outstanding court vision, strength, anticipation, feel and a shot that seems forged in heaven with its accuracy and range. These gifts more than compensate for his relatively slow foot speed and mediocre jumping ability, but they alone do not define the man. Purified in the clear atmosphere of the lonely gym, developed over countless hours of thought and practice and application that have become all but legendary, these gifts have been refined to the perfect point where form and content become one, where you cannot tell where talent ends and hard work begins. As impressive as his ability is, it is all the more amazing that he has taken the time to make himself an even better player, to master the fundamentals to such an extent that they are as much a part of his game as any talent he was born with.

John Lucas: "They talk about Michael Jordan, Magic Johnson, and whoever. But Larry Bird is the best player. He does everything on the floor. Every single thing."

He performs the routine with expert efficiency, lapsing so rarely that an audible, collective gasp of breath fills the Garden at the most minor transgression. He boxes out, makes the correct pass, sets the right pick, moves expertly without the ball, plays defense with his feet, employs a truckload of masterful fakes, concentrates for all he's worth—all with a steadiness that is textbook and inspirational, a steadiness that he, and not God, created.

But even after factoring in Bird's God-given talents and tremendous mastery of basketball basics, we still have an incomplete equation. There is still the x factor, the attribute that brings all the others together and places him in roundball Olympus alongside the small, select pantheon of the truly great. That attribute is easy to define but difficult to interpret; it is his intensity, his drive, his burning desire to win. Of course, it is there when he practices—why else would he apply himself so thoroughly unless he loved the game and loved to win? But this intensity is most dramatically exhibited during the 48 minutes on the court, when Larry dives after a loose ball when the outcome of the game is already obvious, or battles in the trenches at full tilt though injured or exhausted, or demands the ball when the game is on the line and drills a winning shot while wearing two defenders. These are the moments when those of us who have been lucky enough to follow Bird's career know we are witnessing greatness. And even though we've seen enough of those incredible plays to fill hours of videotape, we can't help but ask ourselves over and over again: Where does he get such competitiveness, such zeal, such overwhelming *need* to do anything he can to win? Part of that question can never be answered; any human personality has depths that cannot be plumbed, and Bird is a particularly complex, private man. But what we do know of the man's background and temperament goes a little towards explaining his inner strength, his ferocious will.

Every Celtics fan is familiar with the legend, the apotheosis of the Indiana past. The trick is to sift the real from the ideal, to realize that we are dealing with a man, not a poster image or a comic-book superhero. Bird's home town of French Lick is often described with the kind of nostalgic, soft-focus imagery thought suitable for the home of a basketball legend from the Midwest: a rusted, netless hoop nailed to the garage, an old pick-up parked outside the diner, the local team winning tournament games in the big city while the entire populace tunes in on the radio. Well, those details happen to be true, but what the legendmakers often leave out are the harsher aspects of French Lick, aspects more difficult to see from the comfortable vantage of an Eastern city. It may be situated in the gentle hills of southern Indiana, but the town has hardship beneath the surrounding beauty. Orange County is one of the poorest in the state, and Larry Bird experienced enough of that poverty to give him the drive to overcome it. In the 1930s French Lick was a rather famous resort, known for its mineral springs and fine hotels, host to Presidents and Chicago gangsters, but for the Bird family of later decades it was a setting for financial difficulty and occasional emotional turmoil—no more than many families, perhaps, but enough to shape the rather brooding, temperamental boy who would become the Great American Hero. Small-town America has been good to Larry Bird, and he still makes his home in French Lick, but it also

kept him cloistered from the rest of the world for longer than a man with his talents and temperament perhaps should have been.

By all accounts his father, Joe Bird, was a generous, firm-principled man who worked hard and did not shirk his duties, but debts and alcohol led only to family tragedy when he committed suicide, saddling his hard-working wife with sole responsibility for their children. Georgia Bird worked hundred-hour weeks as a waitress to support her family and channeled a determined, moody personality in the positive direction of survival and support. With his mother's schedule, Larry spent much time with his grandmother, Lizzie Kerns, a woman he still admires tremendously, and tried to find an outlet for the stubbornness, passion and shyness bred by heredity and circumstance.

He found that outlet in Springs Valley High School, where his older brother and role model, Mark, had also been a hoop star. Larry's first coach there, Jim Jones, has said that from the beginning Bird was one of the most competitive kids he had ever seen. He always needed to win, always did his best to develop his game. As he discovered his passion and started the journey that would lead to greatness, he drove himself ceaselessly. He lived in the gym and had to be thrown out after practice. When he broke an ankle during his sophomore year, he used the time to observe team play carefully, to develop a wider, deeper vision of the game. Sprouting from 6-3 to 6-9 between his junior and senior years and turning into the finest player in the region, Bird became a local hero, a basketball giant in a place where basketball was revered. The attention he could have done without, but the satisfaction of excelling at his passion was its own reward. Though he didn't even think about college while in high school, he couldn't help but attract the interest of recruiters and coaches, including Bobby Knight, the crown prince of Indiana college basketball. He became the talk of the area, and fans from all over looked forward to French Lick's star making his stamp in the big-time world of Bloomington and Indiana U.

But things were not to be as many thought. Looking back, it is clear that the same traits of temperament and background that helped create the star also cut short his time as a Hoosier—shyness, lack of money, loneliness. He moved to Bloomington carrying the expectations of a region; he returned in a matter of weeks, overwhelmed by the huge campus and the glib intimidation of a well-heeled roommate. The fate is a common one for freshmen; but unlike most frosh Larry had to deal with the pall of small-town embarrassment that enveloped his return, the closed-mindedness of the few who saw him as only a basketball star. He had never asked for, never wanted the celebrity; now he felt its double edge.

Then came the oft-celebrated job with the city (including a weekly stint on a garbage truck), the decision to attend Indiana State, the bad marriage (which he still maintains was the biggest mistake of his life), and the birth of his daughter after the break-up. Five years later, when Bird was hoisted into national fame with the Celtics, many people commented on his shyness and defensiveness, as if eloquence were a requirement of fame. But Bird's public persona had been formed in response to the hardships of those early years—many of them associated with his basketball ability. And yet his tenure at Terre Haute turned out to be a positive

experience. Terre Haute was where he met his longtime companion Dinah Mattingly—and where he turned from a local legend into a national hero.

Somehow it seems appropriate that a small school became the collegiate testing ground for this great player, whose hallmark throughout his career has been to raise dramatically the level of play of anyone fortunate enough to share the court with him. Known primarily as the site of John Wooden's first collegiate coaching job, Indiana State would rise through the magic of Bird's touch to do what no college team had ever done before—win 33 straight games in a single season. Ten years later the record amazes, stands outside of time. And for those who disparaged the Sycamores' conference and schedule, even in Bird's Herculean senior season, there was the consistent magnificence of the 1979 NCAA Tournament, culminating in the splendid final that reached 25 million homes. What must Bobby Knight and other Indiana University fans have thought after that performance? What had they let slip away? Of course, for Boston basketball fans, watching Bird's progress while their beloved Celtics stumbled through another embarrassing season, the college season was a double treat: Bird's greatness was a ticket to the next ten years, a promise of redemption. There were many in Boston that year who praised Red's foresight and rejoiced in the irony of Bird's initial failure at Indiana U—because of his decision to return to French Lick back in 1974, he had become eligible for the NBA draft after his junior year.

But as the Celtics' choice of Bird in 1978 makes clear, he did not wait until his senior year to show his greatness. Bird starred immediately for the Indiana State

Sycamores, resuming what could only be called a career of destiny after his brush with disillusion. And he did it with style, with grace, and with completeness. His position was forward, but he used his dominating basketball skills in any way and in any place that could give him an advantage. He developed an adamant post-up game, modeling a center, but he did so much more than the conventional center. Once he had the ball he was able to choose from a powerful range of options he had perfected steadily since his freshman year in high school: he could hit the quick turnaround jumper; he could circle past his man with an assortment of power drives; he could throw one of his precision passes to an open teammate. In the paint or on the wings, he was dangerous, with a nose for the right play, a new fake whenever required and a shot that had the world of college basketball talking, a perfectly arced, radar-guided shot with faultless backspin off his succinct fingertip release. And then there was his stamina, his quickness, his perception, his uncanny instinct for every aspect of the game! Where had this guy come from, and why was he at Indiana State? Yet there were still those who said State had an easy schedule, that the Sycamores were not to be ranked with the cream of Big Ten, ACC and SEC schools. These critics managed to ignore Bird's ability to singlehandedly dominate a game, no matter who the opponent. And those naysayers were still there after his junior year, by which time he had proved to the majority that he had dramatically altered the fate of this small, unassuming school from a forgotten conference.

But as meteoric as the Sycamores' rise to prominence was, the team did not emerge from a vacuum. Bird was work-ing within a tradition, and not just the broad tradition of Hoosier basketball. Indiana State had been, after all, a star in the constellation of John Wooden's career, and though the Missouri Valley Conference did not rank high in the eyes of hoop junkies in the 1970s, older fans did not have to think back too far to remember the time when it was one of the finest conferences in basketball. In the late 1950s and early 1960s Missouri Valley consistently sported top-ranked teams that did well in the national tournaments, including Bradley, Wichita State, St. Louis and the University of Cincinnati. Many distinguished players came out of the conference (Bob Ferry, Chet ''The Jet'' Walker, Paul Hogue), and the University of Cincinnati achieved a remarkable double by winning back-to-back NCAA championships in 1961 and 1962 against an Ohio State team that featured John Havlicek, Jerry Lucas, Mel Nowell and Larry Siegfried. But history will record that the conference's most lasting contribution to the sport (at least until Bird's appearance) was the example of a remarkable individual, a player who singlehandedly changed the nature of the game and paved the way for the type of all-around player Bird was to become— the Big O, Oscar Robertson.

Robertson had it all. A 6-5 guard who could score, rebound and pass with equal facility, he set the standard for the complete player. His defense was superlative, his playmaking immense. He was beautiful to watch, the raw power of his game always contained within a form that wasted no motion. Like Bird he raised the level of all his teammates and focused everyone's attention on winning. Like Bird he also had the x factor, the intense drive and ability to take over a game that mark the truly great. He dominated basketball awareness during the late fifties, and though UC's NCAA championships came later, his contribution after his departure was tangible, both in the example he set and in the quality of the players his presence attracted to the university. More than anyone else, he set the stage for the emergence of great black players in the sixties and seventies and the corresponding dramatic changes in the game. Through high school (where he led the black Indianapolis school, Crispus Attucks, to a state championship that galvanized the Indiana black community), college and an outstanding pro career, the Big O was the consummate player, and it is significant that Jerry West and Bob Cousy—no slouches themselves on the court—have said that Robertson was the greatest all-around player they have ever seen.

In a very real sense Bird is part of the tradition Robertson created, and it is fitting that he used his broad range of skills to bring prominence back to the once-great conference of Robertson's past. If anything, Bird's impact was greater, since his college career came at a time of intense media and fan awareness created by the rapid expansion of television and print coverage of college basketball during the seventies. As Indiana State reached the top 20 during his junior season, *Sports Illustrated* and *Sporting News* did major pieces on the team. Professional scouts were taking close notice, labeling Bird one of the best passing forwards ever and comparing him to Rick Barry and Bob Pettit. The team upset Purdue, led by Joe Barry Carroll and Jerry Sichting, 91-63, and landed an invitation to the NIT. The NIT was a more prestigious tournament ten years ago. Because the NCAAs were

Bill Russell on the Big O: "Oscar Robertson was so brilliant that he could orchestrate his team's offense and pump so much energy into it that, by himself, he could push a game into a high—if we could respond."

limited to 32 teams, with no more than two per conference, the smaller invitational could feature some fine competition. But a season that attracted so much attention ended in frustration: a key player encountered drug problems; the Sycamores suffered a tough second-round loss in the NIT to the University of Houston and Otis Birdsong, 84-83. Bird had stunned the crowd at that game in Hofheinz Pavilion with his artistry, scoring 44 and doing everything but hitting the winning shot. Asked for a comment afterwards, he angrily refused all statements. Was he already preparing for the following year? To most observers, it seemed logical that he should pursue the goal of a college championship during his senior season, in spite of his eligibility for the pros. This was his choice.

The Celtics' pick of Bird in June made Indiana State's next season even more of a fishbowl, but in typical fashion Bird managed to concentrate on basketball. His ability to focus on the task at hand is preeminent, and Bird has said that he gave very little thought to the Celtics during his senior season. He was too busy winning with the Sycamores and proving they were one of the country's best teams. Preseason expectations focused on the good teams from the big conferences: Duke, Notre Dame, UCLA, Louisville and Indiana. The media's interest in Indiana State seemed to have waned, perhaps because Bob King, who had assembled the team, stepped down for health reasons. But even with rookie coach Bill Hodges, the Sycamores put together their incredible 33-game streak and a number-one ranking in the polls by season's end. Bird was everything, though he did receive excellent support from backcourt star Carl Nicks and a corps of consistent contributors.

The 1979 NCAA Tournament was one of the greatest ever, and Indiana State proved its mettle to even the most skeptical observers by playing consistently first-rate basketball. They advanced to the Final Four by beating Virginia Tech, Oklahoma and an outstanding Arkansas team featuring Sidney Moncrief. Bird, playing with an injured thumb, dominated. In the national semifinals the Sycamores showed the country how great they really were. Playing an extremely balanced, well-coached DePaul team that outshot and outrebounded them, the State players still managed to pull out a 75-74 victory, with Bird scoring a hard-earned 35 and playing at the top of his game.

It is an unfortunate irony that this splendid team should be remembered primarily for its tough loss in the finals to Magic Johnson and Michigan State. Under coach Jud Heathcote, MSU was a team that peaked at the right time. Coming out of an excellent conference, honed by the rigors of the regular season, they dominated the Mideast Regional, winning three games by 59 points behind the play of Johnson, Greg Kelser, Terry Donnelly and Jay Vincent. Magic, of course, was another all-around star in the tradition of the Big O, a 6-9 point guard who could post up or operate from the baseline whenever the occasion demanded. Who can forget the intensity of that final, Magic scoring 24, the Spartans utilizing a match-up zone that keyed on Bird and held him to 7-for-21 shooting, as Michigan State went on to a 76-64 victory? That loss was far tougher to take than even the NIT loss the year before, and the image of Bird hanging his head for ages provided a closing signature on that season and his college career. But it must have made Bird all the more hungry for championship rings once he came to Boston, and the match-up between Magic and Bird was not the last.

The tournament certainly proved to Celtics fans that they were welcoming to Boston a kid who wanted to win, who knew how to win, who had all the tools necessary to lead by example and effect a return of the greatest dynasty in American sport. But even the most casual of them knew that there was a big gap between college hoops and the NBA; only a fool would take anything for granted. As any real Celtics fan knew, that dynasty, that tradition of winning with great individual effort and even greater team play, had been the result of Red Auerbach's philosophy, a big part of which was the belief that you can never rest on your laurels, you can never stop trying to improve. Larry Bird had proved that he was an excellent college player, one of the best perhaps, but if he was to help extend the Celtics' tradition, he was going to have to prove himself on the parquet floor, on that battered checkerboard that had absorbed the pounding of so many great players. It was time for a second transition. Bird was moving out of one great tradition and into another.

2

CELTICS JOURNEY

One theory of human personality suggests that at any given point in our lives we are the sum of all we have experienced, all we have lived through, seen, heard and imagined. Facing every new moment with the subliminal wrap of the past pressing in around us, we make our decisions, develop our attitudes and determine our values within this cocoon of identity, spun out of experience from the moment of birth. In the age of immediacy that is 1980s America, when the demand for instant gratification and the cult of youth devalue experience and tradition, it is easy not to see the significant connections, the lifelines that link past and present and allow us to fulfill whatever role destiny has chosen for us. Ignoring all that has gone before, assuming nothing but the moment is relevant to who we are, we often fail to take advantage of all that self-examination and

careful consideration of the past can bring. Settling for easy solutions and superficial pleasures, we fail to match our potential, discovering too late that life has passed us by.

A sports team also has its own personality. A collection of individuals (like the conflicting impulses peopling any single person), it functions best when the separate parts fulfill their roles, transcending individualism in the pursuit of its end. Of course, a sports team has a far simpler purpose to its existence: it must win. Everyone hopes along the way that the game will foster a sense of fair play, provide entertainment for fans, build character and contribute to the community, but these secondary motives are always tarnished by defeat—and at any rate are usually invoked by those with a need to justify the monstrous overindulgence of sports in our culture. The most successful men and women in sports are those who win and win consistently, and history shows that the biggest winners are the coaches and players who learn from experience and value tradition without being afraid of innovation. Teams, like people, have lives; they have individual histories, good times and bad times, habits and traits that develop over the years. This personality is subtly passed on and carried into performance, affecting every game, every minute, every team response to a situation. A team with a solid tradition, one based on a sound philosophy, good coaching and hard work, will always have an advantage. Its personality, by building on what it remembers, by maintaining a tradition, has a maturity that will never leave it. Even when playing poorly, the team's players will know something is wrong and, it is hoped, make the necessary adjustments. They have a sixth man better than any brilliant player, home-court advantage or natural talent. They have an identity that is focused and secure.

At any given moment there are 276 active players in the National Basketball Association: 276 very different individuals who happen to be the best basketball players in the world. To put it in the simplest mathematical terms, this number represents *one millionth of 1 percent* of the population of the United States. Every player in the league has been a high school and college star: all are oversized men of exceptional ability who can do amazing things with that round orange ball. Yet in spite of the incredible level of talent, most NBA teams remain mediocre. They struggle to .500 records, make the playoffs by virtue of the league's money-directed structuring of the postseason, do the best they can before

becoming sacrificial lambs to the Celtics or Lakers, the only two clubs of the last decade that have managed to construct a winning tradition. No, talent is not the problem. These teams go nowhere because they are the logical results of scattered, directionless pasts. Like the Nets and the Cavaliers in the early years of the Bird Era, these teams, unsure of their identity, carry into the future a philosophy based on gaining immediate success. *We want to win and we want to win now*, they seem to be saying, and their expectations seem more the product of hype and hedonism than any firm notion of what it takes to win. They lack vision, coherence and character.

Of course, the league itself is relatively young, and many of the franchises, even some of the better teams in the league, are less than a decade old. Even in the best of times it would be unrealistic to expect an average NBA club to win championships consistently, and the current environment—where youth and money and the unrelenting need for press and fandom to have it all create the worst kinds of pressures for a group of athletes in their twenties—is an environment particularly unsuited to the establishment of a winning tradition. Larry Bird has frequently commented on how tremendously difficult it is to win an NBA championship, and everyone knows that since the 1969 Celtics only the L. A. Lakers have won back-to-back titles. But how many fans know that in the 42-year history of the NBA only two teams have *ever* won consecutive championships? However difficult it has been for Bird or Magic and their teammates to win, it has been virtually impossible for anyone not fortunate to play for the Celtics or Lakers. Of those 42 titles, 27 have been garnered by different versions of these two clubs. In this context, the Celtics' tradition moves into the realm of the extraordinary.

Building a winning tradition demands talent, time, luck and leaders of outstanding discipline and vision—all occurring at the same time. Only this combination of virtues, a combination of great rarity, creates the maturity needed to win repeatedly. It is not surprising then that the Celtics' achievement over the last four decades is unparalleled. The talented players have certainly been there, but there has always been talent aplenty in the NBA. You have to look beyond individuals to understand the Celtics' success; you have to look into the personality of the team, a personality at ease with itself, sure of its purpose. Boston teams,

on and off the court, have almost always functioned with unity, informed by a team personality that is consistent, balanced and focused. And this unity has not been a benison of the hoop god; it has been earned.

While the cliches surrounding the team's success over the years have grown tired, they still have meaning because they reflect an essential truth: the Celtics, more than any other team in professional sports, have an identity that is directed almost perfectly towards the expression of the true end of all athletic endeavor. Two men in particular created that identity; two men collaborated in the construction of this dynasty. Is it significant that a Jewish man from New York and a black man from Oakland should lead a team with an Irish

Bill Russell and K. C. Jones, 1988. "K. C. and I would talk for hours about basketball tactics," Russell wrote in Second Wind. *"We concluded that if you fix your mind on the goal of winning and stay honest with yourself, you'll come to realize that winning isn't about right and wrong or the good guys and the bad guys or the pathway to the good life and character. Winning is about who has the best team, that's all."*

nickname to this lofty position? Yes, because from the beginning the philosophy of the Boston Celtics organization has been concerned with nothing less than sports excellence, and sports excellence, as Russell and Red knew better than anyone, means winning. It matters not a whit who is pounding the parquet as long as the players remember this truth and work their hardest to bring it to fruition. And as long as the men in green keep hiking championship sheets to the rafters, as long as the Garden reverberates with the confidence of fans who know their team is better, as long as the Celtics remember who they are and where they came from, those cliches will ring true.

Yet it wasn't always this way. It is hard to imagine now that there was once a time when the Boston Celtics basketball team was mediocre. Certainly the dreadful interlude of the late seventies was a time of despair for Celtics fans, but for the most part those two seasons have been seen as an aberration, a lamentable and temporary departure from the tradition caused by the whims of an errant owner and his wife. For most fans the Celtics' domination stretches back in time to the hazy beginnings of the NBA, when running hooks and two-handed set shots were *de rigeuer* and shooting percentages over 40 were considered excellent. But the fact is that for the first four years of their existence the Celtics were a poor team that lost over 60 percent of its games to the likes of the Tri-Cities Hawks and Fort Wayne Pistons. The Celts were a second-rate team in what was considered a second-rate professional sport, and in only one of those years did they manage to make the playoffs. It wasn't until Red Auerbach's arrival in 1950 that Boston ever saw the sunlight of a plus-.500 record, and it would take ten years and the arrival of Bill Russell to bring Boston its first championship.

Nevertheless, the late forties were a not a bad time for professional basketball in Boston. Spurred by the collegiate success of the Holy Cross Crusaders, who won the national championship in 1947 behind the play of George Kaftan and Bob Cousy and the coaching of Alvin "Doggie" Julian, New England fans were reluctantly ready to support a pro team in a fledgling league. In spite of the early losing seasons, those fans had the good fortune of seeing a solid foundation being laid for the team by one of the best owners in the history of the game, a man who helped bring the NBA into being and saw the Celtics through the first two decades of their existence. Willing to devote his life to professional basketball, Walter Brown had vision and dedication, attributes that were to serve the organization long after his death in 1964.

Brown's involvement in pro basketball, like so much of the history of the Celtics, was indirect, almost accidental. The late twenties and early thirties had seen the rise in the United States of the big indoor arena. Boston Garden, Chicago Stadium, Madison Square Garden and the Milwaukee Arena were all examples of the sporting side of the urban boom that carved American cities out of the sky, filling the heavens with huge structures for the work and play of the metropolitan masses. In those days the most popular indoor sport was boxing, and huge audiences let men like Joe Louis and Willie Pep and Sandy Sadler dispel Depression blues by slugging it out beneath hot lights

Walter Brown, one of the founders of the NBA and the original owner of the Celtics, was renowned for his generous spirit. "Walter loved to win," Bill Russell said, "but I believe that he liked us whether we won or not."

and blue cigar smoke while the crowd screamed with vicarious enthusiasm. Hockey was also popular, and college basketball was getting more and more attention, but towards the end of the Second World War, a war that had siphoned off so many athletes and fans, the arena-owners started looking for a professional sport that could fill the gaps in the calendar and help get these cavernous, costly enclosures to pay for themselves. As owner of the Garden, Brown became one of a group of men who saw professional basketball as part of the answer. These men formed what would go on to become the National Basketball Association.

The game was much different then. Slower, less creative, it featured tight zone defenses and cautious, plodding offensive set-ups that look almost comical forty years later. (The 24-second clock did not come into effect until the 1954-55 season.) Players were only beginning to discover the staples of today's game: the jump shot, pivot play and the fast break. Many of the teams in the new league were manned by returning servicemen, older men who saw the sport as an avocation, a diversion after the rigors of war, rather than a profession. With franchises in remote parts of the country, the league had difficulty attracting the good college players. As Bob Cousy said about being drafted by the Tri-Cities Hawks, "I had a business ready to get off the ground in Worcester; the Tri-Cities Hawks? You had to be kidding me." Credibility in the new league was going to have to be earned; the game was going to have to change.

And in parts of New England after the war it was beginning to change, at least at the college level. Frank Keaney's Rhode Island Rams featured a "firehouse-style" fast break that won games with speed, endurance and hustle. Holy Cross could not help but construct an innovative approach with Cousy as quarterback. The flamboyant Frenchman from New York City had uncanny court sense and wonderful speed and quickness, and he opened up the game completely with his blind passes and streaking moves to the hoop as he led the Crusaders to the 1947 NCAA championship. The Crusaders' success was such that in 1948 Brown, fighting for the team's and the league's credibility, hired coach Julian to head the Celtics. A stern disciplinarian, Julian did not succeed in the professional ranks; frustrating records of 25-35 and 22-46 forced him out of the pros in two years. For all Brown's success in bringing professional basketball to Boston, he had yet to see a decent team play a home game on the parquet. But it was at this point that he made the wisest decision of his career—and arguably the wisest decision any owner of a sports franchise ever made.

Tom Heinsohn on his brilliant teammate: "Cousy was ordained from above as the best guy in the history to run a fast break. He had everything—imagination, intuition and desire."

Searching for Julian's successor, Brown brought a group of advisers and businessmen into his office, as was his custom, to ask for ideas. His partner and friend Lou Pieri recommended a 32-year-old man who had left Tri-Cities the previous season because the team owner, Ben Kerner, had not given him the control he felt he needed to build a team. Unlike Julian, however, Red Auerbach had already proven himself in the professional game. At age 29 Auerbach had walked into the office of Washington Caps owner Mike Uline and talked himself into the position of head coach of the Caps for their maiden season. He delivered. The Caps put together a 49-11 mark, an .817 winning percentage that would stand as an NBA record until the great 68-13 record of the Philadelphia 76ers 20 years later. The Caps' 18 straight victories that opening season stood as a league record until 1970, and though it exited early from the playoffs, the team had one of the finest seasons in NBA history. Arrogant, knowledgeable, intimidating, shrewd and loyal, Auerbach had proven immediately that he had a mind for the game well ahead of his time. But neither Washington (where Auerbach lost a power struggle with player Bob Feerick, who would become player-coach after Red's departure) nor Tri-Cities, where he moved in 1949, had owners who were prepared to give Red the freedom he needed to fulfill his vision.

Red built the Washington team by carefully judging the limited talent and schooling his players thoroughly in the pressing, fast-breaking, aggressive brand of basketball he had learned from his former coach and mentor, Bill Reinhart of the University of Oregon. Then, as always, he saw the future of the game and found creative ways of bringing it into being before anyone else. As the war receded and the younger collegians, strengthened by a better diet and more leisure time, entered the new league, Auerbach expanded his system, emphasizing discipline, controlled defense, the fast break, teamwork and conditioning. Yet he also felt occasionally frustrated by the caution of owners who knew much less about the game than he did, and by the time the Celtics hired him he needed more control. Brown gave it to him, and Red responded with loyalty, working for a time without a contract and treating the financial burdens of the team as if they were his own. He was going to prove to New England that basketball could be its favorite sport. He was going to bring excitement to the Garden. He was going to construct a dynasty by choosing the best players and then teaching them how to win. And he knew it.

But many Bostonians were not ready for the arrogance of this young man, no matter what his background, and Red's vision of what the team should be was not always shared by the press and the people of the city. Still considered a small-time, almost local sport, pro basketball often attracted a provincial attitude. Red ran into it immediately. In 1950, the year of Bob Cousy's graduation, most locals wanted the Celtics to draft the Holy Cross star, if only because he would be such a gate attraction. But then, as always, Red was a purist. Seeing the future of the game, he thought the Celtics' biggest need was height and used the first two picks to draft 7-0 Charlie Share of Bowling Green and 6-5 Chuck Cooper, the first black to play in the NBA. Cousy, meanwhile, was drafted by the Tri-Cities Hawks. The picks caused an uproar. Pressed for an explanation, Red turned to Brown at the drafting table and blurted the famous line: "Walter, am I supposed to please the local yokels and take a player I don't want?" The following day the press bannered the statement, and the long, complicated relationship between Red and the city had begun.

Cousy, of course, came to the Celtics that year by the luck of the draw. Temporarily forced out of business, the Hawks traded their rights to him to the Chicago Stags. When the Stags disbanded soon afterwards, their players were distributed throughout the league, and Boston was fortunate enough to receive a guard who would go on to be one of the greatest players in the game. In retrospect, Auerbach's draft-day attitude towards Cousy seems a huge oversight—Share never played for the Celtics, and Cooper played four good but undistinguished seasons. But in the context of Red's complete commitment to winning, the attitude makes sense. First of all, it is very difficult to know whether a good collegian will make it in the professional ranks, especially if the player lacks commanding height. Furthermore, in spite of Cousy's greatness he failed to bring Boston a championship until the arrival of Bill Russell six years later. The lesson here is not that Auerbach was mistaken, but that he saw that the key to success in the NBA was having a dominating center. That insight may have caused some initial misdirection—but look at the final results.

Cousy was joined by a corps of outstanding athletes, including Bill Sharman and Easy Ed Macauley. With all three stars consistently averaging around 20 points a game, the team was always among the league leaders in offense throughout the first half of the fifties. Cousy turned in some heroic performances during those years, including a 50-point night against Syracuse in the 1953 Eastern semifinal in which he made 30 free throws as the Celtics won in four overtimes. But for six straight seasons Boston lost in the postseason to either the New York Knicks or the Syracuse Nats. Neither Cousy's wizardry nor the accurate shooting of Macauley and Sharman could compensate for the lack of a good big man, and in spite of their tenacity and great running game—perhaps almost because of it—the Celtics always seemed to fatigue by the end of the season. The dominant team of that era was the Minneapolis Lakers, who featured one of the greatest players of all time, George Mikan. Like Dolph Schayes of Syracuse and Paul Arizin of the Philadelphia Warriors, Mikan controlled games with size, strength and stamina, and until the arrival of Russell the Celtics could not match the success of these center-oriented teams.

Red was certainly successful during those six seasons: not once did the team finish below .500; not once did it miss the playoffs. But he knew during those years that something was missing, and he always kept a close eye on the college ranks, where that something might show up. When Bill Russell came to national attention at the University of San Francisco, Auerbach called Bill Reinhart and asked him to scout the big man personally. Reinhart phoned him back soon afterwards and told Red to land Russell whatever way he could. Unfortunately, Boston's consistency meant that it would never be able to land a draft pick high enough to get Russell. But Red has never let conventional barriers stop him, and he watched Russell's situation closely. The St. Louis Hawks drafted Russ, but they were worried that St. Louis would not accept a black player. Red jumped right in, cleverly offering the Hawks Ed Macauley, a native of St. Louis who had averaged nineteen points a game for the Celtics over six seasons, and the draft rights to the fine collegian Cliff Hagan for the rights to Russell. The deal was consummated and history was made.

Russell's arrival completed the equation. The greatest player in the game was now playing for the greatest coach, and together they defined success in profes-

sional basketball for the next thirteen years and beyond. As K. C. Jones has said in his autobiography, "I believe the Celtics' success comes from the character of the people who began the winning tradition, and those are the two big R's— Red and Russell." An important thread himself in that tradition, no one is in a better position to assess basketball influence than K. C. Certainly no one knew Russell's play any better.

Russell had to be seen to be fully appreciated, but the bald facts proclaim his greatness. Never mind the 21,000 rebounds. Ignore the 14,500 points. Disregard the 40,000 minutes. After a while these statistics, impressive as they are, have a way of spinning off into the stale atmosphere of after-dinner encomium.

"Nobody is as good as Bill Russell," John Thompson said in 1985. "You count Russell, then you skip three or four places, then you talk about the rest of the people."

Besides, both Red and Russ would tell you to look at the only statistic that counts: Bill Russell played for the Boston Celtics basketball team for 13 seasons. During that time the Celtics won 11 NBA championships, including eight straight. No sports team of any significance can make such a claim; no one who has any idea of the difficulty of winning even *one* championship can fail to be impressed. And though Russell was surrounded by a cast of great players, the parallel between his presence and the team's record is not accidental. He fleshed forth Red's vision. He permanently altered the team, the league and the game of basketball. He put together a record of individual brilliance, team leadership and dedication to winning that would make it very easy to say he was the greatest ever if it were not for the existence of Larry Bird. Russell was the man.

Like Bird, Russell was a complex player, a man whose skills were broadened by his very personality, a man whose generosity was as deep as his aversion to hypocrisy. He too made his fellow players shine; he too could not brook a losing attitude, a half-hearted effort or an excuse for poor play. On and off the court he personified dignity, and his belief in himself was perhaps the most important ingredient in his success. He had no time for the off-court niceties, the politics of being liked, and if he felt his privacy was in danger he could be cool. In spite of his achievement and his legacy there are still many in Boston who think he treated fans with disdain—as if he owed them anything more than those 13 magnificent seasons. But Russell's reserve—some would say haughtiness—can only be understood in the context of history: the history of racism in the United States and Boston,

and the history of Russell's own battle against it throughout his life. Let those who shared his battle assess his attitude; the rest of us should consider ourselves lucky that we got the chance to see him play.

And what a player he was. Six-nine, blessed with a sprinter's speed and tremendous leaping ability, Russell possessed a blend of physical skill and basketball instinct rarely seen before or since. Like Cousy (and unlike so many players of that era), Russell was constantly in motion, allowing his instincts to direct him, using his natural gifts and flawless fundamentals to become the most complete defensive player ever to grace a court. No one established position more effectively; no one read an offense with more accuracy; no one helped out his fellow players more quickly. He refined shot-blocking to an art, anticipating, jumping and avoiding contact with perfect timing. A left-hander, Russell had the added advantage of his stronger arm matching the shooting hand of the usually right-handed offensive player. His rejections were the stuff of legend—and must always remain so as blocked shots did not become an official statistical category until 1973, four years after Russell's retirement.

Russell was also one of the smartest players ever, a man who understood perfectly what K. C. Jones has called "the moves, counter-moves and strategies" of the game. His court awareness was as complete as Bird's. His defensive responses were exact and timely because, like Auerbach, he was always one mental step ahead of his adversaries—and because he had the physical tools to transform his instincts into action. He was always analyzing the game, visualizing his

25

opponents' moves and his own reactions as he prepared for play. In his autobiography, *Second Wind*, he tells of how he often dreamt of matching his defensive prowess in flight against attacking players. He lived basketball; he lived winning.

His record speaks for itself. The Celtics won their first NBA championship in 1957, concluding a dream season by blowing out the Syracuse Nats in three straight games to win the division finals, and then besting the St. Louis Hawks in one of the most dramatic finals ever. According to Tommy Heinsohn, Game 7 of

When Bill Russell coached Satch Sanders, he said: "It didn't matter so much why I yelled at Satch; I just had to do it at certain intervals, the way you take vitamin pills. After only a few months as player-coach I found myself thinking, 'Okay, it's 7:20. Time to yell at Satch.'"

that series was the greatest game ever played, a two-overtime affair that was not decided until an Alex Hannum-to-Bob Pettit pass bounced awry in the waning seconds. The image of Red being swarmed at the end of that game, arms stretched out, cigar clamped in a victory smile, is one of the highlights of Celtics history. Though the Hawks came back the following year to beat Boston, 4-2 (Russell injured his ankle in Game 3 of that series), the dynasty had begun. The march of eight straight championships began in 1958-59, and until Russell's retirement ten years later the Celtics would lose a postseason series only once, to the great 1966-67 76ers team that won 68 games and swept to the NBA crown.

It was during this decade that the team's personality, the collection of traits that we all associate with the Celtics, found its full expression. During the latter half of the 1950s Auerbach assembled some wonderful talent around his star center: Sharman and Cousy remained, and the 1957 draft yielded Heinsohn and K. C. Jones in addition to Russ. Frank Ramsey, Jim Loscutoff and Sam Jones completed what had to be one of the most balanced basketball teams ever. Their defense was tenacious and fundamentally sound. Their offense was stylish, fast-paced and totally team-oriented. Each of these men was a fierce competitor; each wanted to be there when the game was on the line. And yet all of them thought of the team first and foremost. Imbued with Red's sense of discipline and dedication to teamwork, they all knew their roles and performed them to the extent that the team became virtually unbeatable. But Red and Russell never allowed them to think they couldn't lose. Quite the opposite: the drive and discipline of the leaders forced everyone else constantly to evolve, to improve, to work in and out of season at their profession. Scrap and hustle were the dominant virtues; winning the byproduct. These men came to know each other, on and off the court, with the kind of intimacy that transcends ego. They thought and played as one. They brought their experience to bear on every game, every play. Young players sat on the pine for years, so that by the time they started they had developed a maturity and an attitude that befitted playing for the greatest basketball team in the world. And this personality has persisted. K. C. Jones's five-year tenure as head coach was a perfect illustration of how the Celtics approach has extended throughout the team's history. Scrupulous, conservative and tough, Jones brought the classic Celtics virtues of experience, hustle and unselfish play into the high-flying world of the 1980s NBA.

That the Celtics had developed a distinct identity and philosophy became clear as the 1960s arrived. Many of the faces changed, but the championships kept rolling on. Cousy and Sharman retired. Loscutoff and Ramsey soon followed. But the players who replaced them—Don Nelson, John Havlicek, Satch Sanders, Baily Howell—sustained the tradition. Part of it was Russell's presence; he was always the key player, the man in the middle. Part of it was Red's choice of personnel. He always came up with players who fit into what had become the Celtics' system; if they couldn't, they didn't last long. And the Celtics have always had a knack of taking players who have not had success fitting into other teams and making winners out of them. But the main reason was less tangible. The Celtics are a perfect example of how a good sports team is greater than the sum of its parts.

They were always better than their collective talent because they had a coherent, sound philosophy and two men who owned the best basketball minds of the era.

But though the Celtics were dominant during these years, they were not unchallenged. The Lakers, who had moved to Los Angeles in 1959, continued their winning tradition into the sixties behind the brilliant play of Elgin Baylor and Jerry West, two career 27-points-per-game scorers who were also complete players in the Oscar Robertson mold. The Lakers finished first in the Western Division five times in the sixties and reached the NBA finals six times. They lost to the Celtics on all six occasions, a record of futility that goes a long way towards explaining the intensity of the current Celtics-Lakers rivalry and the tremendous pride the Lakers have in the rings they have won in the eighties. Rightly proud of their own tradition, Los Angeles has nevertheless always had the specter of that frustrating decade floating in the background.

In their own division the Celtics also had to contend with the 76ers and Wilt "The Stilt" Chamberlain, the powerful center who had come out of the University of Kansas in 1959 to revolutionize offense in the NBA. Chamberlain's strength, size and extraordinary skill were overwhelming. Will anyone ever again average 50 points a game for a season? Will anyone ever again score in triple figures in one game? Most people know he is the all-time NBA leader in scoring average, but how many know that Chamberlain pulled down more rebounds than anyone else, including Russell? Night in and night out Chamberlain singlehandedly dominated his opponents, and though he did receive help from stars Hal Greer and Chet Walker, he *was* the 76ers. He mastered the game at will; he almost always had total control. Why then didn't his teams win more often?

That question isn't as easy to answer as most people think. Chamberlain was easy to dislike: his size and strength and arrogance made him an easy target for the media, and his rivalry with Russell, the player's player, cemented his image as the bully. It may be true that he did not always play team ball, but he learned how to win during his career and has two championship rings to prove it. And yet his shortcomings (and the shortcomings of his teams) were undeniable: he wasn't quite as coachable as Russell; he wasn't playing for Red Auerbach; and the Sixers teams of that time were not as cohesive as the Celtics. But what teams were? The strategic genius and motivational skill of Red, the great talent he had assembled, and the strength of Russell in the middle gave the Celtics an advantage that Wilt

could overcome only once in a decade. But the Lakers, Warriors, Hawks, Knicks and everyone else in the league had the same problem. The Celtics were that good. (In Philadelphia, the 76ers organization still argues that Wilt was a better player than Russell.)

Red retired from coaching in 1966 with 938 regular-season victories, still tops in the NBA. He continued working for Boston as general manager, ensuring continuity and maintaining the tradition. Russell became a player-coach and led Boston to two more championships before abruptly retiring in 1969. His departure signaled the end of an era. His leadership, ability and influence were so crucial that the Celtics virtually collapsed after he left, failing to make the playoffs two straight seasons and losing as many as they won over the two-year period. Meanwhile, the Lakers, Knicks, Baltimore Bullets and Milwaukee Bucks had moved into the upper echelon of the NBA, and it is signifi-

John Havlicek Day, 1987. Both Havlicek, normally detached from his emotions, and Red Auerbach, of the gruff exterior, wept openly that afternoon.

cant that each of these teams had a dominant center—Chamberlain, Willis Reed, Wes Unseld and Kareem Abdul-Jabbar, respectively.

But Red was not sitting on his laurels. In fact, for the Celtics it was a time of rebuilding. Using John Havlicek as the key figure—an ironman of great will who, until the arrival of Bird, was the best multiskilled player in Celtics history—and retaining veterans Don Nelson and Satch Sanders, Auerbach reconstructed the team in a leaner, seventies mold, with coach Tommy Heinsohn providing the courtside link to the past. Heinsohn was an outstanding tactician who knew fundamentals as well as anyone. He and Red assessed their talent and constructed the team accordingly. Dave Cowens, a diminutive 6-8, became the center. "Bill Russell told me he would be a center," Red said in 1988, "just by looking into his eyes." In the era of the giant pivotman, many critics said he was far too small, but Heinsohn created a system (spreading players geometrically over the court, with Cowens at the high post and the guards on the wings, a system Nelson would use later in Milwaukee) that played to Cowens's strengths: his speed and quickness, his hustle, his fullcourt play. The team featured an explosive running game keyed by Jo Jo White, Boston's number-one draft pick in 1969, and Paul Silas, a dynamic blend of muscle, guile and winning spirit, who complemented Cowens perfectly in the frontcourt. This edition of the Celtics dynasty finished in first place in the tough Atlantic Division five straight years and won two NBA championships in dramatic fashion, a seven-game classic over the Bucks in 1974 and a thrilling win over John McLeod's Phoenix Suns in 1976. And there was a double thrill for Boston fans in seeing their team both as a manifestation of the Celtics tradition and a team very different from its predecessors.

Dave Cowens defends against Robert Parish of Golden State, 1978. When his number 18 was retired in 1981, he told the Boston Garden fans: "From the people in the choice seats to you people up there in the heavens, you made it easy for me to play hard."

The league was much broader by this time, its talent far more evenly distributed, and in the new environment the Celtics' early seventies achievement was significant, a great tribute to the staying power of Red's basketball vision and his ability to move with the times. But after that 1976 championship something went wrong. Perhaps the game had changed too quickly. Perhaps Red had reached a point where he allowed these changes—huge salary demands, big-business attitudes in the front office and among owners (a charge Tommy Heinsohn levels in his forthcoming book), greater involvement in the sport of people with no real knowledge of the game—to rankle him so much that he lost perspective. Whatever the case, he made his only major mistake as curator of the franchise by failing to keep Silas on the team. And yet his approach was entirely logical, completely within the tradition.

It was the heyday of free agency, and Auerbach had met with Silas to work out a new contract. Silas was proud and independent, willing to voice his displeasure over coaching or money. His demands after the 1976 championship exceeded Cowens's salary, and it was Celtics policy not to alter the team's salary structure for

"We envisioned Jo Jo White to be the leader of the team in the seventies," Tom Heinsohn wrote. "He was a tremendously proud guy... temperamental. It took time, but Jo Jo eventually reached the top."

one man. Cowens was the star, and according to David Halberstam the Celtics were not going to pay anyone on the team any more than they paid him, just as today they would not dream of making Larry Bird the second-highest paid player on the team. Silas had his own ability and the strength of the marketplace on his side, and the negotiations became an ego struggle. Cowens, who knew better than anyone how important Silas was to his own game, asked the Celtics to pay Silas whatever it would take to keep him in Boston. But in an eleventh-hour move Auerbach traded Silas's rights to Denver in a three-way maneuver that brought former UCLA stars Sidney Wicks and Curtis Rowe to the Celtics. That trade marked the beginning of the worst period in Celtics history.

Without Silas's physical support Cowens fatigued quickly, and ten games into the 1976-77 season he left the team, burned out, determined not to return. He was 29 years old. He ended up staying away three months, and though Auerbach never tried to get him to return, he did leave the door open, knowing that Cowens's pride and competitiveness would bring him back if it were at all possible. Cowens now regrets the move, and though he went on to have fine statistical seasons after that hiatus, the team's fortunes deteriorated. The tandem of Wicks and Rowe never clicked in Boston, and as the stars of the early seventies aged and declined the team went from good to mediocre to downright awful, bottoming out in 1978-79 with a 29-53 record under the ownership of John Y. Brown, who, in an unparalleled example of misguided management, had given up three first-round draft choices to bring Bob McAdoo to Boston on the strength of his wife's whim. McAdoo only played 20 games for the Celtics, but his presence on the parquet had significant symbolic importance. Among the fans and the press the acrimony was thick, and not even the expectation of Larry Bird could stop the boos and catcalls tumbling from the balcony. Unlike the two-year down spell earlier in the decade, this period of failure did not seem to contain the seeds of rebuilding, and the fans, hypercritical at the best of times, held out little hope. Wicks and Rowe became scapegoats. Brown forced Auerbach out of the decision-making process (for a while Red even pondered retirement). Jo Jo White, unable to adjust to his own declining abilities after an extensive heel operation, became argumentative and uncooperative. Cowens himself coached the team for most of the 1978-79 season, finding out quickly that Russell's achievement as player-coach was no mean feat. The Celtics had very quickly come to lack the very ingredients that had underpinned their success: cohesion, leadership, team spirit. The situation was so bad that when Brown announced he was selling his interest in the team, Cowens declared to the press, "That's the best news I've heard all year!" A change was in order.

In the meantime Philadelphia's star had risen again. Flying on the wings of Dr. J, the Sixers embodied an energetic, elegant brand of play that made the Celts look anachronistic. As the eighties edged close, more and more people saw the future in players like David Thompson and George Gervin, outstanding athletes and one-on-one stars who could carry a team. Well, Dr. J was a lot more than a one-on-one player, just as the latest incarnation of the Sixers was much more than a collection of good players, but it was

David Halberstam said of Paul Silas: "He became the embodiment of what being a Celtic meant, playing with intelligence, sacrificing his personal game for the benefit of his teammates; he was not only an exceptional player himself but an important positive influence on younger players." Silas made $175,000 in 1976, the final year of his contract.

easy to simplify when your team was losing 65 percent of its games. Boston's doldrums just did not seem right. There was too much lost too fast; the championships were still too fresh in people's minds. But things would have to change drastically if Philly was to be challenged and that great Eastern Division rivalry to resume.

They did, of course. Everything that goes around comes around, and the cycles of the seventies helped lay the psychological groundwork for the team's resurgence. Who else but Red would make the difference? Who else but Red could fashion a phoenix out of the ashes of mismanagement and despair? But even during that worst of seasons Bird was in the fold, legally if not in person, and Red's mind had returned to the game with renewed vigor. By the time he had finished the job he had begun on draft day 1978, the Celtics were set to pursue excellence for another golden decade. Has it really been as good as we remember? Have there really been that many terrific plays, wonderful games, nail-biting series? Has the French Lick-Boston lifeline really been that good to us?

You bet it has.

3

ROOKIE YEAR

Winters in Boston can be long and bleak—not the intense, shackled bleakness of the frigid Midwest, but a raw city chill that fringes the streets with dirty snow and frays the nerves of the already surly waitresses and taxi drivers. There is no beach, baseball or Concerts on the Common. No fall colors or spring flowers. Night falls before work is over, and the wind off the Atlantic has an edge like bad beer. People take warmth where they can find it, and in the long nights between Thanksgiving and the Boston Marathon, NBA basketball is at least as good as whiskey and cigarettes for keeping malaise at bay. And when the team you support is as good and as consistent and as smooth as 12-year old Jameson, it goes a long way towards loosening winter's grip.

The miracles of television and satellite dish have made the modern game of basketball an intimate diversion. The flickering, sculpted bodies of huge young men dance across the wide screen nightly, performing amazing feats of athleticism in replay after replay while we shake our heads in wonder. Where do these incredible players come from? How do they do what they do? Michael Jordan and Isiah Thomas and Magic Johnson and Akeem Olajuwon and a host of other splendid players from Brooklyn, Des Moines, Seattle, St. Louis, *Nigeria* if you can believe it. Gliding, skying, rejecting; slamming home dunks and scooting up the floor with behind-the-back dribbles and look-away passes; transforming that rectangle of contained energy into an aerial circus of ability and grace. The perfect escape from a cold night. The ideal antidote to winter. Like spirits from another world, like a vision of what the ordinary person can only dream of doing, these

33

brilliant young athletes, the best the world of basketball has to offer, brighten the dark night as they shake their fists in triumph and peer from the television with the easy smiles of the young, the famous and the gifted.

At its best, the inspired choreography that moves across the television screen is a transcendent, poetic statement of the grace that man can physically achieve. But the knowledgeable Boston fan, secure in his team, appreciative of what the Celtics do to brighten every winter, knows not to trust the promises of the highlight film. Television tends to mask the hard work, discipline and lonely hours that give rise to consistent excellence. Every NBA team has incredible talent, individuals who on any given night can do something you have never seen before. But after the hype and glitter have worn off, most clubs end up trading missed jump shots and self-defeating one-on-one play. In the eighties NBA very few teams rise above the skills of individual players. The Celtics, on the other hand, because they've paid their dues and worked their butts off, play a brand of basketball that does more than keep the chill from your bones—it gives you the warm certainty that you'll still be rooting for them in the leafy days of June.

Ten years ago, however, the only certainty in the Celtics' organization was change. When Larry Bird arrived at training camp in 1979 he was only one of many new faces. M. L. Carr had come to Boston after playing out his option with Detroit; journeyman center/forward Eric Fernsten had emerged from Europe; Gerald Henderson had come out of the Continental Basketball Association to sign as a free agent.

Veterans Don Chaney and Cowens maintained a link with the last championship team, but the other faces were relatively fresh. Tiny Archibald and Chris Ford, though longtime employees of the NBA, each had but a year with the Celtics on his resume. Rick Robey, obtained from Indiana in exchange for Billy Knight, had been in Boston less than a season. Cedric Maxwell, the number-one draft pick of 1977, was considered a veteran after only two years on the club. Curtis Rowe, media and fan scapegoat of the previous season, was trying to keep his spot on the roster, but the atmosphere was one of renewal, of new blood and a new attitude.

The media center of this patchwork team was Bird, who carried whatever muted expectations Celtics fandom had during that hot summer. But ironically, the press coverage during camp was meager, especially by the standards of a decade later. So low had the Celtics fallen in the hierarchy of local loyalties that they were being written up beneath the schoolboys. In a critical, sports-mad city they were being told that they would have to prove themselves all over again, that they would have to rebuild the faith of their supporters as well as the team. A tall order, but who could blame the Boston basketball fan for being spoiled? For 20 years he had been given nothing but the best the sport had to offer; now the benefits of those two decades seemed squandered in two years of poor management and selfish play. It would take more than a cocky rookie and a collection of free agents to convince him the good times had returned. It would take more than training camp promises and new faces. The drafting of Larry Bird was old news by now, and his stilted, media-shy arrival in Boston had people making cracks about the Hick from French Lick. Also, the involved, sometimes heated negotiations between the Celtics and Bird's agent, Bob Woolf, had some fans wondering just how much this new guy was worth. Sure, he had done it all in college. Sure, he had the skills and the physique. Sure, there were those touting him as the franchise savior, the hottest player to grace the Garden in years. But these fans had just seen John Havlicek close out one of the finest NBA careers ever; they had seen Dave Cowens rise from the ashes; they could remember Russell in his prime.

They knew it was a long way from the Missouri Valley Conference to the NBA, where Bird would be competing with the likes of Julius Erving, Bobby Dandridge and Paul Silas. As far as the informed fan was concerned, this new kid had some dues to pay.

But there was another Midwesterner in town, another product of the American basketball heartland who was going to be just as important as Bird to the most dramatic transformation in NBA history. Bill Fitch *had* paid some dues, and he brought many years of coaching and

Larry Bird and Bill Fitch, 1980. "There are guys who have success and smother the people around them," Fitch said then. "But Larry is not that type of individual. Besides, there is no room on this club for 'I people.' We've got 'we' people on this team and Larry is just an important part." Fitch had foes here, but Bird wasn't one of them.

managerial experience to Boston, experience that helped him become the immediate architect of Boston's return to respectability. Fitch knew basketball. *NBA* basketball. He knew a system that—with free agency, the draft, the overly frequent bartering of players, the huge salaries and egos—militated heavily against the team unity that is so essential to success in such a highly talented league. He proved this in Boston more quickly than anyone could have, and yet a decade later too many commentators look back at those early years as if the team were in incubation, as if the success were a prelude to the dominant years of the K. C. Jones Era.

That simply isn't so. Recently Bill Fitch's reputation has suffered unfairly for behavior that has to be seen in the context of the time to be fully understood. The common perception of Fitch is that he was a martinet who drove his players with repetitive, unnecessary drills and saturated them in the video room with ceaseless viewings of recent games. His well-publicized beefs with K. C. Jones, a noble, extremely likeable man, never helped that reputation. Fitch drove people hard and had the kind of personality a person in his position needed. That personality did not earn him too many admirers in Boston, at least after the euphoria of his championship season wore off. But as with Red, Russell and Bird, the facts speak for themselves. Fitch engineered a magnificent turnaround and led the Celtics to perhaps their sweetest championship of the Bird Era, and he did it with the very tactics that led to his dismissal later on. Larry Bird has said more than once that Fitch was the best coach he ever worked under, and though most Celtics who played for Fitch do not

share that opinion, Bird's view in this matter has to be respected. When all is said and done, Fitch has that achievement to point to, that championship ring and those 242 victories in four seasons. And he was very much what the Celtics needed in 1979, with or without Bird.

Fitch already had a substantial legacy by the time he arrived in Boston. For most of the seventies he had been the guiding light of the Cleveland Cavaliers' franchise, ushering them into the NBA in 1970 and leading them through the growing pains of expansion to a Central Division crown in 1976. Domineering, intelligent, experienced, Fitch liked power and knew how to use it. As both general manager and coach, he had been involved in all decisions with the Cavaliers, and the club's impressive development was largely the fruit of his hard work and ability. He oversaw the club's move in 1974 from the old Cleveland Arena to the beautiful Richfield Coliseum, a change of scene that symbolized the team's coming of age in the NBA. He was an excellent tactician, a good judge of talent and a diehard disciplinarian. Above all he knew how to win.

Fitch came up through the ranks. Some people say that his problems communicating with the NBA athlete have been the result of his grooming at the college level, where players were more in need of his demanding, paternal style. The Cavs were not his first project. In the sixties he built programs at North Dakota, Bowling Green and Minnesota, recruiting and coaching with an intensity that was the natural product of his ambition and Spartan philosophy. He won a Division III championship with North Dakota and laid the groundwork for a championship program at Minnesota by recruiting players like Jim Brewer, Ron Behagen and the baseball star Dave Winfield, who played basketball at Minnesota. He asked for a lot and expected even more, an attitude that bred mixed feelings among his players. Phil Jackson, a star at North Dakota and later with the New York Knicks, recalled in his book, *Maverick*, how extremely persuasive Fitch had been when recruiting him, but he implied that Fitch had further goals that he used Jackson to achieve. Yet in 1982 Jackson said that Fitch was "tough, demanding, insulting even. But I appreciated him later in my career. His stress on discipline had a benefit later. I still keep in touch with him."

Reaching the Big Ten was Fitch's dream, and players like Jackson helped him get there—though he certainly helped them in turn. Fitch himself said that he never thought about coaching in the NBA, that the Big Ten was "the ultimate coaching goal." But the money, the allure and the opportunity to build a franchise brought Fitch to Cleveland, and he has been in the NBA ever since. Here too he paid his dues. Every expansion club has its problems, and Fitch struggled through seasons where he won as few as 15 games. He learned to mask his intensity, hiding behind a media persona of stand-up comic. He was quick with one-liners, quick to point fun at his team and himself. But in the meantime he was working hard behind the scenes, assembling the disciplined, well-conditioned talent he believed in. His coaching style featured the liberal use of substitutes and an offense based on cutting, picking and jump-shooting accuracy. He loved size and demanded pressure defense. On and off the court he knew how to build a team. His drafting was exceptional: Austin Carr,

Jim Brewer, Campy Russell, Foots Walker and Mike Mitchell all came to the Cavs in the seventies. The team's poor records helped its drafting position, of course, but Fitch had an excellent eye for players who would fit into his system, and he always brought players together whose abilities seemed to mesh well. Cleveland missed the playoffs by a single game in 1975. The following season they finished first in the Central Division and advanced to the conference finals before losing to the Celtics, eventual champions. Fitch had arrived.

There is a school of thought in the NBA that says a coach's life span of effectiveness is five years. Red Auerbach notwithstanding, the evidence over the years suggests that the pressures of maintaining 50-to-60-win seasons for any longer is too great, that after that time the lack of quality draft choices and fresh ideas inevitably brings a team down to the level of its rivals. This has certainly been the working principle of the Celtics brass during the eighties, and it seems to apply to Fitch's tenure in Cleveland as well. Nineteen-seventy-six marked the limit of his success there. The Cavs made the playoffs the following two years, but dropped to a 30-52 record in 1979. Attendance fell by almost 50 percent during that time, and the sports talk shows, always a barometer of local opinion, called repeatedly for Fitch's resignation. After ten seasons in Cleveland he resigned; leaving must have been tough, but he could point with pride to his achievement there.

It was perhaps inevitable that Fitch should come to Boston. His philosophy and coaching method were very close to Auerbach's, and he was available at precisely the time when Red was looking for someone who could bring the Celtics back to the basics that had established a dynasty. In fact, by 1979 the two men had been friends for several years and frequently talked about their similar approach to the game. They met at the Hall of Fame induction ceremonies in Springfield, Massachusetts, in May of 1979 and had a long talk about their respective situations. Red saw a coach with the know-how and discipline to pull the Celtics out of their slump and restore their confidence. Fitch saw precisely the position he was looking for: a solid franchise which was in the doldrums where he could concentrate on coaching and shed the general managerial duties that had begun to wear on him in Cleveland. With Red he would have the best GM in the business, but one who would allow him considerable input into decisions about personnel. It was a script written in hoop heaven, and with Bird waiting in the wings the stage was set for success.

The collaboration was perfect, at least at first. Auerbach and his new coach put together a team that rivaled the greatest NBA teams of all time. Even before the legendary deal that brought Robert Parish and Kevin McHale to Boston, they effected a complete turnaround in method and attitude that was to pay off with a full return of confidence and a 61-win season. And they did it by drawing out the potential of players already on the club and combining their skills with those of the new players. Cowens, was the key figure in the opening weeks of the season, leading by example and showing the new players that even someone who had won almost every basketball honor imaginable could submit to the rigors of a Bill Fitch training camp and approach that camp with the attitude that he still had a place

on the team to earn. Cowens was living proof of Red's pride in building from within. Proud of the fact that he rarely traded a player, Red had a philosophy that was nevertheless tough to maintain in the modern environment of competing leagues, free agency and compensation. But typically, Red adjusted, bringing players to Boston whom he recognized as having the potential to fit into the system and contribute. Recognizing the potential of Gerald Henderson, the unselfish play of M. L. Carr and Chris Ford, the flowering of Cedric Maxwell and the ability of Tiny Archibald, he and Fitch built a team around Bird and Cowens that combined the qualities of the past with a blueprint for the future.

Perhaps the best example of this new vision and the way it produced winners was the case of Archibald. The Celtics have always had a way of transforming men who have struggled with controversy into productive team players. Charlie Scott, thought by many to be uncoachable, had been a key element in the 1976 championship. Kermit Washington's brush with infamy had rendered him untouchable until Red gave him life in Boston. Dennis Johnson would become the finest example of all, the supposed problem player who would mature and blossom under Red's system. But very few people could have predicted the way in which Nate Archibald filled his role to perfection for the Celtics for four years. An established All-Star, he had come to Boston after eight years as one of the outstanding guards in the NBA, with the distinction of having been the only player in history to lead the league in scoring and assists in the same season when he averaged 34 points a game and 11.4 assists in 1972-73. Like Cowens, he was a major force in the NBA in the early seventies. Like Cowens, he was a player who helped define the game during that period. But Tiny's career was mottled with tough injuries and losing teams, and by the time he came to Boston most people thought he was never going to be a winner.

Tiny had come out of the University of Texas at El Paso in 1970, a second-round draft pick of the Kansas City-Omaha Kings. His basketball roots, however, always remained in the playgrounds of the Bronx. Under coaches Floyd Lane at El Paso and Bob Cousy at K. C., Tiny had learned the finer points of playing point guard at the college and professional levels, but his basic game—free-wheeling, one-on-one, with a blurringly quick move to the hoop and an uncanny feel for finding the open man after a switch—was faithful to the urban style of play that has made the game so entertaining over the years. Through all his years in the Midwest, Tiny never relinquished his links with the East. An intensely dedicated, competitive man, his life off the court was crucial to his play, and he has said that two very personal aspects of his life, the death of his brother as a result of a drug overdose and his devotion to his mother, fueled the fires of his competitiveness. On the court, however, he shielded that intensity with an impersonal stare. He preferred to let his game be his means of communication.

In Kansas City Tiny was a scorer, consistently averaging over 20 points a game. Cousy knew that a team that was as short on talent as the Kings were in those years had only the excitement of Tiny's brilliant one-on-one play to attract fans to the gate, so he encouraged his diminutive point guard to attack the defense constantly. No

doubt Cousy saw a lot of himself in Archibald, and no doubt Tiny enjoyed the glory; but the competitive side of Tiny wanted to get away from losing, and the personal side of him wanted to get back to New York. The opportunity to satisfy both sides seemed to arise in 1976 when the New York Nets, darlings of Long Island and two-time American Basketball Association champions, acquired Tiny from the Kings in exchange for Brian Taylor and two first-round draft choices, just as the two leagues were merging. Archibald was coming home, to a winning team no less. But the move was star-crossed: Julius Erving, the man who had led the Nets to its titles, became disenchanted over, among other things, the way

"I've led the league in scoring, assists, all those things," Tiny Archibald said of his earlier years. *"Now I don't have to do that anymore. I let the younger guys worry about those things."*

Tiny's arrival had disrupted the salary structure. He entered into a protracted holdout that eventually led to his trade to the 76ers. As the Nets struggled at the beginning of the 1976-77 season, Tiny became the target for scorn. He played well enough but failed to sparkle as much as he had in Kansas City. The season bottomed out when he broke his foot at midseason. During the 1977 preseason the Nets traded him to Buffalo where, after a promising start, he went down again with a torn Achilles' tendon. Most observers thought his career was over, and following Archibald's transfer to Boston in the swap of franchises in the summer of 1978, Boston fans saw Tiny as a symbol of failure.

Of course, failure and indifference were the dominant feelings among Celtics fans in 1978, so perhaps they could be forgiven for failing to notice Tiny's major comeback that season. He had not played in 18 months—for Tiny, you might as well say he had not lived during that time. "I love to play...watch...teach," he said. "It's what I care about." Here was another chance, another opening. But he had come at a difficult time, and much of that season sent him into a confused, unhappy state. He had problems maintaining consistency on the floor while working his body back into shape. He had trouble teaming with both Jo Jo White and Billy Knight, who wouldn't or couldn't accept him as point guard. His minutes were often limited to single digits, and his sporadic playing time did little to improve his physical condition. But the toughest fight was mental, as it always is, and Tiny agonized during the first half of the season. Following a rough game against Chicago at midseason he lashed out, "I just want to be moved. I just want out of Boston." The Celtics were reportedly doing everything possible to accommodate him. Privately, it was being said that Cowens had told Red that either Tiny or White would have to go—neither would surrender point guard duties to the other. At the end of January White was traded to Golden State in exchange for a first-round draft choice. Did the Celtics keep Tiny because he was their future? No. White went because his market value was greater—that was how far Tiny's stock had fallen.

But around the time of White's trade, at what was probably the franchise's lowest point in its history, there was a brief respite from the horror of that terrible year as the Celtics played a stretch of basketball that, for one short week or so, looked forward to the renaissance that was to come. Significantly, Tiny was at the point during that stretch, directing a starting five that included Chris Ford at off guard, Cowens at center and Rowe and Maxwell at forwards. Finding the kind of team rhythm essential to success, the Celtics won six out of seven in late January (one-fifth their total victories that season). Two offensive sets were particularly effective during that streak: a wide alignment, with Cowens at the high post looking inside to feed Maxwell, who had become a star in the league his second season; and a one-four set, which gave Tiny the freedom to operate one-on-one and to create. With Tiny up top and Max down low, the Celtics had a couple of powerful offensive weapons, and for that short period fans unwittingly saw two elements that would become key to Boston's future success.

The cheerless acquisition of Bob McAdoo quickly stifled whatever promise those six games held out for the Celtics, but the departure of White and the short spell of success gave Tiny new hope. Though he welcomed the end of that awful season (as everyone did), he looked forward to the following and arrived to camp in excellent shape and even better frame of mind. In the general purge of the off-season, Auerbach and Fitch had refused to prejudge their feisty point guard, and Tiny responded well to their faith in him. What he needed, what he had always needed, was direction and leadership—exactly what Red was looking for from Fitch for the team as a whole. The new coach provided both at once. He began by releasing Rowe and continued by conducting one of the most demanding training camps ever. Red, of course, had always run his players hard: the Celtics teams of the fifties and sixties were always the best-conditioned teams in the NBA, conditioning that always paid off. While other teams played themselves into shape, the Celtics were usually bolting from the blocks, establishing a margin of comfort that would carry them into the playoffs. At the end of the year, when the most important games were on the line and the competition was fiercest, Red's teams always seemed to have a little bit more to give, even though the starters usually played 40-plus minutes a game all year long. Motivation and conditioning—these were the muscles for the bones of Auerbach's system.

Fitch carried on the tradition. From the beginning the Celtics had two-a-day practices, morning and evening. Each practice consisted of extensive running, including mile runs, wind sprints and "lines," exhausting sprints one-quarter, halfway, three-quarter and fully back and forth across the court. This running took place in the full summer heat, and even those men who had come to camp in good condition, like Tiny and Bird, showed the pain in their faces. Basketball drills followed immediately: standard full-court figure eights, controlled fast-break drills, set offense practice. Fitch has always advocated a motion offense that depends on weaves and passes to set up an inside game, so his drills concentrated on passing, learning offensive patterns and establishing a rhythm reflective of team unity. His approach required time, patience and the cooperation of every player. It was mentally and physically demanding, particularly for a team with so many

Gerald Henderson. The team announced his signing on Draft Day, 1979, calling him "the equivalent of a first-round draft choice." After he was traded in 1984, Larry Bird, referring to Henderson's famous steal in the 1984 finals that turned the series in Boston's favor over Los Angeles, said, "He saved our ass."

new faces. As floor generals, the point guards came under a lot of pressure, and Fitch was constantly pulling Tiny and Gerald Henderson aside, emphasizing the little things, reinforcing their roles. That the veteran, the All-Star, showed as much enthusiasm and respect as the kid from the CBA who was trying desperately to impress was a testament to Tiny's desire and character.

The atmosphere in camp was excellent. Bird set the tone with his unstinting effort and relaxed attitude. He came to camp willing to play his own game, making creative passes and responding to the one-on-one challenges of the veterans. "That white boy can play!" Cedric Maxwell said after one vigorous battle, and M. L. Carr noted that this rookie acted like a veteran, playing with poise and confidence, joking with the others in a way that was natural. Not that he was perfect. Bird had to adjust to the new faces himself, and at times he had difficulty connecting with his passes or knowing where other players would appear in the new offense. He also suffered from a heavy cold throughout camp and went home each day exhausted, thinking only of sleep and practice the next day. He knew he had a job to do; he knew expectations were high. So he worked hard and watched the other players closely, learning from the veterans Cowens and Chaney, getting used to the moves of Max and Tiny and M. L.

Much of the renewed spirit and determination of that first Bird Era training camp was due to the presence of M. L. Carr, who had come to the Celtics from Detroit in a move that seemed destined in the stars above Boston Garden. A fan of the Celtics since his youth in Wallace, North Carolina, Carr had achieved the dream of playing in the NBA the hard way. Injuries, poor advice and deceptive coaches had kept him from making the league when he was first out of college, but he refused to lose his dream and worked his way through the old Eastern League, Israel and the ABA before landing a job with the Pistons. Once there he became a standout role player, a man who knew his strengths and weaknesses so well he always seemed to get the best out of himself. Full of determination and hustle, he was a defensive specialist who could also explode for quick offense off the fast break. In a noteworthy feat for a forward, he had led the league in steals in 1978-79. He was a smart player who knew his limitations and strengths better than anybody, and he always played with fire in his eyes.

Red had had his eye on M. L. for years, so his move to this new Celtics team was not a surprise; he would fit Red's blueprint perfectly. But the nuances surrounding Carr's acquisiton were manifold and tell us much about Auerbach's ability to judge character. The words "chemistry" and "character" are bandied about so much these days that it may seem strange so few teams actually have those traits. The Celtics' team personality has always been unique, mostly because of Red's keen sense of these extremely important qualities, a sense that informs every move he makes for the team. The Carr deal was a good example of Red's vision, but it was also a perfect illustration of how Red, in this new age of free agency and high-tech negotiations, had moved with the times and turned into the canniest ringmaster in the league.

Under league rules of the time, an NBA team that signed a free agent was required to give compensation to the old team (this

M. L. Carr with Larry Bird on the Celtics' bench. "They talk of Celtics pride, mystique, loyalty and so on; well, M. L. Carr happens to have all these wonderful characteristics," Red Auerbach said. Bird called Carr his "best teammate."

rule later changed to the current Right of First Refusal). But because the terms of the compensation were worked out after an agreement had been reached with the individual player, negotiations could be difficult for the new team. They obviously wanted the free agent, otherwise they would not have signed him. That put the old team in the position of being able to demand a good player in return—with the commissioner serving as arbitrator. Red, however, managed to turn the tables, investing the compensation discussions with the complexity of a trade and extracting the maximum benefit, as usual, for the Celts.

Auerbach knew that Detroit coach Dick Vitale craved Bob McAdoo, so he offered the star to the Pistons. Perfect: the Celtics rid themselves of a major liability just as they acquired a player who was a real Celtic. But Red didn't stop there. Never a man to judge players by their statistics, he was suddenly very keen to point out that McAdoo was a three-time NBA scor-

ing champion, a former league MVP (1975) and the proud owner of an impressive 27.4 career scoring average. Carr's 14.8 career average and thin NBA experience looked puny by comparison—on paper anyway—and Red used the discrepancy to wheedle the Pistons' 1980 first-round draft choice out of them. Knowing that the lowly Pistons were likely to have a poor season, Red must have known how valuable that draft choice would become. As it happened, he would use it to create one of the biggest deals in Celtics history.

But the McAdoo deal had further ramifications that are not as easy to delineate because they involve one of the most complex and controversial issues in the game. That McAdoo did not have an easy time with Celtics fans is understandable. Like Rowe, he was a scapegoat of sorts, and it is probably safe to say that he did not give 100 percent during his brief time in Boston—after all, what incentive did he have? Boston fans are known for their hard-nosed, heckling style, and McAdoo must have gotten exasperated with many of them, especially the fan who repeatedly yelled, "McAdoo, McAdon't, McAwill, McAwon't." But this kind of derision, as hard as it can be to put up with, comes with the territory, and if McAdoo or anyone else couldn't take it then he shouldn't have been making a living in the NBA. But occasionally this attitude became unacceptable by any standard, moving into stereotype and shading close to racism, particularly when people started talking about the "negative influence" of McAdoo and other black veterans on young players like Cedric Maxwell.

Max had emerged as a real star in his second year on the club, averaging nearly 20 points a game and developing an inside game so tenacious that Bob Ryan of the *Boston Globe* would later describe those who had to defend him as entering "Cedric Maxwell's low-post house of horrors." The brass saw Max as a very important part of the team's future, and they were worried that the team's poor attitude during the 1978-79 season would have a detrimental effect on the young player. McAdoo, while he may not have been an ideal role model, was a natural idol for Cedric: both were from North Carolina; both played in McAdoo's summer league; McAdoo was one of the premier stars in the NBA when Max was cutting his teeth in college and looking forward to a pro career; both were black. McAdoo naturally drew the respect and emulation of Maxwell, and there was concern inside and outside the organization that the veteran's transient situation and perceived lax attitude might affect the franchise's key player.

As long as concern for Max stayed in the realm of individual influence, this worry was certainly legitimate. But when uninformed fans and observers moved beyond the individual case and started making judgements on the basis of a stereotype, then there was a problem. As it happened, many of the unhappy players on the Celtics during those years were black—not surprising in a league that was 80 percent black to begin with. McAdoo, Jo Jo White, Curtis Rowe, Sidney Wicks, Tom Boswell and Charlie Scott—all important players, all veterans—often made no secret of their dissatisfaction with the team and their places on it. And when veterans are dissatisfied they usually don't

Cedric Maxwell, University of North Carolina-Charlotte, 1976. A superstar at the amateur level, Maxwell carried UNCC to third place in the NIT, where he won MVP honors, and took Charlotte to the Final Four of the NCAA in 1977.

have a positive effect on the younger players around them. But to move beyond this simple observation of fact to the blanket generalization of "negative influence" along racial lines is very dangerous, and many critics went even further, implying that not playing a team game was a black characteristic. This kind of prejudice, though it might never be expressed openly, communicates itself quickly, and the players, who already felt defensive about living in a city not known for its benign racial climate, usually responded with belligerence. The vibes were not good.

The whole situation was exacerbated by the league's position at the time. The NBA was certainly not doing very well. Many teams were struggling to stay solvent, and fan interest had ebbed considerably. While pro football and baseball were booming, pro basketball was having trouble promoting itself as a major league, with several league cities televising The Finals, the pinnacle of the NBA year, on a tape-delay basis. The league's image was not moving forward, and it was difficult to say why. Revenues were desperately needed, but the league had a lot of problems landing a CBS contract. Meanwhile, there was a peculiar brand of logic invading discussions of the situation, a logic that argued that the league was not doing well because the prominent players were chiefly black. In the three decades since Chuck Cooper's signing with the Celtics, the NBA had gone from 100 percent white to nearly 80 percent black. Just as play had evolved from a plodding Midwestern style to a free-flowing urban game, so too had the league's major category leaders and stars tended to be almost exclusively black—Marques Johnson, Kareem Abdul-Jabbar, Moses Malone, George Gervin, Elvin Hayes, Julius Erving. Fortunately, NBA coaches and owners remained committed to winning, committed to drafting the best players available, regardless of race. But the reasoning persisted.

As it happens, the whole notion of race being the reason for the league's decline has been seriously brought into question by the events of the last ten years. In that span, the NBA has turned around fully, proving it is a major league. Using modern marketing techniques, wiser money management and knowledgeable use of new media technology, the league has refurbished its image and built itself a sound fiscal base. While it may not rival football, it has increased its popularity and generated the belief that the finest athletes in America play basketball. In the meantime, of course, the percentage of black players has remained about the same, suggesting that the league's former woes have been badly misrepresented.

But this analysis begs a very important question. If the racial composition did affect the popularity of the league, what difference would it make? Who could possibly advocate a quota system designed to improve attendance? Who would ever suggest that the number of white players be arbitrarily increased? Because unless you're willing to make those kinds of changes, you're not going to alter the league's racial balance—if that is what you want. But the pursuit of the best players possible is the *minimum* we as fans have a right to expect. Anything less is compromise. Anything less is racism. This does not mean that race is not a factor when putting a team together. As the history of the Celtics clearly shows, the personalities and cultural backgrounds of individual players are important to on-court performance, and a wise coach or general manager must consider everything. But racism is not only morally repugnant—it is damaging on the much less important level of winning basketball games as well.

Red Auerbach presents the classic winning attitude. Always color blind, he goes after the players he feels will best fit the Celtics' system. The black players mentioned above were, for a variety of reasons, not fitting into the system, so they had to go. But Tiny stayed; Chaney stayed; and M. L. Carr replaced McAdoo. Red probably saw that M. L., a true Celtic if ever there was one, might also exert a positive influence on Max. He too was from North Carolina. He too was black. Being a realist, Red knew that black players hang around with each other more; there is a shared core of custom, language and culture that goes a long way towards keeping the strangeness of an alien city at bay. As it turned out, Maxwell willingly ceded his uniform number to Carr—the 30 that Carr had worn since high school. Max and M. L. did become close friends. But Carr was also close to Chris Ford and Dave Cowens. Any attempt at dividing that team into separate groups always broke down. A big part of the success of that first Bird Era team was its closeness, its blend of players who respected themselves and respected each other, without regard to age, background or race.

The respect grew even before the final cuts. As the scrimmaging began and the intensity heightened, Fitch kept his crew working constantly. Before the cuts there were four teams, and the games continued well into the late summer nights. It was here that Fitch made his final decisions about who would stay; it was here that the rookies and free agents showed whether or not they could cut it on this new, vigorous Celtics team. As the first camp came to a close the eleven who would stay emerged: Cowens and Chaney, Ford, Tiny, Henderson, M. L., Maxwell, Robey, Fernsten, Jeff Judkins and a solitary rookie by the name of Bird.

After the final cut the drills, running and scrimmaging did not let up. Fitch was even harder on the players who had survived, and the second camp continued at the same intense pace as the players worked themselves into outstanding shape and learned Fitch's motion offense by heart. For 14 straight days they kept at the two-a-days, supplementing their workouts with sessions in the weight room, extra shooting or treatment. It was soon clear that there was a cohesiveness and spirit to this group in keeping with the Celtics tradition, and though the fans may not have known it the players did. With what little free time they had, the new men in town found homes and tried to get to know Boston, but the most important matter at hand was the approaching preseason, and their initial game with the Philadelphia 76ers, the Atlantic Division's reigning powerhouse.

That game was important on several levels: it was the first game of the Bird Era; it was Fitch's first game as the Celtics' coach; it was the first game of what would become a renewed Celtics-Sixers rivalry; and it was Larry Bird's first game as a professional basketball player. Played in Madison Square Garden, in the heart of the sports media capital of the country, the game was a showcase of sorts. On display were the two teams that were going to dominate the Eastern Division for the next five years, and the two players who carried most of their club's expectations: the most highly touted rookie to enter the NBA since Lew Alcindor, and the preeminent player in the game—Julius Erving, Doctor J.

It was inevitable that Larry be compared to the Doc. Anyone with Bird's background could only be expected to measure up against the best in the business, and in 1979 there was no one better than Erving. Elegant, hard-working, his ego always under control, Julius Erving brought a touch of class and a talent as smooth as a fingertip roll to every game he played. From his rookie season with the ABA Virginia Squires, when he averaged over 33 points per

Doctor J and Larry Bird, 1980 playoffs. As the Sixers extracted revenge in the postseason for Boston's regular-season triumph, Erving declared, "Boston won the regular season. Now it's our turn."

game in the playoffs, to his move to the NBA after the merger, the Doc was always a force. He had not been without struggle—after his move to Philadelphia he had had his differences with the spectacular Sixer guard Lloyd Free, and he had suffered a tough knee injury. But in 1979 he was at his peak: the star of one of the best teams in the league, healthy, 29 years old. Teams were adjusting to *him* as his talents fit into the new environment. Like all the greats, he came into the league with immense talent and proceeded to work at his weaknesses as if he were a 12th man. His hang time and creative stuffs are legendary, but his outside shot, team play and tough defense made him a complete player. Winning was number one with him, and like Bird he always brought out the best in his fellow players. For Bird to have to guard Doc that first night was a true baptism, and Larry was equal to the task.

Though fans did not know it yet, Bird had already made the transition to the pro game. As Fitch said many times, Larry Bird was never a rookie. The instincts, work ethic, fundamentals and raw talent ensured his success, and the ease with which he fit into the system was matched only by the hours he put in. He was the first to arrive to practice, the last to leave. Even by Fitch's slavish standards he worked very, very hard. The trauma of moving to Boston was not as great as that first move to Bloomington in 1974, but it was still an intimidating experience to an Indiana boy, in spite of the paternal guidance of his agent, Bob Woolf. Bird compensated as he always did, by channeling his energy into the steambath of Fitch's practices. But the true test for any rookie is on the court, and Bird must have felt some apprehension as the preseason approached and he contemplated guarding the greatest player in the game while the New York media watched every offensive move of his own. It was time to prove himself.

He acquitted himself well. The Sixers beat the Celtics soundly, 115-90, but the preseason is the one time in the basketball year when "W"'s and "L"'s are less important than self-discovery. Coaches are testing their players and their systems. Players are testing themselves and their opponents. It was time for Bird to see what he and his rivals could do. He started the game cautiously. "I went out there and all I could think about was stopping Julius Erving," he said after the game. "I wasn't thinking about my offense at all." But when Erving missed his first three shots Bird began to feel more self-assured. The first basket of his pro career came 4:19 into the game, a high lay-up off the glass, in traffic, which foreshadowed the thousands of perfectly timed field goals he was going to cash in over the next decade. The flashbulbs snapped, the crowd let loose a *whooooo*, and the Bird Era was christened.

Bird finished with 18 points and a respectable defensive job on the Doc. After the game Erving had this to say about the new kid on the block: "I guess the best thing to say is that he can play. He's what he's supposed to be; what you've read about. You feel the intensity he has. He moves; he can create his own offense. And he was talking all the time out there. I have a very favorable opinion of him as a player." Bird's own reaction as the media blitz enveloped him? "I'm just glad it's over."

Bird's modesty and obvious respect for his opponents were an important part of the maturity he brought to the pro game.

Whatever troubles he may have had with the media, or with adjusting to the harassed life of a public figure in a big city, on the court he always had poise. It helped that he was 23 years old, but his attitude would have been excellent at any age. As the preseason continued, it quickly became apparent to anyone who knew anything about the game that this attitude was characteristic of the team in general. This was a team that, from very early on, had a clear self-image and a knowledge of exactly what it had to do to win. Each player knew his role. Maxwell, recognizing Bird's prowess from the outside, further refined his inside game and his skill on the offensive glass. Cowens, in the final year of a stellar career, continued to be outstanding on the boards. Chris Ford became the ideal off guard—tough defensively, with a deadly three-point shot and an excellent feel for being at the right place at the right time. His role freed up Tiny, who finally had the starting unit he needed, one that allowed for one-on-one freedom and a range of effective offensive alternatives. With the benefits of Fitch's tough practices in their legs and the knowledge of his system in their heads, this starting five had the potential of being one of the best in basketball. Off the bench, M. L. Carr gave hustling, quality minutes, and Rick Robey, perhaps the biggest surprise of the preseason, was a 6-11, 230-pound rock underneath with an unusually dextrous touch.

The team's most important virtue, though less tangible, was just as easy to see. As the preseason's good news continued, reporters remembered, perhaps with some embarrassment, how they had laughed back in May when, at Fitch's first press conference, Red Auerbach had said, "There's a whole new *spirit* here! We have it in mind to turn everything around.'' Why, they asked themselves now, had they doubted Red this time? As usual, his prognosis had been correct, and they started to look at the upcoming regular season with anticipation. They were not going to be disappointed.

The NBA of 1979 was a lot different from the league of ten years earlier, when Russell's retirement closed the book on the Celtics' 13-year domination and Red Auerbach was scouting a red-headed center at Florida State. The decade of the seventies was not a bad one for Boston—the team won two championships, something only the great Knicks team of that era was also able to achieve—but not even Red's genius could overcome the peculiar parity that existed for ten years in the NBA. In the forties and early fifties, it was the Minneapolis Lakers who dominated play; the late fifties and sixties belonged to Boston; and the eighties have been all Boston and L. A. But in that interim decade a parade of teams claimed the NBA crown: Milwaukee, L. A., Golden State, Portland, Washington and Seattle joined the Celtics and Knicks as champions. And the turnstile at the top was not an accident: the league had changed significantly. Some of the changes were part of the natural evolution of the game; others were the result of outside cultural and economic influences. Some purists have argued that these changes were not for the better, claiming that the decline in fan interest during this period was a direct response to a decline in the league itself. But there is no doubt that this era saw some of the most exciting basketball ever played, and played by men who will go down as some of the game's greatest all-time stars.

There was certainly more talent in the NBA than ever before. The rise of corporate sports in America in the sixties and the opening up of the game culturally had ensured the league of bigger, better players. Pro basketball had become very physical, and the men providing the muscle were not clumsy giants with hands of stone—they were big, quick, strong players who combined brute strength, speed and excellent athletic ability in a way that transformed the game. As Auerbach had realized as early as 1950, when he drafted seven-foot Charlie Share, having a dominating big man had always been a key to success in the NBA. But now size was essential at every position. The 1978 Finals had featured two teams with bullish frontcourts, and Seattle's rocklike line of Jack Sikma, Lonnie Shelton and Paul Silas had simply worn down Washington's Wes Unseld, Elvin Hayes and Bobby Dandridge. Every quality team had its Moses Malone or Maurice Lucas or Truck Robinson, and success in the league meant having at least one top-notch power forward as well as a center with muscle and finesse.

But the forwards weren't the only players getting bigger. The NBA backcourt was also undergoing a transformation, with men as tall as 6-8 or 6-9 taking the ball upcourt, running the offense and knocking home long-range jumpers. Unless he had the exceptional playmaking ability of a Tiny Archibald or a Gus Williams, the six-foot guard was suddenly a rare commodity, and you almost never saw two small men on the court at the same time. David Thompson, George Gervin and Dennis Johnson set the standard, and the arrival of Magic Johnson in 1979 gave the league its quintessential modern guard—a big man with all the skills of a point guard, off guard and power forward. In an age of specialization, the reverse was happening in the NBA—the game was moving towards the era of the complete player, reflected in the sudden popularity of the triple double (double-figure stats in three categories for a game) and the freer use of players in different positions.

Where had these new players come from? How had big men developed such abilites? The evolution of the college game had a lot to do with it. During the sixties and early seventies college basketball had become big business, with lucrative television contracts stoking the fires of an already blazing college sports system. In an era of academic decline to begin with, many colleges found it conveniently easy to ignore the academic requirements of their athletic recruits, many of whom came from deprived educational backgrounds as it was. Virtual professionals, these college stars took advantage of the generous facilities and excellent training that their scholarship-rich schools provided, and comprehensive recruiting programs and booster-fed budgets brought the best athletes in the country into the nation's schools, where they usually didn't have to spend much time studying. Such a system fed the NBA with better, bigger athletes—at the expense, of course, of the 99 percent who could not make it into the NBA, many of whom left college with a poor education and no skills to fall back on.

The economic environment of the league was also changing, attracting better athletes. Earlier in the decade, salaries had shot up when the ABA provided market competition for the older league. The trend continued, aided by better player organization and the general socioeconomic surroundings of American

sport. David Thompson, then at the height of his game, reportedly received an $800,000 per-year contract from the Denver Nuggets during the 1978 postseason. Suddenly, an athlete making a million dollars a year—an unheard-of figure just a few years before—became a very real possibility. Boosted by this rise (and smaller rosters compared with the other major sports), the NBA's average salary quickly became higher than either football or baseball, and the nation's best athletes looked to the NBA first.

But the rise in salaries also brought disruption, and the absence of a dominant team in the seventies was due in good part to a more sophisticated business environment, the development of sounder player representation and the rise of free agency, all of which had a dramatic impact on an NBA team's operation. More than ever before, a team's ability to win depended as much on off-court business as it did on on-court performance. Acquiring the right players, keeping them contractually satisfied and assembling a sound fiscal structure became of paramount importance. There were important new questions: How would a coach exercise authority over a player who earned ten times as much as he did? How would the team as a whole react to a high-priced free agent? How would labor-management relations affect the game on the floor? The seventies was very much a decade of transition, and the best teams of the eighties had general managers who could answer these questions and act on their answers with the minimum friction on the court.

Finally, the NBA was much different in 1979 because of the successful creation of the American Basketball Association earlier in the decade. Having an alternative market for their skills gave the good players coming out of college an ideal negotiating tool, which they and their agents used to get more money, freedom and clout. It also forced the NBA to modify its relationship to the college game. Colleges have always been a kind of minor league for the pros, but before the ABA came along the NBA was able to make the rules, forcing players to stay in college before they could play pro ball. To the NCAA's horror, the new league successfully challenged the status quo, invoking the principle of the free market as it went after players in the midst of college careers—even players just coming out of high school. College recruiters now had rivals with the benefits of the marketplace and without the hypocrisy of the NCAA. Off the stars went, and the NBA, after paying lip service to their old policy, quickly followed suit, disguising their capitulation under the euphemism of ''hardship cases,'' a term that fooled no one.

The ABA had a big effect on the court as well. Part of the new league's success had been its ability to attract some of the top players in the game, even though the overall standard lagged behind that of the NBA. Doctor J, Gervin, Thompson, Artis Gilmore, George McGinnis, Marvin Barnes and Larry Kenon were definitely as good as anyone in the NBA. Against the weaker competition of the ABA they looked even better, and a freer game, with balletlike flights through the air, stylish dunks and spirited running, developed. After the merger in 1976, these players brought that style, with its great fan appeal and its roots in urban playground ball, into the NBA. The game has been better for it.

All of these changes were neatly symbolized by the Celtics' first regular-season opponent of the 1979-80 season, the Houston Rockets, and by the Rockets' finest player at the time, Moses Malone. One of the new breed of big, rugged players with all the offensive skills needed to dominate, Malone has always had the ability to carry a team. Since joining the ABA directly out of his St. Petersburg, Virginia, high school in 1974, he has had the classic post-Russell career, moving from club to club through the lucrative route of free agency or its threat, playing the kind of power post-up game for which he is perfectly equipped. Even before he went on to become the classic Celtics nemesis, Moses was one of the most feared players in the game. Big, strong, relentless underneath, he was the best rebounder in the league. His prowess off the offensive glass and his array of inside moves sent him to the free throw line constantly, and he complemented his inside game with a delicate, accurate outside shot that belied his size. With the exception of Wes Unseld, no center had his combination of strength and touch and size.

Long celebrated for his move to the pros out of high school, Malone proved that college experience was not essential. Unlike Darryl Dawkins, another celebrated high school graduate, Malone was mature enough to handle professional competition at that young age. From his beginnings with the Utah Stars, he was able to keep pace with the stars of the ABA and soon became one of the new league's top players. But he did not do well in other respects. The media onslaught that accompanied the age of hype was not kind to someone whose communication skills did not match his physical ones, and as a result Malone was often misrepresented in the press. Self-conscious, unsure of himself, he turned surly and defensive under the inevitable pressure of stardom. In a way, his predicament represented the clash of cultures that afflicted the NBA in the seventies and contributed to the occasional lapses into racism. Very much the product of his rural, cloistered background, Malone entered the heady world of professional basketball at precisely the time it was becoming all glitz and glitter. Not content to let his game speak for itself, the media often chose to ridicule Malone. It was a tough situation for someone so young, and judging from the problems many men still have entering the NBA, it is still not something the league or our culture has sufficiently addressed.

Naturally, his problems affected his play, but when the leagues merged and Moses came to Houston in 1976—by means of a complex trade involving Portland and Buffalo—he rejoined coach Tom Nissalke, who had had a lot of success with Malone in Utah. The Rockets, who had gone 40-42 the previous season, flowered with Moses in the pivot and won the Central Division in 1977 with a 49-33 record, only to lose to the 76ers in the playoffs. The next few years were erratic, but Malone remained outstanding, consistently putting up excellent stats and winning the MVP award in 1978-79.

In spite of having the strongest player in the league at the center position, the Rockets, like every NBA team in the seventies, found it hard to win consistently. They too were trying to adjust to the free agent system, the escalated salaries and the disruptions brought on by the frequent movement of players. It was around this time that the term "chemistry" started to pop up in pep talks and sports columns all over the country, as if the concept had never existed before. In other language it had always been a working principle of Red Auerbach's, as any Celtics fan knew. But in the new NBA its absence was so obvious that it became an obsession—at least in what people *said* about the game. On the court the unselfish play, group experience and good coaching that creates winning chemistry was harder than ever to achieve. The new environment often brought out the selfish streak in players and moved them around at a clip that made team experience a scarce commodity and coaching an even more difficult task. For example, the turnover of personnel in Houston during those years was considerable, and when the Rockets arrived in Boston to face the Celtics in the opening game of the 1978-79 season Malone's support was a patchwork of rookies and free agents. But then didn't that describe almost every team in the league around that time? Didn't it describe the Celtics themselves? In the new NBA, where tradition was harder than ever to maintain, success had become very unpredictable. As it happened, these two teams were two short years away from a classic showdown in The Finals. This game would serve as a foreshadowing of a new rivalry.

Before the game the lockerroom was a mixture of established ritual and new detail. Tense and anxious, players reviewed videotape of a previous Houston game while they wrapped limbs, read fan mail and changed into the traditional green and white. Anticipating the media attention that would surround the rookie star, Dave Cowens changed his locker from the corner, near Bird's, to the opposite side of the room. To people who had been around the Celtics over the previous two years, there was a discernible change in atmosphere, a confidence and sense of meaning derived from steady practice and a rising recognition of team identity. By the time Fitch walked to the front of the small room to deliver his first regular-season pregame talk, the players had assumed the blank game faces that masked an intense focusing on the task at hand.

Fitch detailed strategy and spoke briefly about the league's new three-point rule (during the game, Chris Ford would score the first three-point goal in NBA history). Turning to the chalkboard, he went through the Rockets' personnel—Malone, Rick Barry, Calvin Murphy, Rudy Tomjanovich, Tommy Henderson, the rookie Robert Reid. Then he named the Celtics' starting line-up: Cowens, Ford, Maxwell, Archibald and Bird. He paused briefly before mentioning Bird's name, then added that the rookie had earned the spot during the preseason. Nothing would be assumed under the Fitch reign but the need for hard work. The athletes gathered around their coach, joined hands and shouted, "*Let's go!*"

The Celtics jumped out to a quick 13-6 lead that night and maintained a comfortable margin through three quarters behind the fast-breaking attack of Bird and Archibald. Cowens did what he had to do against Malone, using his own strength, quickness and experience to position himself and make the big man work for every point he scored. Going into the fourth quarter with a ten-point lead, the Celtics hit a dry spell, and the Rockets rallied behind Moses, who would finish the night with 31 points. With 8:43 left in the game the lead stood

at four. It was at this critical juncture that the practice and emotion invested during the five weeks of training camp and the long preseason paid off. With Cowens working with five fouls, M. L. came off the bench to spark the club, hitting two key baskets and feeding Maxwell for another big hoop. Milking the lead they had again expanded to double figures, the Celts went into the lockerroom with a 114-106 victory, whooping and high-fiving as if they had won The Finals.

Auerbach joined the team in the lockerroom immediately. He had seen the season's keystone laid, and he was looking to the future, to the building of a champion. "What we're trying to do here is rebuild our image. We're going to be competitive...Whether it will happen for us today, tomorrow or down the road I don't know, but we're heading in the right direction."

For the time being the direction was on the road, where the Celtics, so inept in enemy arenas the previous year, would play seven of their next nine games. The following night's game was in Cleveland, a homecoming of sorts for Fitch and another critical test for the team. Boston went right at the Cavaliers, led by Bird and Cowens. The rookie shot 11 for 15 from the field, mostly long outside jumpers. Cowens, who had recovered his old agility and confidence in his shot, scored most of his 20 down the stretch as the Celtics won convincingly, 139-117. Carr again played a key late-game role as Fitch showed a confidence in his bench that would become a pattern that season. After two games the Celtics had arrived.

In those early games a number of things became clear. Cowens had emerged as a leader, playing with scrap and hustle and setting an example for the rest of the team.

Bird was obviously no rookie: the confidence he had exhibited in the preseason carried over into the regular season without a hitch. The team's confidence was there from the start, and it quickly established an elegant perimeter passing game and a sticky defense. Fitch's liberal substitution encouraged the kind of offense he liked, one that was also superbly fitted to the team's personnel: a fast-breaking, motion offense that allowed for a number of options off the set. Fitch was not afraid to go with the tiny tandem of Henderson and Archibald on occasion. Running and discipline—these were the linchpins of Fitch's philosophy.

The early season was one test after another for the reborn Celtics, and a pair of contests against the Washington Bullets sandwiched around that first road trip were particularly important. NBA champions in 1978 and Eastern Division champs the previous season, the Bullets had a big veteran club, with Wes Unseld, Elvin Hayes, Kevin Grevey and Greg Ballard leading the charge. The fervor with which the Celtics went after the Bullets in the first game further contributed to the "image" Red had described. Cowens was all over the court, diving for loose balls, whipping around Hayes with his classic reverse spin move in the post. Behind Archibald, Boston ran at every opportunity and took the Bullets apart, 130-93.

There is a certain intensity surrounding championship-caliber teams, an aura that sets them above their rivals. It is what Bobby Knight was referring to when he said, "Great teams play against the game, not against their competition." In only four games, the Celtics had demonstrated that intensity, playing with the high pride the Bullets had displayed the two previous

seasons. The second game against the Bullets concluded a successful road trip (after losing to Indiana and San Antonio, the Celts had run off three straight against Houston, Atlanta and New Jersey, with Maxwell playing superbly and Bird continuing his mature play), and brought the Celtics to the Capital Centre averaging 119.8 points per game, second in the league. The players were proud of the wins—"We took a lot of bad beatings on the road last year," Chris Ford said—but they saw the second Bullets' contest as crucial. "A victory over the Bullets," Fitch remarked, "might have a lasting consequence...for the entire season." It was a test.

Chris Ford, Detroit, 1974. Asked about the trade that sent him from Detroit to Boston in 1978 in exchange for Earl Tatum, Ford replied, "I was glad to go to Boston, but don't ever believe any player is fully happy about being traded. There's a feeling of rejection."

54

The Celtics passed easily—in both senses of the word. Registering 40 assists out of 50 field goals, they ran the veteran club off the court, finishing off the Bullets with a 12-2 run late in the game. Maxwell led the scoring with 22; Bird, according to Fitch, played a "fantastic" game with 18 points and 11 rebounds. "I'm starting to believe we're for real," Red said. It showed. In the *Boston Globe* Bob Ryan wrote, "Red Auerbach looks as if he just discovered oil oozing out of his kitchen tap."

Off to a 9-2 start, trailing the first-place Philadelphia 76ers by half a game, the Celtics were authentic, proving they could win on the road against the best teams in the league. Defeating Kansas City and San Antonio the following week, they prepared for their next test—a game at the Spectrum against the Sixers. If the early part of this new season had shown the Bullets as a team in decline, then it had also established the Sixers as the team to beat. Boston would join them as the cream of the East by season's end, but at this early stage no one had any idea of the rivalry this game was about to kick off, a rivalry which would generate both respect and violence, which would extend from the floor to the press to the front office, which would involve the best players in the game over the next seven years.

This first game, intense and well played, set the tone for the years to come. The Sixers led throughout the contest, extending their lead to 15 early in the fourth quarter as Fitch searched for a combination that could battle back. A unit of Bird, Maxwell, Robey, Henderson and Judkins finally clicked, reeling off 13 unanswered points in four minutes to close the gap to 82-80. Now, in a way that would become so familiar in the years to come, each possession became focused and precise. Again the 76ers pulled away; again the Celts came back, using two jumpers by the seldom-used Judkins to pull within one. Boston stopped Philadelphia next time down but betrayed their inexperience by waiting 13 seconds before calling a timeout and then failing to convert. Erving then backed Bird in and scored on a jump hook to give Philly a 95-92 lead. Bird answered with a leaner in the lane, and when Cowens pulled down his 14th rebound on an Erving miss the Celtics had the final shot of the game and a chance to win.

How many Celtics games would come down to the wire over the next decade? How many times would fans hold their breath as the inevitable pass went to Bird and the inevitable creative shot found its way to the net or the back of the rim? Even this early in the Bird Era the Celts knew whom to go to. When the Celtics had trailed, 82-67, Fitch had turned to Robey on the bench and said, "We're going to win." Now, during the timeout called after Cowens's rebound, Fitch plotted the winning strategy: a sideline jumper for Bird. But with Bobby Jones in his face, Bird could not square himself for the shot, which hit the front of the rim. Cowens rebounded with two seconds remaining, shot while still in the air...and missed. Caldwell Jones gathered in the ball as time ran out. Philly had taken the first game of the new rivalry in classic fashion. Erving had led the team with 37 points, ten rebounds and eight assists. But Boston had proven that the run for the Atlantic Division crown would be well contested.

A year before, such a defeat would have demoralized the team; this year it strengthened its determination and unity.

Boston went on to win nine of its next 11 contests, including an important pair of road wins in Indiana and Atlanta. Carr continued to excell under pressure, making a key defensive play and snaring a big offensive rebound in the closing moments of a win over New York. Against Detroit, in one of the most dramatic plays of the whole era, he pulled down a missed Cowens three-point attempt with 11 seconds left and the Celts trailing, 108-105. Racing the clock, he dribbled into the corner and fired up another three-pointer. This one riffled through the net as time expired, and Boston went on to win in overtime.

Those early games in Year One of the Bird Era had a level of excitement completely free of expectation. No one thought the Celtics would do *this* well. As the wins mounted up, the team's confidence grew, and its ability to perform well in close games grew with it. The Celts had proven to themselves and to the city they represented that they were for real, that the spirit was there. Capturing the imagination of Boston, they brought basketball back to the Garden and passion back to the fans—what *Boston Globe* columnist Leigh Montville called "the passion of first love." Looking to the years ahead, Montville captured the wonder of the first year, pointing out that "no matter how good this team might become in the future, the atmosphere will not be as exciting because the standard will be so much higher."

With each win, the team grew more certain of its destiny. When Ford sank a buzzer-beater from near halfcourt to beat Don Nelson's own resurging Milwaukee Bucks, 97-94, the players returned to the lockerroom shouting at the tops of their voices. That win gave them a 23-7 record and a one-game lead over Philadelphia. Not only was the team doing well—the players were enjoying themselves. Every game seemed to have a dramatic finish; every player seemed to have his day. But as the All-Star break approached, the leaders who emerged were the rookie and the veteran, Bird and Cowens.

Cowens was pushing himself to the limit and beyond, and no one appreciated this more than Red, who knew a winner when he saw one. After the center clinched a win over Phoenix, Auerbach sought him out in the hallway between the lockerroom and the training area. Grabbing him by the arms he said, "Dave, you're playing beautifully!" The significance of the veteran giving it his all in the last year of his career was not lost on the Celtics' guiding light.

Nor was the effort of Bird. He had already established himself as the controlling force on the team (his role would expand even further when Cowens went down for six weeks with an injured toe). He was looking to shoot the ball; he was creating opportunities for his teammates; he was setting up shop underneath and battling for boards. The stats were there—32 points and 18 rebounds against Cleveland; 31 points and 13 rebounds against New York; 19 points and 16 rebounds against New Jersey—and were certainly appreciated by the fans, but the biggest thrills came during those moments when he revealed his unerring basketball sense, his uncanny feel for the perfect move at split-second opportunities: the no-look pass to the teammate at the hoop; the touchdown pass following an opposing team's basket; the drive through the lane when, as he discovered himself covered, he bounced a pass to himself off the backboard or squeezed a shot off under a defender's arm. Solid *and* innovative, Bird was a leader by example on the court from the start.

The first half of the season was highlighted by a win over Philadelphia at home in late December, the first significant victory by the Celtics against the 76ers in nearly three years. Sparked by Archibald's masterful playmaking and brilliant team defense, Boston shot out to a 37-20 lead, which they maintained throughout. The 112-89 win increased their divisional lead to three games and convinced even the most cautious that this was a dream season. "I was very skeptical about this team," Maxwell said. "I mean, we were looking forward to turning things around, but this...this is just a plus, everybody coming together this way. All the turmoil, all the animosity of those two years is gone. It's beautiful."

The next test facing the Celtics was a pair of nationally televised contests against the best of the West: Magic Johnson and the Los Angeles Lakers on one Sunday, and the defending champion Seattle Supersonics the following Sunday. Boston had already lost to the Lakers earlier in the season, a 123-105 drubbing in the Forum. With newcomers Johnson and Michael Cooper, L.A. was in the middle of its own resurgence and well on its way to an NBA title that year. And the Magic-Bird matchup was newsworthy long before the two players ever donned pro uniforms. Who could forget the classic NCAA confrontation at the end of the 1978-79 season? A renewed rivalry was in the making, and Boston was eager to even the season series.

The Lakers had stiff competition in the West from Seattle. In spite of rumored tension surrounding guard Dennis Johnson, the SuperSonics seemed as strong as the previous year. Anchored by center Jack Sikma and forwards Lonnie Shelton and Paul Silas, Lenny Wilkens's champions played a physical game without sacrificing finesse. DJ, in spite of his problems, was already one of the premier guards in the league, a clutch player who played superb defense and had ice water in his veins during crunch time. Seattle would provide another challenge to the reborn Boston squad.

Boston prepared for these games with predictable enthusiasm and intensity. Most of the players had never been involved in a chase for the flag at this level,

Dave Cowens driving past Darryl Dawkins in a 129-110 victory over the Sixers in 1980. That year was a classic comeback season for Cowens, then in a veteran role. He would retire during the 1980-81 preseason and make a comeback with Milwaukee two seasons later.

and as it became clear that there fast start was more than just a fluke, the pressure—positive and negative—began to build. On a few occasions it blew up. In San Antonio, after a tough loss to the veteran Spurs in what is probably the most raucous arena in the NBA, Cowens and Bird ran into problems with some fans on the way to the bus. The game was the last of a two-week trip, and the players were tired. After listening to several shouts from drunken fans, Cowens asked some of them why they bothered harassing athletes. He should have known this was no place for reason—an alleged scuffle involving Cowens and Bird meant a return trip to San Antonio later in the season to settle the affair.

In January Cowens locked elbows with Tree Rollins during a game in the Garden. Heading up the floor, Cowens suddenly swung intensely at the big Atlanta Hawk, and the two of them were ejected. Though video evidence suggested that Rollins had provoked the fight, Cowens received a one-game suspension. Rollins, of course, had not had his last scuffle with a Boston player.

Bird and Cowens were tough competitors, and their scuffles were the by-product of their intensity. But the pressure to win in the NBA can be almost overwhelming, and the Celtics' enthusiasm at midseason was tempered by the realization that the greater their performance, the higher the expectations—of their fans, their coaches, themselves. In a business where success or failure is determined by the score of the game, the high of winning can be very fragile, especially when a team is young and inexperienced.

Boston lost both of those crucial Sunday contests, defeats that shook their collective confidence and called into question the surge to first place that had defined the first half of the season. Both losses were heartbreakers. Against L. A. the Celtics had a 16-point first-half advantage erased by a classic Lakers blitz of 21 unanswered points in the third quarter. Stabilizing their offense, the Celts stayed with the eventual champions to the end, tying the game behind Bird's heroics at 98-98. On the final possession, the Lakers isolated Norm Nixon on Tiny, who fouled the quick L. A. guard on his way to the hoop (Fitch was upset—he thought it was a touch foul). Nixon sank the two free throws, securing the win. The Celtics filed into the locker room absolutely silent. Before the game Tiny had jumped on a stool and shouted "blowout city," an expression of confidence rarely heard from the usually silent ballhandler. Now he watched Bill Fitch storm into the lockerroom with the tape of the game and play the final foul over and over again. Auerbach walked over to the coach, attempting to console him, but Fitch insisted on reliving the defeat.

The next day Fitch ran a strenuous practice and a long session at the VCR, trying to keep the championship aspirations alive and the anger fresh. But the following Sunday Boston lost another tense duel to Seattle, even though they did play well. Leading through most of the game, the Celts seemed to have victory sealed when Cowens hit a jump hook with ten seconds left, giving Boston a three-point lead. With a foul to waste, a big advantage when they knew the SuperSonics had to try for a three-pointer, Boston sweated through a confused timeout. After Cowens deflected the first inbounds pass, Seattle got the ball to Dennis Johnson as Carr and Archibald were entangled on a switch. As he would do more than once

DJ, 1980. Coming off his 1979 playoff MVP season, Johnson hit crucial shots in both meetings against Boston in the 1979-80 season.

for Boston in later years, DJ hit a clutch trifecta from the corner near the Celtics' bench. Seattle went on to win in double overtime, and suddenly the dream season was invaded by serious doubts.

Throughout the euphoria and occasional uncertainty, Bill Fitch was professionally steady, concentrating on doing his job and running the club the way he thought it should be run. In the general enthusiasm over the Celtics' rebirth, many fans failed to notice how well Auerbach and Fitch worked together in what could sometimes be a very delicate situation. Fitch was the first head coach in the Auerbach Era to come from outside the Celtics family. He brought a strong will and a calculated independence to the job; he respected tradition, but he also knew exactly what he wanted to do, what he *had* to do, to turn the team around. Red was eager to give Fitch room to work, but he also had the benefit of 30 years of Celtics experience that he knew could help the club. And yet what could have led to conflict went very smoothly that first year, with Fitch and Auerbach collaborating effectively as the team motored along near the top of the Atlantic Division.

The personnel decisions that Auerbach and Fitch made together usually turned out very well. Signing free agent Gerald Henderson was a big success. As a star of the Tuscon Gunners of the Western League, Henderson had come to the Celtics on draft day 1979—a year in which the Celtics did not have a first-round draft choice. Auerbach's claim that Henderson was the equivalent of a first-round pick may have been an overstatement, but it reflected the commitment of the team in the back-up guard.

Henderson was Fitch's type of player. He worked incessantly at practice, pushing himself through extra laps, lifts and shooting drills. Content with his reserve role, he played hard during his ten minutes or so per game and ran the offense well enough that Tiny wasn't missed. Sometimes he teamed with Archibald and adjusted well to the off-guard role. Personable and wry, he got on well with his teammates, and soon people were wondering how he had ever ended up in the minor leagues.

But the flip side of Henderson's success was the fading of Jeff Judkins. A second-round draft choice out of the University of Utah in 1978, Judkins was an angular, tough player with an accurate jump shot. As a rookie he had played well, averaging 8.8 points per game and impressing fans in an otherwise awful season. But Fitch was not the coach for him. After pressuring him in training camp over missed shots, the new coach never seemed to warm to the young player and buried him on the bench. His minutes cut by almost two-thirds, Judkins grew more and more frustrated. "I'm losing it," he complained to Maxwell, "and there's nothing I can do to change [Fitch's] mind."

Understandably, Fitch was thinking only of winning. He ran the team like a general, expecting his charges to do what they were told. His expectations could be unreasonable. Judkins would fade from the scene, a casualty of the reality of professional basketball. But without faith in Judkins, Fitch needed a guard off the bench, preferably a veteran with scoring punch who wouldn't object to a limited role. Auerbach gave him exactly that in February when he signed one of the legends of basketball, Pistol Pete Maravich.

It was both sad and ironic that Maravich should finish his career with the Boston Celtics: sad because he did not stay long enough to fulfill his dream of a championship; ironic because the man who many felt was the greatest individual guard in college basketball history ended his playing days with the quintessential *team*. And though Pistol Pete came to Boston eager to do his part, he too would run afoul of Fitch's expectations, proving long before it became obvious in Boston that Fitch was not the ideal coach for veterans.

Anyone who saw Maravich play at Louisiana State University will never forget it. His long hair hanging over his forehead, his white socks drooping around his ankles, he scored every which way and then some as he became a symbol of the era and the greatest gunner in college history with a 44.9 points-per-game average. Coached by his father Press, an intense man who some say used his son as a vehicle for his own ambition, Pete had free rein during those glory years and never saw a shot he didn't like or couldn't make. With Cousy-like moves, a lithe 6-4 body and tremendous court sense, Maravich played with audacious confidence and amazing control. He was glamorous, eccentric and bold.

Perhaps no player in NBA history arrived to the league surrounded by more controversy, envy and suspicion. He was

The late Pistol Pete Maravich, here scoring against Mike Newlin of Houston in 1978. Playing for his father and idol, Press Maravich, Pete averaged 44.2 points per game at LSU and went on to become a two-time NBA First Team All-Star. Though he failed to win a championship with Boston, he found inner peace through religion.

too good, prevailing opinion seemed to suggest; how could he possibly play a team game with those college numbers? How could he ever adapt to the rigors of a professional team after being babied by his father for four years? Maravich graduated at the perfect moment contractually—with the bidding war between the leagues at its height, he signed for big bucks with the Atlanta Hawks—and the handsome contract buttressed the envy of his critics. And the transition to the pro game was not easy. Although he did average over 23 points per game his rookie year, he struggled defensively and never got out from beneath a spotlight that did more harm than good. Atlanta traded him to the expansion New Orleans Jazz in 1974. He grew as a pro but never fully escaped the gunner rap, even when he won All-Pro honors in 1976 and 1977. A crippling knee injury in 1978 brought his career to a sudden stop. He was never the same player again.

After the Jazz moved to Salt Lake City and Maravich's knee improved to a point where his old form was evident, he ran into problems with Coach Tom Nissalke during the 1979-80 season. On a night when Maravich was to oppose the rookie star Magic Johnson, Nissalke benched him, commenting afterwards, "He can't run, he can't play defense, he can't help us." During a two-month exile on the bench Maravich negotiated for free agency. Like many veteran stars with outstanding individual careers, he wanted a ring before retiring, and he placed himself on the market with an understanding that he was willing to subordinate his own minutes for the sake of a share in a title.

Philadelphia and Boston, locked in a battle for the best record in basketball, became Maravich's final options. He passed a physical in Philly, and after several meetings the Sixers were so confident of signing him that they reportedly had a jersey made with his name sewn on the back. But as Billy Cunningham was on a local radio show discussing Pistol's probable role with the team, Sixers GM Pat Williams was trying to get him on the phone to tell him that it appeared certain that Maravich had changed his mind after meeting with Red Auerbach. The rivalry that had already been established with such intensity on the court was now moving to the front office, forming a tone that was to become more and more competitive as the years went on.

The Celtics players greeted the news with skepticism, but Fitch was convinced he needed another guard. He also insisted that Maravich work himself back into condition over two weeks before joining the roster, a move that left important questions hanging in the air longer than a Maravich dipsy-do: Who would be placed on the injured reserve list to make way for Maravich? How would the new guard fit into what had become a very successful unit? Would Pistol Pete's style disrupt the rhythm the team had worked so hard to achieve? As the team worked at overcoming the doubt bred by losses to the Lakers and SuperSonics, these questions increased the pressure of the race with Philadelphia over the second half of the season.

The way in which Boston continued to win, going on to garner the best record in the NBA that year, was a tribute to Fitch's coaching and the inspired play of a young team. Ironically, the night Maravich was signed, Cowens injured his toe in a game against the

Rockets. The leader on and off the court that season, the essential link with the Celtics tradition, Cowens was a tough man to lose. But his absence was amply compensated by the excellent play of backup center Rick Robey and the leadership and scoring prowess of Larry Bird.

It is easy today to think of Robey as an injury-prone big man who never fulfilled his NBA potential; as the second-rate center Red so skillfully used to bring Dennis Johnson to Boston in 1983. It is true that, as one Celtics executive put it, Robey "never *loved* the game enough to stay in game condition all the time." But in 1980 Robey was hungry, and when Cowens went down Robey established himself as a force, setting mountainous picks, taking up room underneath, pulling in bushels of rebounds—21 against Denver, 19 against Detroit. He ended up that season with career highs in points scored, minutes played and rebounds, and his contribution was key as the Celtics continued winning and maintained a slim lead over the 76ers in what had become the league's toughest division.

Bird, meanwhile, was lighting up arenas all over the league. Already a shoo-in for Rookie of the Year, he was proving to opponents that he owned an offensive arsenal second to nobody's. He scored 36 against the Clippers in Boston; he sparked an incredible 129-110 win over Philadelphia after Boston had trailed by 12; he established a career-high 45 against Phoenix. He led the team in scoring 18 times down the stretch and assumed the mantle as the next Celtics superstar. Cowens recognized the transition and gave it his blessing. "I remember Dave coming over to me," Bird said, "and telling me that I was playing some of the best basketball he'd seen *anybody* play. For a

veteran to tell a rookie that…well, that just lifted me right up. I never forgot that."

Bird, of course, was lifting the Celtics up, leading them to a 3-2 Western road trip and a gutsy victory over the Sixers in March. With the starting unit playing with renewed confidence and Maravich averaging over 11 points per game off the bench, Boston overcame its doubts and continued its winning ways. When Cowens returned for the final month of the season, the team's prospects looked very good. But after back-to-back losses to Cleveland and New Jersey, the division lead was down to two games with four to play. The final game of the season was in Philadelphia, and the Celtics feared having to clinch in the enemy arena. In its next game, against the veteran Bullets, Boston played like a champion, resisting an attacking Washington team all night and producing a big victory under pressure. The game ball (and perhaps the sole moment of true Celtics glory for the aging star) went to Maravich, who fired in 17 fourth-quarter points, including a game-winning three-pointer. For one night, at least, he felt close to that championship he so badly wanted.

Wins over New York and Cleveland seemed almost automatic now, and as the seconds wound down in the clinching victory over the Cavaliers, the bench stood, clapping, cheering and waving. Fitch and K. C. Jones embraced briefly, and then the head coach, a son of a truck driver and a former Marine, cried. It had to have been one of the best moments of his distinguished career (he would later be honored as Coach of the Year), but he was too conscious of what lay ahead to celebrate long. After the irrelevant season-ending loss to Philly (and a tribute from the Doc—"They were the best team"),

Fitch looked to the nine-day layoff and the prospects of steering a talented but inexperienced team into the first postseason of the Bird Era.

The layoff was welcome. Fitch himself—as intense a man as you'll find in the world of the NBA—was exhausted. Cowens had reinjured his toe in the game against New York and, like Bird, had lost weight in the season's final month. Archibald, after establishing himself as the league's best point guard, also suffered from fatigue. So the coach granted two days off before gathering the team beneath the 13 championship flags suspended from the rafters of the Boston Garden. Asking them to rededicate their energies for one month of their lives to the pursuit of the championship, he pointed upwards: "That's what those flags were all about."

Looking back, it is clear that the 1979-80 playoffs were a dress rehearsal for the following year, a necessary rite of passage for a young team with a future. For the sake of Cowens and Maravich, perhaps, the failure was sad; but for the team it was a painful and worthwhile lesson in self-discovery. They learned what it was like to play with everything on the line. They learned the real meaning of pressure. And while their effort was never anything but the best, they learned that experience is a factor in winning, a factor that cannot be enthused into being.

Moses Malone led the Rockets to a 2-1 Central-Division victory over the San Antonio Spurs in the miniseries, but Houston was heading to Boston to play a team that had defeated it in all six meetings that year. Though nervous, the Celtics had plenty of confidence against Houston, and their four-game sweep was proof that having the most dominant center in the game was not nearly enough in the NBA. With Cowens playing good defense against Moses and Chris Ford leading the team offensively, Boston showed that their regular-season record was no fluke. Bird, who had an off series offensively as fellow rookie Robert Reid defended him well, demonstrated a quality that Celtics fans would come to expect over the years. Recognizing his difficulties, he turned to his defense, rebounding and passing to compensate, firmly establishing himself as a worthy successor to another Celtics all-around great, John Havlicek, with whom Bird had missed playing by a year. Symbolically, Havlicek scrimmaged with the Celtics during the 1980 playoffs, and it was intriguing to see him with Bird, teaming on the break, running a give-and-go, as two eras brushed briefly.

But the Rockets were an uncontested lay-up compared with the 76ers, who had disposed easily of the Bullets and Hubie Brown's Atlanta Hawks as preparation for the Eastern Conference championship round with Boston. Behind the imposing play of Doctor J and Darryl Dawkins, the Sixers were doing what an experienced team should do—peaking at playoff time, pulling it all together for a do-or-die run at the crown. For the Celtics, the first year of the Bird Era would end as it began, with an educational loss to a very good 76ers team.

The home-court advantage actually worked against Boston that year because it created expectations that were shattered in an opening game loss. After bolting to an emotional first-half lead, the Celtics settled down to face a poised and confident Philadelphia team. Erving scored 12 straight points in the third period, and

Caldwell Jones blanketed Bird down the stretch. Boston rallied and played well, but Henry Bibby's clutch scoring decided the issue, and Philly stole the treasured home-court advantage. The team was shocked as it filed into the lockerroom, with Fitch storming about, vowing he would take official action against the referees. Down the hall the Sixers celebrated with self-contained, realistic joy.

Game 2 gave Garden fans a taste of the future as Bird played a masterpiece, a 36-point, 14-rebound virtuoso performance in a tough 98-94 win. But one play said more than all the stats put together. As a loose ball rolled down the parquet in the third quarter, Bird gave chase. Hopelessly beaten by the simple physics of the play, he nevertheless gave it his all, diving headfirst and sliding 15 feet before disappearing beneath the press table and into a realm occupied by only the most dedicated, intense players.

That play, and that game, encapsulated the drive and skill that the Celtics were just short of perfecting in 1980, and as the series moved to Philadelphia the odds shifted to the older team. Boston's best opportunity came in Game 3, when they rallied after a hard fight throughout to close to within 99-97 with possession of the ball. The Celtics then ran an outside weave in which Carr passed up an easy shooting opportunity and the team ended up with an uncertain shot. That indecisive play was the season's death knell. In Game 4 Erving dominated, sweeping to the basket repeatedly and scoring 25 in the game's final 24 minutes. Boston's composure suffered, and Carr and Erving nearly fought after M. L. contested a Doctor J transition with a lot of force. After Philly's 12-point win, a mirror fell in the Celtics' lockerroom, cutting Carr severely and symbolizing Boston's shattered self-image.

The return home was resigned and hopeless, in spite of the optimistic cliches thrown to the press. On the same afternoon that the Lakers took control of the Western Conference championship with a 23-0 run against Seattle, the Sixers went out and controlled Game 5. Behind by 12 with four minutes left in the game, Fitch removed the starters and conceded the season. He had a lot to be proud of, as everyone on that team did—but he would have to wait another year before seeing a miracle finish.

4

THE FIRST CHAMPIONSHIP

On a muggy afternoon in August 1980, the sound of a solitary bouncing basketball echoed among the trees of Brookline, Massachusetts, home of Michael Dukakis, Larry Bird and the quiet campus of Hellenic College. When they are not working out on the parquet of the Boston Garden, the Celtics practice here, amidst the hilly, bucolic woods behind Jamaica Pond. The atmosphere couldn't be more different from the girders and concrete of North Station; it was the last place you would expect to hear that distinctive sound, especially three weeks before the opening of preseason training camp. But it had been three long months since elimination from the playoffs, and Larry Bird for one was eager to get back to the business of doing what the Celtics organization was paying him so much to do.

Not that Bird had been fishing all summer. In those three months he had done his share of relaxing, certainly, but the long hours of pick-up ball and solitary shooting had continued without a break on the tarmac-covered, regulation-sized court he had built himself beside his mother's new house in French Lick. A year as a professional had improved significantly the standard of living of Bird and his family, but the summer routine remained the same—hoop, hoop and more hoop, with occasional timeouts for beer and chat with friends. The big city, they were happy to see, had not changed Larry Joe; he was still the hard-working perfectionist who would spring for the Thursday night beer tab just as long as his friends didn't expect him to. He was still at home in French Lick.

Rick Robey and Larry Bird. Robey's friendship was an important source of security early in his career. "I was just this kid from a small place like French Lick. Playing in Boston? I didn't know what to expect."

But in August he was in Brookline, working on his conditioning, shooting and timing, developing a personal cycle of preparedness that would peak before the season started. He was joined by the big Kentuckian Rick Robey, the Celtics' backup center and Bird's closest friend on the team. They had visited each other in the offseason, playing golf and hanging out. If Robey lacked Bird's total dedication to the game, he shared a wry, country sense of humor and a dislike for formality. They liked to horse around and kid each other. Today Bird challenged Robey to a game of one-on-one, and the big center accepted the challenge with a smile.

They followed playground rules, shooting free throws to see who would start the game (Bird won with mocking ease) and retaining possession after every basket. Bird scored at once with a long set shot, then pumped in the exact same shot to go up, 2-0. "Game to 15?" Bird asked. Robey nodded and stepped closer. A little head fake, a jump shot, all net. Four...five...six-zip. Nothing but the twine every time. "You in this, Rick?" Robey's eyes narrowed in concentration, but Bird's perimeter shots—the perfect arc, the sphere spinning backward in ideal rotation, the sweet silky swish of the net—kept falling like summer rain. At zero-eight Robey turned to an onlooker. "OK, watch me stop him now." Wrong words in front of Larry. Without moving from the outside he tossed in three more. Smelling skunk, he continued to run the rack. As shot number 15 left his fingers he turned away. Pale, frustrated, Robey watched the ball fall true and bounce to a stop. He looked at his friend and walked away. To the small audience he seemed to be thinking, "At least he's on *my* team."

In later years anything but a championship would be considered failure to the Celtics and their fans, but in the fall of 1980 the players returned to camp happy with their performance the previous year and confident about the year ahead. The convincing loss to the 76ers still did not sit well, but Boston had every reason to believe the coming season would be better. With the best record in basketball in 1979-80, the Celtics saw now that lack of experience, fatigue and a less-than-overpowering inside game had kept them from a championship. Experience would come—had come—with time; the sustained mental pressure of inexperience, which adds so much to physical fatigue, would also be lessened with the years; and the team's inside game was helped immeasurably by an offseason maneuver that was the greatest steal in Boston since the Brinks Robbery.

All last season, when he wasn't watching the Celtics return to winning form, Red Auerbach was keeping tabs on the Detroit Pistons, noting with glee their league-worst record and thinking of the draft picks he had obtained in the Carr-for-McAdoo compensation deal. The Celtics now had the first pick in the 1980 draft. So what do Red and Fitch decide to do? They trade it away! They give Golden State the number one in exchange for the young and inconsistent center Robert Parish and the Warriors' first-round pick, overall third in the draft. Fine. Red must know what he's doing, he must have some secret scheme. But then what does he do? He tells Sam Goldaper of the *New York Times* why he did what he did so that the sportswriter has time to get the story into his paper *the morning of the draft!* "There are three superstars in the draft," Red said. "When we traded

choices with the Warriors, we knew they would take Joe Barry Carroll. Utah, with the second pick, will take Darrell Griffith, even though they shouldn't. That means we'll be able to take Kevin McHale from Minnesota, who we think is the best player anyway." And, to take the logic of the deal to its conclusion, get Robert Parish for nothing.

Red was obviously playing mind games with the Warriors and the Jazz, but the braggadacio of that statement was incredible. Red's confidence was such that he could get away with it, however. Eight years later we shake our heads in wonder, but at the time Red was giving his rivals credit for making the obvious choices. Carroll, a very talented seven-footer, had led Purdue to the Final Four with some spectacular play. Griffith, aka Dr. Dunkenstein, was the Final Four MVP. McHale had been hampered by a knee injury in the last half of his senior year. The choices seemed pretty clear (and when the time came they went as predicted, though the Jazz deliberately hesitated through their full allotment of time while Auerbach did a slow burn). But Red is famous for seeing through the obvious and into the future. He saw what McHale would *become*, and he saw with time-proven accuracy.

Credit for seeing Robert Parish's potential, however, has to go to Bill Fitch, who had been impressed with the man ever since he blocked 11 shots against Fitch's Cleveland Cavaliers in a 1978 game. Fitch, according to Rick Robey, always "preferred grace," and Parish has certainly been one of the most graceful big men to play the game. The eighth choice in the 1976 draft, he came into the league with all the skills needed to dominate: strength, court sense, impressive speed

"I've had the zeroes since junior high school. We didn't have enough numbered shirts to go around, so my shirt was called double zero. I liked it, so I kept it."

for a man his size, good fundamentals, an excellent outside shot and a number of sweet moves to the hoop. But Golden State, in a slow downward slide after their 1975 championship, did not provide the incentive Robert seemed to need, and he never fulfilled his potential in the Bay Area. Fitch, knowing the Warriors were keeping Parish out of games, had kept in touch with general manager Pete Newell during the '79-80 season. Meanwhile the Warriors plunged to a 24-58 record, and Parish was a convenient scapegoat. "They had their favorites," he claimed. "But when it came time to support the other players such as myself, nothing ever happened." His concentration waned, but Fitch did not forget him.

McHale looked like the perfect frontcourt mate for the Chief. In spite of his

injury history, he was a very confident player with a surprisingly complete game and a relaxed approach to the sport. He played "because basketball is fun," and although his attitude could cause problems, at 6-11, with long arms and a good sense of timing, he was just what the Celtics needed in the frontcourt. MVP of the postseason Hawaii Classic, he impressed the scouts, including superscout Marty Blake, who pointed out that the Minnesota star was a "great battler" who "will make the play inside and can hit from outside." Auerbach and owner Harry Mangurian had scouted him in December and come away impressed, so the deal of the century should have been no great surprise. On Draft Day, with Parish and McHale safely in the stable and the finest frontcourt in NBA history about to assume its beginnings, Fitch and Auerbach enjoyed their coup at a press conference. Red deferred to Bill; Bill to Red. "*You* tell them," Red said, "*you're* the articulate one." Fitch laughed and pointed at the legend. "What can I tell you?" he said. "Red has done it again."

Fitch's laughter sprang from his pleasure at a job well done. He and Red had done exactly what they needed to strengthen Boston's inside game and enter the 1980-81 season as one of the favorites to go all the way. But in the modern business environment of the NBA it is not enough to get players into the fold—you also have to negotiate their contracts, and that can be difficult. During training camp three members, a quarter of the team, were holdouts: Archibald, Maxwell and McHale.

Tiny had played the previous year with a "make good" contract, with the understanding that he would be compensated for a job well done. And he had clearly made good, averaging over 14 points and eight assists per game. Money was an important issue to Archibald. He had struggled with his finances after his return to New York, and he literally lived the game, deferring plans for the future to work on his moves continually in the schoolyards and gyms of New York and Boston. As the Celtics found out without him during the preseason, Tiny was an essential cog in the system. His ability to push the ball up the floor opened up the game and gave the team more offensive options. Creative and tough, he gave all he had, and he wanted to be paid well for his efforts. And others appreciated his worth. As the inevitable trade rumors circulated, Bird was asked who he thought could help the team as a point guard. "There is *nobody* better than Tiny," he said.

Max was in a similar position. A free agent, he was coming off a season when he had led the league in field goal percentage and demonstrated his team consciousness by adjusting perfectly to Bird's commanding offensive presence. A dominant force underneath, the perfect complement to Bird, he was also turning into one of the outstanding defensive specialists in the NBA, a role he would refine as the years went on and the list of offensive forces on the team increased. He wanted his reward, and he was willing to sit to get it. During the preseason his lively conversation was missed almost as much as his ability on the court.

Time brought Max and Tiny back to the team—time and the evidence of their absence during the preseason. In a game against Milwaukee at Hartford, Quinn Buckner did to Boston what Tiny had been

doing to opponents all last season, threading the defense and finding inside men easily against the weakened Celtics inside. When Bird fouled out, the moves of the two holdouts were sorely missed. Maravich had already left the team, walking out of training camp without telling anyone. Though no one but Red Auerbach and Dave Cowens knew it, the two men had met during the summer and discussed the possibility of Cowens's retirement. And Parish, the heir apparent to the big redhead, was struggling. Unused to a Fitch training camp, he was having trouble with his conditioning. He had never had these kind of problems at Golden State. "We had always played our way into shape," he said. "I don't know if I'll make it."

Meanwhile, McHale, even after Max and Tiny had signed, continued to hold out, making the deal of the century look like a failure. Unlike the veterans, he had no part of the previous great season to use as a negotiating tool, and his agent, Ron Simon, was getting nowhere with Auerbach. "Red's out of touch," he said. The situation reached a crisis point late in the preseason when McHale went to Rome to meet with representatives of the Italian League while Simon desperately tried to reach Fitch. McHale would play in Italy for a year and then reenter the draft if Fitch couldn't work something out. Red seemed happy with the frontcourt. In spite of Parish's slow start, the general manager was still hoping Cowens would decide to play, that Parish would come on, and that Robey and Maxwell would continue to do as well as they had the previous season. Bird had been sensational in camp—enough to make Red indifferent to McHale's whereabouts.

Rookie Kevin McHale. He had an immediate impact as Fitch used him in the fourth quarters of key games so often that Johnny Most dubbed him "Kevin the IV in the fourth."

But not Fitch. A stockpiler of big men since his early days, Fitch had always liked twin towers. In Cleveland he had had success pairing centers Nate Thurmond and Jim Chones. Later, Chones and Elmore Smith teamed well together. He could never have a team that was too big and he coveted McHale. At the eleventh hour Simon finally reached the coach and the two men hammered out a deal. Red, supporting his coach, consented.

McHale flew in from Rome happy and held an immediate press conference. He seemed indifferent to playing with the Celtics, saying that the Italian representatives had been "generous and fair." Fitch took him immediately over to Hellenic College for practice, where McHale faced a cool reception from the

veterans, particularly Robey. Donning number 32, the number of his idol, Bill Walton, he played spectacularly—after being halfway across the globe just 12 hours earlier. Crashing both boards, blocking shots, playing excellent defense, he proved himself at once. Bird had three shots rejected by the rookie. The veterans saw they had a player here, and a grudging respect developed. Fitch had another tower.

The bus moved down the highway with the same steady monotony of a thousand previous rides. Dave Cowens watched the road slide by from his seat at the back, thinking, perhaps, of how his own career was threading its way to a close. Wasn't it just a week ago that he had ventured into the Rucker League as a rookie and awed writers and veterans of that circuit with the best jumping ability of any white player *ever*? Hadn't only two days passed since he was drinking champagne in the dressing room of the Mecca, celebrating the 1974 NBA championship and a personal seventh-game highlight film of 27 points and a defensive job on Abdul-Jabbar that held the star to no field goal attempts over an 18-minute span? Wasn't it just yesterday that he had shrugged off fatigue and led the Celtics to their 13th championship in the 1976 finals against Phoenix (and this despite a cold war with Coach Tommy Heinsohn, so icy Cowens would not listen to him during timeouts)?

He had known the highs and lows. He had left and returned. He had played and coached. Never easy to figure, he had always followed the direction of his own inner voice. And now, as the bus sped through the basketball back country of

70

Indiana, he was preparing to stop the trip for good as the end of the 1980 preseason approached.

Though Fitch would not have admitted it, Cowens had been playing well. The summer of rest had sharpened his running and helped his power game. And his heart—well, Dave Cowens's heart would never leave him while he had a basketball in his hands. He would walk off the court first. But insiders reported he was exhausted by Fitch's camp. The Spartan coach had not let up this year, and the regimen did not sit well with the veterans. Maravich had already left. Cowens and Fitch had had their arguments, and Cowens gradually saw that it wasn't worth it. The fighting spirit that had marked his game for an even ten years was not as strong as it needed to be for Dave Cowens to continue.

As the bus pulled into Terre Haute he stood and faced the team. None of the other players knew what he was about to say, and the shocked stares said these men did not believe, as Dave himself did, that he had lost the competitiveness he had to have to be his best. He was retiring. He offered advice to individual teammates: Bird should assume team leadership; Robey should become more committed to the game. It was an emotional scene, one that grew into an awkward silence before M. L. Carr barked from the rear, "If that's all you have to say, then get your butt off the bus." In the laughter that followed, M. L.'s point was not lost— we've heard what you said; we'll go forth as a team, conscious of your leadership, knowing that of all your contributions to us, this may have been the most important.

As Bill Fitch assembled his charges for the 1980-81 season, he was beginning his most important year in a head coaching career that spanned a quarter century. He was not going to change his methods now. The son of a military man who had gone into the trucking business, Fitch came from what he described as "conservative Republican stock." Though the native Iowan had considered careers in law and the clergy, he decided early to apply his staunch outlook on life to the world of sports. He had lettered in four sports in high school and played basketball for Coe College in his home town of Grand Rapids. Upon graduation he prepared himself immediately for a coaching career, starting as an assistant in basketball and baseball at Creighton University. While there he earned a master's degree in educational psychology, which he applied to his coaching. "Some of the psychology really does fit in with coaching," he said years later. "It is really interesting if you get behind all the big words and get into the cases, like ego defense mechanisms. Certain 'uncoachable athletes' would be coachable if not for their egos."

Throughout his successful years in college and the NBA, however, Fitch was known more for his ability to build a program than to maintain it, and in spite of his knowledge of psychology, his leadership was autocratic and tough. In the years following his peak 1976 season with the Cavaliers, he had often raised players' ire and engaged in confrontation. In one newsworthy incident he had argued strenuously with Terry Furlow on the bench. He knew he was not popular with his players, but he accepted it as part of the job. "I didn't take that personally," he said about the Furlow fight, "I take it as part of the job. You can't be concerned with friendships on a team. The day a team comes up to me and gives me a Christmas gift I'll have cardiac arrest...My job is to make players better than they think they can be."

In spite of the tremendous success of his first season in Boston, Fitch was not free of controversy. He had problems with assistant coach K. C. Jones that had been publicly aired by the *Boston Herald*. Fitch viewed K. C.'s attempts at establishing an active coaching role as an intrusion on his authority, and they often had sharp words. Fitch and Jones would never get on, and the seasons ahead only worsened their relationship as Fitch retreated behind the stone wall of his control. K. C. was close to many of the players, and they would seek counsel from him when Fitch's insensitivity got to be too much. Yet when it came time to divvy up playoff money, the players voted against Jones receiving a share. Trainer Ray Melchiorre was also excluded, and he complained in the press. Finally, there had been bruised feelings when players were left unprotected in the expansion draft for the creation of the Dallas Mavericks. Only eight players could be protected, and the juggling act was not easy, but in an era when coaches, in spite of their authority, receive much less money than the team's stars, these slights can be blown out of proportion.

Training camp had its problems as well, with the holdouts, Maravich's sudden departure and Parish's problems. With McHale arriving late, Robey hampered by leg and thigh injuries, and Cowens "disappointing" Fitch with his performance, the coach thought he had frontcourt problems and pushed Parish very hard. The two men would always have a complex relationship, but that training camp established the tone for years to come— Fitch treating Parish like a "project"; the proud Chief not allowing himself to be intimidated; Fitch cajoling, negotiating, usually failing to establish rapport. During that season Fitch and Robert lived in the same apartment building, and they would occasionally have dinner together. Parish was deeply skeptical of Fitch's methods, and yet the coach would bring out the best in Parish, who would perform as he never had at Golden State. Who deserved credit? In the wake of Parish's Boston success, the press often gave Fitch more than perhaps he was due. Look what he's made of the Chief, it liked to say. Look what he's done with this project. Later Fitch would say that Parish needed a kick in the butt. But Robert himself had a more balanced view. "I did as much for him as he did for me...I certainly never had the players around me [at Golden State] as I did in Boston. He may have made me, but I sure made him, too."

But Fitch was determined to put problems behind him as preseason ended and the long-awaited regular season approached. The first game was against the Cavaliers. It was an important game for Fitch and an important game for the players and fans, who were looking forward to this season with an anticipation unmatched in the city's history. Advance sales were excellent. The press was having a field day. And as opening night approached, any team acrimony disappeared in the general feeling that *this* was the year. There was an atmosphere of renewal, of picking up where the miracle team of last year had left off and going all the way.

There were noticeable differences. The certainty of last year's starting lineup was lost in the confusion of training camp. Fitch decided to start Gerald Henderson and M. L. Carr in the backcourt on opening night, a choice dictated as much by his infatuation with that pairing as by Archibald's late entry into camp. Fitch conceived of the backcourt rotation in duos; he had been pleased with the job Tiny and Ford had done the previous year, but he was eager to bring the younger backcourt along in the hope of getting more significant minutes out of them. With Cowens gone, the nucleus of the team was both young and inexperienced, but the awe in face of professional suc-

Archibald held out during the preseason, 1980-81. Asked about rumors that the team was trying to acquire a replacement, Bird replied "They shouldn't. Tiny's the best there is."

cess that had marked the team in 1979-80 turned now into an attitude that combined aggressiveness, determination and individuality. Bird was a constant joker in the lockerroom; Archibald's confidence had returned full force; Henderson's rookie jitters were now a thing of the past (though it would still be a while before Bird completely accepted him as a player); and Maxwell was the court jester, holding court in front of his locker and playing the music *loud* (until Fitch banned music from the lockerroom following a disastrous loss in Hartford in November).

The Celtics routed Cleveland, and the team's skill and confidence was obvious. With M. L. scoring 25 and Parish playing an outstanding overall game, the long exhausting practices under Fitch were forgotten. The demands, insults and unstinting drills were easy to accept when the wins rolled in. And whatever anyone said about Fitch, he was completely dedicated to winning. He pushed himself as hard as he pushed any player. He religiously studied tapes of every game the team played, as well as tapes of other NBA games. He was a scout, a technical advisor, a father figure (whether the players wanted one or not). At least for that season, he scrutinized his own role carefully, admitting that he could overvalue the extent of his influence, forcing himself to communicate better with the team as it developed a more secure team ego, doing his best to recognize that the team had grown much larger than him. Led now by Bird, it was creative, powerful, intimidating and able to play its best under pressure. Fitch was never a better pro coach than he was that season. And he certainly never had as good a team to work with, before or since.

The level Larry Bird had reached after only a year in the National Basketball Association can be judged by the expectations the basketball cognescenti brought to the new season. Most observers thought from the early stages of the year that the race for league MVP would be between Bird and Doctor J. Both brought a measure of talent and intensity to the game a cut above anyone else in the league—and this in an era when centers were supposed to dominate the sport. Both were franchise players who made fans think they were seeing a style of play that was unique. And both raised considerably the level of play of those around them.

The balance in ability between these two men was perfectly matched by the teams they carried. The resurrected rivalry of the previous season would settle into consistent high drama in 1980-81, with tremendous heroics, off-court intrigue and a parity so pronounced the teams finished with identical 62-20 records and then battled each other in a gasping, tense seven-game playoff series for the Eastern Conference championship that no one in either city will ever forget. Ideal rivals, the Celtics and 76ers had exceptional talent that matched up physically and mentally. They relished the competitiveness and forced each other to play at the highest level.

Coming off a tough loss to the Lakers in last year's finals—a series they felt they should have won—the 76ers had the prototypical eighties team: a superstar in Erving; a completely team-oriented point guard in Mo Cheeks, who always thought *pass* before *shoot* and was quicker than a state employee at five o'clock; twin towers in Darryl Dawkins and Caldwell Jones, who complemented each other in range and ability; and a steep bench of talented role players, paced by the supple Bobby Jones, who many said was the best defensive player in the league, and an eerily confident rookie from Southwestern Louisiana named Andrew Toney, who had a Lloyd-Free in-your-face jumper and such an unerring ability to hit clutch shots against the Celtics (and others) that he soon became known as the "Celtic Assassin." They had a fine coach in Billy Cunningham, a man who combined a good basketball mind with a searing intensity to win and a sense of loyalty to the 76ers organization that went back to his days in the sixties as a star for Philly. Without a doubt they were the team to beat.

Or at least it looked that way for the first six weeks of the season. After losing two of their first three games, the Sixers reeled off 12 straight wins that included a contest with the Celtics at the Spectrum on All Saints Day. That game, dominated in the early going by Bird, evolved into a classic. After trailing by 15, 82-67, late in the third period, the Sixers rallied furiously, led by Erving and veteran guard Doug Collins. Bird, on his way to 36 points and 21 rebounds, continued to play brilliantly, but the lead melted from 13 to seven to two. The game came down to one play: ahead by two, the Celtics had to halt a final 76er possession if they were to win the game. An Erving try failed, but Dawkins rebounded and powered gracefully into the lane and laid the ball in. The Sixers went on to win in overtime as Erving scored a career-high 45 points before more than 18,000 roaring fans.

Though they lost two days later to the Knicks, Cunningham's crew resumed their winning ways, taking ten in a row before an overtime loss to the Hawks, and

74

then *another* ten in a row to bring their record at Christmas to 33-4. A nice gift for Philly fans and a daunting bolt from the blocks for the other fillies in the league.

Not that the league couldn't provide competition. The Celtics, after floundering around .500 for the first dozen games, stayed within striking distance during those opening weeks. The Milwaukee Bucks had to be considered contenders for the title, with Bob Lanier and Marques Johnson anchoring a quick team featuring the excellent guard combination of Quinn Buckner and Sidney Moncrief. The defending champion Lakers brought the same team back, though Magic Johnson did go down with a knee injury that would keep him out of 45 games. In the Midwest, Moses Malone and George Gervin led contending teams out of Houston and San Antonio, and in Phoenix an already strong team became stronger when the Suns traded Paul Westphal to Seattle for Dennis Johnson. Widely publicized as an "impact" trade, there is no doubt whom it benefited: the Suns went on to record a 57-25 record, the best in the Western Conference, while the Super-Sonics started a slide that took them out of contention until Bernie Bickerstaff brought them back in the late eighties.

But it was the Sixers who were winning, and winning with intensity. Thought to be down and out in Indiana late in the fourth quarter, they outscored the home team, 15-3, to win going away. Against a hungry Bucks team at the Mecca they scored 136 points and won by 15. Down by eight with four minutes to play in Seattle, they rallied to win in overtime. They had talent; they had a killer instinct; they beat you in many different ways. "They're better than us," Fitch confided.

In the meantime the Celtics, for all their talent, were still trying to uncover their own team identity in the early going. The offseason acquisitions and holdouts had made the transition to the new season more difficult than it had been for Philadelphia, and matters weren't helped when Carr suffered a fractured foot in a late October game (he would not play effectively for four months). Parish was a strong contributor, keying an important early win over Milwaukee, but a couple of early losses created some doubts. In Hartford, the Celtics' home away from home, they squandered a sizeable lead against the Knicks and lost in overtime. Fitch lashed out against the team, singling out Maxwell as the main villain in a general lack of concentration (the music was officially shut off after this game). Embarrassed and insulted, Max stopped speaking to the press. The Knicks' trick-or-treat point guard Ray Williams had overpowered Henderson down the stretch, and Fitch admitted to the press that Gerald had been "disappointing." Two days later, Archibald and Ford were starting again.

The second defeat came in a return match with the Bucks, a tense game in which Fitch, ejected late in the game, had to watch the dramatic conclusion on a video monitor in the the lockerroom. Resisting the temptation to send plays in to assistant coaches Jones and Jimmy Rodgers (K. C. would probably have ignored them anyway), Fitch watched Bird match Marques Johnson and Bob Lanier shot for shot down the stretch. After a pair of free throws by Lanier gave the Bucks a one-point lead, Boston set up to try to win the game with 17 seconds left. The ball circled, time ticked off, and Fitch softly whispered, "Please, Larry," as

Bird launched a soft jumper from the left sideline. The shot missed and Boston's record fell to 7-5.

But the NBA season is a long one, and success usually goes to the teams that work through the difficult cycles and maintain confidence in themselves. The Celtics, once they got over their early-season problems, settled into a winning pattern that kept them within striking distance of Philly even as they struggled. These men would not give up. In Boston, trailing Bernard King and Golden State by 18 points at halftime, the Celtics roared back behind Bird's 27 and Tiny's playmaking, winning, 108-106, as Maxwell garnered a key offensive rebound in the closing seconds. This team had too much talent and too great a belief in themselves to give up, and they put together their own six-game winning streak to stay in the race.

Bird was playing superbly, gaining the reputation throughout the league that he had already earned in Boston. His shooting, rebounding and passing were all excellent, of course, but the way in which he also fit into Fitch's system really enhanced his ability and moved his play to another dimension. Sharing the frontcourt with twin towers, he was the perfect leader, using the threat of his dominating offensive skill to open up Maxwell's game (Bird fed the post-up star perfectly, passing at just the right moment and keeping his own defender from double-teaming) and Parish's (Bird and the Chief ran the pick-and-roll to perfection, and Bird's penetrating ability created all sorts of scoring opportunities for the center). He was fast becoming known as the best shooter in the league, but his power game inside was just as effective. He led the Celtics in rebounding a dozen times through early January, including 20 against Chicago, Cleveland and New York on Christmas Day. His determination on the boards seemed to strengthen his offensive game. Against the Bulls he scored 18 in the first quarter and went on to tally 35. "People talk about Bird and ask whether he's the best I've seen," Fitch said. "I tell them there hasn't been any better in the 11 years I've been coaching in the NBA." For a second-year man these were high words of praise from a coach who has never been liberal with compliments.

Fitch was seeing Bird (aided ably by Archibald in the backcourt) successfully running his motion offense as well as flying high as a superstar. Heading into a January 2 game against the Warriors, the Celtics had won 13 straight, giving the Sixers something to think about as the long winter months began. That game, Robert Parish's homecoming, was the most passive of Bird's professional career—he was held scoreless as the Celtics never threatened and Bernard King scored 30. But Bird and the Celtics rebounded. Two nights later they dismantled Jack Ramsey's Portland Trail Blazers as Bird scored the first five times he touched the ball—all jump shots of 20 feet or more. After the game Dr. Ramsay declared flatly that Bird was the best player in basketball and that "the Celtics are the best team." Losing was not contagious on this club—it made the players try harder the next time out, and the player who set the tone down the line was Bird.

Larry Bird was very much on Red Auerbach's mind as he flew from his home in Washington, D. C., to Boston in January 1981. His team had 18 home games that month, including a critical meeting with the 76ers, and Red had to be happy with the 30-9 record and the play of his star forward. Bird prompted memories of Bill Russell; he was a self-motivator of the highest phylum, a man who blended grace and power, an individual hero who would dive to the floor to save a loose ball. The press had already started badgering Red about the two greats, asking who was better. As he would for many years, he shunned comparisons. "I live in the present," he would insist.

Red was also happy with the outcome of the big preseason deal. Parish was developing into one of the finest centers in the game with the ideal Celtics attitude—physical, determined, willing to work. McHale was defiant and determined as well. His shot-blocking ability was excellent, and he wanted the ball in critical situations. In a game against the Bullets he had taken the ball to the hole against the great Elvin Hayes on several key sequences to nail down a two-point win. With Bird and Maxwell, Auerbach had a frontcourt of unparalleled potential.

But as always, Red's mind was also on the future, on the college players he saw as Celtics types. Two impressed him particularly that year, both guards. One was Isiah Thomas of Indiana. Auerbach and Hoosier coach Bobby Knight had been acquaintances for years; Knight often probed Red for insight, and Red respected Knight's knowledge of the college game. Red always believed that, after a center, the most important person in building a team was the point guard. Thomas, who had played in the Pan Am games as a high school senior, had all the tools to be a top point guard in the pros, combined with a fiery will to win.

The other guard Red coveted was Danny Ainge, a 6-4, 175-pound senior at BYU who was probably the finest all-around athlete in the country at that point. A native of Eugene, Oregon, he was reportedly the best end in the history of Oregon high school football—but he was an even better basketball player who had led Eugene North High School to the state title in 1976. Bill Walton, in his professional heyday at the time with the Portland Trail Blazers 110 miles up the freeway, recalled discussing Ainge's exploits in the Blazers' lockerroom. "He could have played with us *then*," Walton said in 1987. But his ability didn't end there. While still attending college he was playing pro baseball for the Toronto Blue Jays; in fact, while Jimmy Rodgers and Red were scouting Ainge his senior year, he was contractually committed to the Jays for the next four years. Rodgers had

Walton on the high school star Ainge: "He could have played with us then.*"*

likened Ainge to the great Doug Collins, perhaps the best off guard in the game in the seventies with the speed of a good playmaker. Red concurred and wanted Ainge in the Celtics backcourt. But what was he to do about the Blue Jays? Could he afford to risk a draft pick on someone who might never be able to play a game? Auerbach thought a lot about these questions that season. The Celtics were never so good that he would stop thinking about the team's future.

But they were *very* good—and Billy Cunningham, coach of an outstanding team himself, pondered that very fact as he stopped for a moment on the ramp leading down to the parquet floor of the Boston Garden one cold night in January 1981. He had just finished speaking to his team about the Celtics. He had done everything this season to establish superiority in the Atlantic Division, and he had the finest stable of talent in the NBA; yet in spite of the Sixers' amazing start they were approaching the halfway point of the season virtually tied with their nemesis from Boston. They watched every hard-fought victory of their own matched by their rivals, and they could not seem to shake this determined Celtics group, no matter what the disparity of talent. Cunningham drew deeply on his pregame cigarette and sipped his Coca-Cola. *Wasn't this always the way it had been?* When Billy himself had taken the court with Wilt, Hal Greer, Chet Walker, Lucious Jackson and Wally Jones—the finest assemblage of talent in the NBA at the time, one of the greatest teams ever—the 76ers still could not dominate as the Celtics dominated. The Celtics always knew how to win. In the

glory years of the dynasty, Boston won the regular-season championship regularly and then used the home-court advantage to bolster their excellent conditioning and intensity in the playoffs. Even when the team aged and slipped into second (or even fourth), they used their experience to win in foreign arenas and take home rings. Now, after the up-and-down years of the seventies, the Boston tandem of talent and discipline was plaguing Cunningham again. He believed he had the better club—yet the C's were coming on.

The Celtics had stayed with the Sixers by winning the games they had to win. Against the Lakers, Bird, Maxwell and Archibald had paced the home team with 22 each and the Centics' defense shone,

Bird grabbing an offensive rebound in the final-day 98-94 triumph over Philadelphia, March 1981. After the Celtics defeated the 76ers in the memorable seven-game playoff, Erving walked into the celebrating Celtics lockerroom to offer his congratulations. The room immediately grew quiet.

22 each, and the Celtics' defense shone, holding the Lakers to 14 in the fourth quarter. Parish had dominating games against center-weak Cleveland, San Antonio and New York. Boston had luck on their side as well. Against Indiana, Max fouled George McGinnis at the buzzer with the Celtics holding a one-point lead. With 0:00 on the clock and the former 76er superstar shooting three to make two, McGinnis missed all three. The team replayed the misses on the lockerroom VCR over and over, Maxwell clutching his throat and screaming, "George, George!" This surge of fine play continued right up to this crucial match with the Sixers in the Garden, with Philadelphia in first place by a half game.

That night, Cunningham's doubts were reinforced. In spite of taking a severe blow to the thigh from Darryl Dawkins's knee (an injury that would plague him for the rest of the year), Bird sparked Boston to a 104-101 win in the face of 35 points by the Doc. It was also in this game that many observers saw the effects of Maxwell's developing defensive prowess. Erving still got his points, but he was becoming increasingly conscious of Maxwell's shadowy presence. As the season went on, the battle between them became a game within a game, and it would reach its zenith in the playoff confrontation in May.

But the Celtics' consistency of December and January faded, and by the All-Star break Philadelphia had taken a lead in the Atlantic Division, giving Cunningham the coaching position in the midseason classic. The break was welcome to most of the players and an opportunity for some of the Celtics and 76ers to be on the same team for once. Cunning-

ham led the East to a convincing win, and Archibald ran the squad with such control and precision that he won MVP honors, even though Robert Parish scored 16 points and pulled down ten rebounds. After the break, Philadelphia opened up a four-game lead as Boston battled through the tough February road swing and Archibald suffered a hand injury. Henderson assumed the point guard role and struggled. Though he registered back-to-back ten-assist games against L. A. and Seattle, Tiny's importance to the team was evident, as the offense often floundered. Still, the Celtics beat the Lakers for the second time that year, while Magic looked on from the sidelines in shirtsleeves, still nursing his injured knee. Bird dominated the boards, and after beginning the game cold went into a zone, connecting on 11 consecutive outside shots. The night before, Bird had played 50 minutes in an overtime defeat at Seattle, but no fatigue was in evidence as he finished has night's work with 36 points, 21 rebounds, six assists, five steals and three blocked shots. Even by the incredibly high standards Bird had set for himself in his short professional career, these were truly superstar stats, all the more impressive because they resulted in a win against the defending NBA champs in their own arena.

The Celtics always expect losses during this road trip, but there were other key wins, including a victory over San Antonio, where Robert Parish's career-high 40 points countered a 49-point performance by the Ice Man, George Gervin. Bird made a special point of crediting Parish. "Our inside game is better this season," he said. "Robert Parish is shooting 60 percent inside. That's a real difference." Earlier, McHale had drilled in 17 fourth-quarter points to help beat

Atlanta, and the Celts also took what Bird thought was one of the biggest games of the year, a 116-97 win over Dennis Johnson and the Phoenix Suns, on their way to a 57-win season. The impressive part of the road trip, in spite of the losses, was how everyone contributed, as Boston proved it could dominate in the West. The season was shaping up as one to move beyond the highs of 1979-80. There was a feeling that this year could produce another Celtics champion.

As they headed into the last two months of the season, the Celtics were above all conscious of the 76ers. With three big meetings left in the regular season (including the last game for both clubs) and the probability of a postseason clash, the importance of the home-court advantage gave every game heightened importance. Everyone was starting to feel the pressure. The NBA season is long, especially when you know who the top teams are and how long the playoffs can extend. There were problems. In a loss against Indiana at Hartford, Fitch became livid at halftime. "Since when are we so talented," he screamed, "that we can afford to be individualistic? Since when are we so good that we don't have to play together?" He followed up with an unusually long practice for late season, a three-hour workout at the Garden in which he forced the team to repeat drills over and over while members of the New Jersey Nets, the Celtics' opponent the next day, were waiting to get on the court.

In a game against the Hawks, the official Jake O'Donnell, who has had an adversarial relationship with the Celtics throughout the Bird Era, ejected Fitch during a bitter contest in the Garden. Eddie Johnson, a brash 6-1 guard who was heroically overcoming cocaine addiction at the time, was on his way to tying a Garden record of 20 points in the third quarter, lighting up Ford and Carr so consistently that when Fitch yanked Carr from the game he followed his progress down the bench and asked, "What's the matter, can't you guard the guy?" Carr ignored him, and a few moments later Fitch vented his anger on O'Donnell and got the heave-ho. Under K. C. Jones the Celtics made a run, but ended up on the wrong side of a 108-97 decision. On the way out, Hubie Brown tried to wish Jones well for the rest of the season, but the assistant coach, angered by the officiating, the loss and Brown's browbeating style, ignored the attempts of the Atlanta coach to shake his hand. Brown was soon shouting, and the two men had to be restrained. "I try to wish the guy luck," Brown roared, "*and he has no class!*" Jones walked into the lockerroom, shouting, "You'd better get back!" The playoffs couldn't come soon enough to the Boston Garden.

But before they came there was a month of regular-season play and three games with the 76ers, games that would act as a dress rehearsal for the postseason and create such drama of their own that people wondered how the intensity could ever be matched (it would be). Against the backdrop of the great Celtic-Sixer rivalries of the past, especially the classic Russell-Chamberlain battles of the sixties, these games offered fans the rich, focused competition of the finest young athletes in basketball trying for their first championship rings. With CBS televising most of the ten meetings that remained, Bill Russell appeared as a broadcaster, a visible link with the tradition.

By March 1, when the first of these games took place, the Celtics had drawn to within two and a half games of Philly and saw this contest at the Garden as crucial. The 76ers were leading the season series, 2-1, but more importantly the Celtics wanted to avoid falling behind by three and a half games with only 15 to play. Riding the emotion and preparedness that led up to the game, Boston did win, 114-107, and three contributors were key: Parish, who ruled the inside with 25 big points (Parish's pattern so far that year was to play well in the Garden and poorly in the Spectrum); Bird, whose tenaciousness got him 15 rebounds and five dangerous fouls; and Maxwell, who had turned into a defensive stopper of the class of L. A.'s Michael Cooper and Philadelphia's Bobby Jones, demonstrating his prowess against Erving. Bill Fitch was again obliged to watch a fourth quarter from the lockerroom after a face-to-face shouting match with Jack Madden got him ejected. Sending messages to the Celtics' bench via the assistant trainer Mike Massman, Fitch played out his Captain Video reputation to the fullest—he intimated after the game that he had observed Philadelphia's timeout huddles on television and acted on his knowledge in his communications to Jones (the Sixers later protested, but Fitch was not fined). The biggest decision, however, was left up to K. C.: whether to leave Bird in the game with five fouls and a full quarter to play. Jones played Bird most of the final period, and Bird did not foul out.

The backstage shenanigans were intriguing, but the message of the game was clear: this season was going to go down to the wire; Boston had not given up. One play summed it all up: Bird, diving for a loose ball on Philadelphia's baseline,

Chris Ford, the starting guard in Bird's first two seasons, recalled, "What I remember most about Larry's early years was his beautiful passing. The way we moved the ball."

initiated a fast break in which all five Celtics touched the ball. The Celtics were contending because they played as a team and wanted to win.

Philadelphia slumped slightly in the ensuing two weeks, allowing the Celtics to take a half-game lead going into their next contest, at the Spectrum. But Cunningham's crew, not allowing its own confidence to ebb, reversed the physical and emotional tenor of the March 1 game and routed Boston, 126-94. Throughout the afternoon, Caldwell Jones and Dawkins dominated the inside, and Cheeks outplayed Archibald. But it was Philadelphia's break that put the Celtics away. Perfectly executed and stylishly finished, they padded the lead and incited the crowd, as Erving and Bobby Jones slammed home one thunderous dunk after another. As was his ritual, Cunningham waited at the entrance of the runway to the lockerrooms and congratulated each man as he walked by. Fitch walked in the other direction with slumped shoulders.

It was fitting and fated that the last regular-season game was the also final game of the year for both teams. Though they trailed by a game, a victory would give the Celtics the regular-season crown by virtue of the tie-breaking rules. And the game was in Boston. But Cunningham had reason to believe his team could take this game in the Garden: the Sixers had prevailed in last year's playoff without the home-court advantage, and they had won the games they needed to win all this season. Cunningham had worked for five years to bring this version of the 76ers to their prominence. When he started, many had seen him as an unsophisticated ex-player, an imposter at worst, who had taken over what Darryl Dawkins in his book, *Chocolate Thunder*, called a "crazy, unpredictable" team. But he had transformed that selfish group into a team that should by rights have won the championship. They had the talent, the teamwork and the fire. And Cunningham worked hard. Fitch, watching a Sixers-Lakers game one day in the lockerroom, had this to say after a close-up showed Cunningham's weary face: "Look at him. You can see the hours he's put in from the eyes. People think [coaching] is fun. But it's not fun at this time of year."

But the season finale had Boston's coach at *his* best—and what better proof was needed than his leading Boston to a season championship and the home-court advantage in the playoffs, which just may have made the difference to that marvelous postseason, which many feel was the best of the Bird Era. When Fitch walked upstairs to the Garden lockerroom that final day, he knew exactly what kind of leadership to provide his weary team. That last week had been tough. Under pressure to win a big game against the Knicks, Boston had ridden the shoulders of Robert Parish, who scored 17 first-quarter points, hit two big buckets in the final minute and then swatted away a Ray Williams attempt from the backcourt to save the win. Auerbach, sitting across from the Celtics' bench, swung a victory punch. The following night, Parish had again dominated, scoring 31 in a victory over the Nets as the Celtics kept the possibility of the divisional championship alive.

But Parish's heroics did not hide the team's fatigue. The year had been physically and mentally exhausting, without respite from the rivalry with Philly, and Bird in particular was worn down. Not quite the same since his collision with Dawkins in March, Bird had had constant whirlpool treatment and plenty of work with Ray Melchiorre's electronic galvanic stimulator. But Bird's unrestrained play simply did not permit the healing process to complete itself, and when he walked into the lockerroom before the penultimate game of the year against Detroit, he had said to no one in particular, "Why is it that I feel so good until the moment I walk in here?" Bird had *identified* himself with the team all year, and Fitch knew he was the key to the Celtics' chances that day. Close to burnout, Bird was conscious of

The Celtics passing style changed with the acquisition of Parish in 1980. Bird and Archibald constantly looked inside to Parish in the low post, and the team utilized Parish's excellent return passing for open shots, an "inside-out" approach. Here he drives on Bob Lanier.

the Celtics' struggles that month and skeptical of the team's chances in the final game—and he had said so to WBZ Radio's Jon Miller.

When Fitch got to the lockerroom and faced his team—the team he could only have dreamed about while eating ham and eggs at truckstops and talking basketball with fellow coaches until four in the morning so many years ago—he was mindful of the state of his troops and determined to say the right thing. It was then that Captain Video, the consummate Xs and Os man, for once kept his sophisticated diagrams off the blackboard. He acted on his instincts and became a championship coach. "I'm not writing a thing

on this board," he told the team. "Just play *your* game. Run the offense. You're the better team now. I think you'll win the game." He may not have known that for certain, but he knew to *say* it, and the team stormed out of the lockerroom intent on dominating the favored Sixers. Minutes earlier, *Boston Herald* beat writer Buck Harvey had walked into the lockerroom and said that the Philadelphia players did not seem too concerned about the game. The Celtics were fired up.

The game was a perfect prelude to the playoffs, a perfect end to a second consecutive dream season. The Garden rocked with the unchecked enthusiasm of an Indiana high school championship as 18,000 fans packed the building and watched the Celtics go through an uncharacteristically intense warmup, replete with crashing dunks and menacing stares at the Sixer players. The opening minutes—when the charging 76ers usually established an advantage—showed Boston at its best, matching their rivals in intensity and keeping the crowd's cheers alive as they grabbed a 14-10 lead. Boston was continually attacking, but thanks to Andrew Toney's hot shooting the teams stayed even through the first quarter.

The game turned as the first half closed and McHale starred. A 7-0 run sparked by Bird's hustle had broken open a deadlocked game, setting the stage for McHale to show some of the shot-blocking ability that had distinguished him from his first practice with Boston. Intent on stopping Boston's surge, Erving flew by Bird and went up for a finger-roll over the front rim. Out of nowhere McHale soared high for a rejection, and Boston scored immediately in transition, Archibald feeding Bird. On the next possession the visitors worked the ball around, setting up the final play of the half. With the clock running down, the Doc drove hard again, flying by Maxwell and pausing midflight to take a little reverse scoop shot. Again McHale came up with the big block, this time sending the ball rolling towards the Celtics' basket with Carr in breakneck pursuit. He grabbed the ball at :03, crossed the timeline at :02, and laid it in at :01. The horn could not be heard above the Garden cheers, and the Celtics rushed into the lockerroom with an 11-point lead and an emotional lift as high as the championship flags.

The adrenalin of that sequence filled the lockerroom. "Those blocks were *nasty!*" Bird exulted. No fatigue now. But the Celts did not allow overconfidence to edge into the room, and by the start of the third quarter they were all business, executing with no wasted motion, tightening the defense to such a pitch that the Sixers

scored only ten points in a ten-minute span. When Ford nailed a three-pointer from the left wing, the lead peaked at 20 twenty. Philadelphia, its season padded with come-from-behind victories, did make a late surge, Andrew Toney hitting jumper after jumper, but they would get no closer than eight. When Tiny sank two free throws at :17, the bench was standing. The celebrations had begun: the Celtics and Sixers had split their six-game season series and finished with identical records, but the Celtics had won by virtue of the tie-breaking rules. The crowd must have been thinking as one, "How could this be matched?" It would be, and soon.

The importance of the home-court advantage grew as the playoffs began. While the Lakers were

The Lakers would use Kareem Abdul-Jabbar on McHale, even as a rookie. Bird said, "There isn't anybody we know about in the league they could get who could stop Kevin McHale. He can score on anybody. Maybe some guys could push him, but usually it doesn't matter who's on him—even two or three guys—he's going to score."

losing their miniseries to the Houston Rockets out West (and virtually assuring the Eastern Conference winners the championship), the Celtics breezed past the weak Chicago Bulls, 4-0. The Sixers, meanwhile, had to go a tough seven games against Don Nelson's Milwaukee Bucks, at that time one of the strongest teams in the NBA (they had beaten the Celtics three times that year). Nelson, whose competitive game had graced the Garden for 11 years, wanted badly to play Boston. "I just want to get into the final series against Boston because I want to have the opportunity to coach against my mentor, Red Auerbach." Every game of that series was tense and emotional as the teams swapped wins on enemy soil. With the series tied at two, the Sixers went into Game 5 with an interesting twist of strategy that showed Cunningham's ability to surprise at even this late date. Philly deviated from its customary "right-handed" offense by having guards Mo Cheeks and Lionel Hollins bring the ball up the left side of the court, confusing the Bucks defense. The Sixers were also helped when Marques Johnson pulled a back muscle, and they won easily, 116-99. But the Bucks fought back to take Game 6 at the Mecca behind a Quinn Buckner-led defense that limited Philadelphia to 86 points, and the Sixers went into the Spectrum on Easter Sunday with their chances of meeting Boston riding on a single game.

Only 7,000 fans showed up for that game, a sad commentary on Philly's fans and a late manifestation, perhaps, of the credibility the 76ers had lost in the tough years before Cunningham's charges jelled into the team-oriented unit they were now. But the game made up for any lack of fan interest in its drama and tension—tension to the point where Quinn Buckner's gut twisted so badly he had to wait for another day. Nelson used Moncrief and Johnson for 48 minutes, and Marques sparked a dramatic comeback that nearly cut the Sixers' season short. Behind by 16 with less than five minutes to play in the third period, the Bucks battled back to take the lead, 80-79. The the last quarter, eight lead changes led to an intense final minute. Caldwell Jones starred, snaring three lifegiving rebounds and preserving a 99-98 win in the more than half empty Spectrum.

So Philly was anything but fresh as the finest series of the playoffs approached, and the schedule was not going to help them. Immediately after the Milwaukee-Philadelphia series, Commissioner Larry O'Brien called the Celtics' offices and informed Boston that because of the demands placed on the league by CBS, the series would open with back-to-back games in Boston on Tuesday and Wednesday, then move to Philadelphia for a Friday-Sunday format. The league decision angered Auerbach and infuriated Fitch. "We've given up our home-court advantage," the coach declared. "All the visiting team wants in the first two games is a split. If Philadelphia is out of it on Tuesday, they could ease up and rest for Wednesday"—when, the implication was, the winning team would still be tired from the full exertion of the night before. Auerbach called the league offices and became embroiled in a shouting match with the commissioner, but the ruling stayed. But Philadelphia stood to lose even more by the decision. The series with the Bucks only ended on Sunday, meaning that the Sixers had to play three games over a four-day span. "Three *playoff* games," Cunningham reminded.

Game 1 introduced the epic series appropriately. Tense throughout, it heightened the heroic plays and stunning failures dramatically before a packed Garden. The Celtics began strong, rushing to a 32-24 lead as Archibald led the break with precision and flair. With the floor open, Bird (back to peak form) started shooting from outside, connecting on seven of his initial ten field goal tries. But this opening 18-minute surge ended when Archibald sat, and the Sixers fought back behind some crafty substituting by Cunningham. Philly took the lead, 49-48, with 2:51 left in the half, a lead they extended after the break to six. But then Tiny took over again: penetrating, drawing Caldwell Jones, then flipping a wraparound pass to Max for a lay-in; driving solo for a transition basket; directing an 18-7 counterattack that gave the Celts a 75-70 lead.

Against a lesser team this rush would have all but assured victory. Against the multidimensional Philadelphia club it only meant a temporary ascension, because the Sixers had so many guns to go to. And who better than Andrew Toney, the Celtic Assassin? "Toney will not beat us in a game," Fitch had declared to the Boston press. Those were apparently fighting words, because Andrew slashed through whatever defense Ford, Henderson and Carr set before him. And remember—Toney was a rookie. In Game 7 against the Bucks he had played only two minutes after getting into quick foul trouble. Cunningham didn't want to end the year with a handicapped rookie at the controls. But Game 1 at the Garden was a new night, and with 11 minutes left in the game and the Celts holding a five-point lead as if it were a priceless vase, Toney caught fire. A quick jumper in the lane; a lofted shot with Carr in his face, and the subsequent free throw; another pair of foul shots—just like that he had thrown a seven-point shutout, and the Sixers had their lead and their aggression back. "We were tired," Cunningham said later. "Our reactions were a half-step slow and the ball seemed to trickle off our fingertips all night. But when Toney came on, he gave us the spark. In the clutch. That's why I love him."

This drama had two more visceral scenes and the key Celtics were Maxwell and Gerald Henderson. First, another Celtics rally got the crowd roaring again. Bird scored on a goaltend. Then Maxwell scored two hoops off excellent defensive plays by Henderson. After the second, on which he was fouled, he waved a clenched

Cedric Maxwell scores over Indiana's James Edwards, January, 1981. Tradition-minded Celtics fans grew to revere Maxwell, who went on to win the MVP of the 1981 championship, the first of the Bird Era.

fist—then missed the free throw. A few minutes later, Henderson also missed a clutch foul shot with the Celtics up by one. After Erving and Bird exchanged foul shots, the second scene unfolded. With eight seconds left and Philly still down by one, they got the ball into Toney's hands. He drove to the right side as Erving set a good pick on Henderson. Toney headed to the hoop, and on the switch Maxwell threw out his leg to stop the Philly guard. The foul was obvious, a weak foul at that. There is something about such a self-defeating move that almost guarantees that the result will be the worst possible. Anticipating the worst, the Garden fell silent as Toney swished both freebies. A last-second heave by Bird only punctuated the loss, and the Celtics filed into the locker-room, stricken.

They sat at their lockers while Fitch watched the VCR replay the final minute. The effort had been there, the clutch plays and winning moves. "I blew it," Maxwell muttered. Later he called it the worst play of his NBA career. Fitch said to the press, "You say, 'Don't foul,' but you can't blame one man or point a finger. But you do want to make them earn it." The Celtics dressed quickly, their only consolation that the chance for redemption was less than 24 hours away. They knew they had lost the home-court advantage; they knew they were already in a hole. But unlike the previous season, when Fitch had stormed into the lockerroom after a crucial loss railing at the referees, this year's atmosphere was less extreme. Stronger physically and mentally, the Celts were already gearing up for the next game.

The cores of the team's identities, Doctor J and Larry Bird, assumed the dominant roles for the next two games, a 118-99 win for the Celtics in Boston and a responding 110-101 victory for the Sixers at the Spectrum the following Friday. After scoring his uniform number in Game 1, he upped that by a point in Game 2, scoring 34 as he also had 16 rebounds in an all-around fine game. Bird was here to play, and the defensive scheme the Sixers had used on him last year (shifting between Caldwell and Bobby Jones) was not going to work this time round. In a crucial sequence, he sparked a 21-6 run with McHale, Parish, Carr and Henderson sharing the floor with him, giving Boston a 59-46 halftime lead and momentum. "When you win the first game of a playoff series away from home," Cheeks said later, "it's always important to get the lead in the second game. When you do…you fight. When you don't get the lead, and you know you've already won that first game, you relax."

Philly did relax and Bird took advantage. "I played as hard as I have all year. There was a lot of pressure on the team because this was a game that we had to win. But the thing that I said to myself was that I wasn't going to think about any of that pressure." Bird's maturity had never been more evident. As the Celtics put their rivals away in the second half, the crowd gave him a standing ovation, insisting that the star stand up and wave. Bird didn't want to. "I was very proud. It gave me a great feeling inside because I had played well and the fans appreciated it. But I hated to get up and wave because this is only one game, and I don't think I should show any feeling until the series is over and we win it." But Fitch had motioned the star to acknowledge the applause. Bird saluted the fans and started thinking about Game 3.

That game was the Doc all the way. Watching the tapes of the first two games with assistant coaches Chuck Daly and Jack McMahon, Cunningham had agonized over Bird's dominance and searched for a way to neutralize him. He decided to have Erving guard Bird in Game 3. Though Fitch later claimed the move did not surprise him, the adjustment was major. Erving was a good defensive player, but most observers thought Caldwell and Bobby Jones were better. The Doc's defensive game depended a great deal on hand-checking and steals—maneuvers that Bird was well equipped to overcome. Also, it is standard coaching procedure not to ask your star player to defend the opposing team's offensive star, lest the strain diminish his own offensive game.

Yet here was Doctor J guarding Bird, an intriguing parallel to the previous season, when the rookie Celtic was asked to defend the superstar. And as Game 3 developed, Cunningham's strategy paid off. Philadelphia broke to a 21-10 lead, and they would not trail for the rest of the game. Erving's tight defense freed up Caldwell Jones to concentrate on Parish. Against the twin towers of Jones and Dawkins, Robert shot one for 14, his season-long woes in the Spectrum continuing. Bird handled the ball only 46 times and scored only 22 points. "I don't think they were prepared for it," Doc said after the game. "Larry might have been surprised to see me fronting him and sticking with him out on the court." Though the Celtics did struggle to within six with four minutes left, Erving capped his best night of the series by leading Philadelphia's break to a 10-2 romp and a 2-1 series lead.

It was a night of redemption for Erving, who had been pulled in and out of the lineup during Game 2 and held scoreless until the game was 17 minutes old. His role in Game 3 was a good example of his flexibility and his importance to the team on every level. But better than anyone, he was aware how long a seven-game series could be, and his comments to the press were characteristically cautious. "Basketball is a team sport. The individual strives to go out and have a great game every night, but it's not going to happen. If a team becomes dependent on that, then that team's not going to win the series."

The Celtics had not won in the Spectrum since January 1979, a span of ten games that did not bode well for a team that had lost its home-court advantage. In the lockerroom after Game 3, the players had spoken of the importance of winning Game 4, breaking the jinx, and avoiding a must-win game in Philly in Game 6. They also thought the series would become more physical. In Game 2 Dawkins had unintentionally elbowed Tiny in the ribs and forced him from the game with 18 minutes to play. Dawkins's strength would have to be matched if the Celtics were to win the key game on Sunday. As Maxwell said, "Sunday means everything to us now."

But Game 4 meant just as much to the Sixers, and the contest was one of the rivalry's most intense and exciting battles. Philadelphia roared away at the start, Mo Cheeks leading the break and Jones and Dawkins dominating inside. The Celtics *appeared* to be playing more effectively, but when the halftime buzzer sounded they were behind, 65-48. Finally, after the lead peaked at 19 in the third period, Boston did what it was fast becoming famous for—it put its own surge together and got right back into the game. Bird (shaking Erving, who continued to defend him), Ford and Archibald brought the Celtics to within three. Boston's desperation was evident in Fitch's substitution strategy: the starting unit stayed on the floor the entire second half except for brief appearances by Robey, McHale and Carr, who came in as the game wound down to its breathtaking climax.

Boston had edged to its first lead, 84-83, with 10:42 left in the game when Bird fed Robey inside for a lay-up. Dawkins then scored back-to-back baskets, fighting off Robey's physical defense. Their battle seemed to lift the level of play. Boston ran off seven straight points to tie the game at 93 with 6:19 remaining. In the ensuing minute and a half, Toney hit two free throws, Carr a fadeaway and Toney a long jump shot. Archibald streaked through the defense to connect with Max for a dunk, and Cheeks answered by overpowering Bird with his body to hit a reverse lay-up. To complete the furious rush of action, Robey missed in spite of heavy contact, and Cheeks scored off an offensive rebound. As the long minutes ticked off, the teams became more cautious, and with a minute to play and the Spectrum screaming, Philly held on to a 107-105 lead. Twice the Sixers mishandled the ball on offense, and after the 24-second clock ran down and Bobby Jones forced up a bad shot from the baseline, the Celtics had the ball, two timeouts and a 20-second timeout with six seconds to go.

The easiest second guess in sports is *Why didn't you call timeout?* Nothing seems more rash than the failure to stop, with the game on the line, to talk things over and devise a strategy. And yet anyone with experience in the matter will tell you that as often as not those timeouts

aid the defense as much if not more than the offense. With a man as creative and as quick as Tiny Archibald at the point, it makes sense to go with the flow and create something on the break. So when Max took the rebound and handed it to Tiny, the guard glanced at the sideline and either did not notice or chose to ignore Bill Fitch's hands coming together in the shape of a T. Bird was pressing up the left sideline, and Tiny was looking for him.

But so was Bobby Jones. As the tumult of the Spectrum surrounded them, the players seemed caught in a frozen moment, so drawn out that, looking back, you wouldn't believe it was only six seconds. Tiny swept through the center of the floor, head up. Bird was angling towards the basket, knowing exactly where Tiny was. But Jones, ever balanced and focused on his defensive game, was heading to a spot midway between the two Celtics. As Archibald aimed a hard chest pass at his teammate, Jones stretched and intercepted. The horn blared and the Sixers were up, 3-1. The Celts had lost their key game.

And so the stage was set for the greatest comeback of the Bird Era.

No one could blame the media for expecting a repeat of the 1979-80 playoff series, when the Sixers took a 3-1 lead to Boston and finished the Celtics off with the kind of flourish you expect from a veteran team. So the Celtics were a year older and wiser; so were the Sixers. So Larry Bird was performing with MVP talent and determination; he had last year as well and still not staved off defeat by the deep, determined Philadelphia team, a team that now had a new Mr. Clutch in Andrew Toney. So in the wake of Game 4 the press made much of the parallel as they walked into the Sixer lockerroom and found a team both exultant *and* apprehensive. In one corner of the room Darryl Dawkins was saying, "The Celtics never die. They don't give up." In another, Chuck Daly and trainer Al Domenico were comparing notes. "I knew the lead wouldn't stand at halftime, but I thought they'd get back into it with six minutes left in the third quarter, not by the end of the third." Domenico nodded. "The fourth one...that fourth win will be murder." "You ain't kidding," Daly said. What did these men know that the press didn't?

The press hadn't *played* the Boston Celtics ten times that year, hadn't learned that this Celtics team had a confidence and an intensity that even a 3-1 deficit was not going to diminish. When the Celtics regrouped at Hellenic College the following day, they were surprisingly loose; they knew their task was formidable, but they were heartened by the way they had come back from a 19-point deficit to nearly win the game. If they could win in the Garden, they reasoned, they could go back to the Spectrum and give the jinx one last challenge. "If we beat them in Game 5 and then get them in the next game," Parish said, "there's *no* way we'll lose back in the Garden." Odd logic from a team so deep in the hole, but it was evidence of the belief the Celtics had in themselves.

Fitch gathered the players in the coach's office to watch a film of the fourth game. Focusing on technical matters—avoiding mismatches, anticipating picks, and so on —Fitch spoke generally from a supine position on the floor (Fitch had thrown his back out so severely he couldn't sit upright—more evidence of the tension and strain of this series). He did not point fingers. The players recognized their mistakes and looked forward to correcting them. At one point Archibald muttered, "C'mon, you guys. We gotta get 'em." Fitch shut off the VCR before the game was over and turned to his team, the team he had brought along so brilliantly to this point in late spring. "I've only been around one team that's been able to come back from a 3-1 deficit," he said. "The team made a total commitment, and it was extremely hard to shake off what looked like a certain defeat. But I'm telling you, it was the most rewarding experience a group of guys can have in this sport. We can do it." The players believed Fitch because they believed in themselves, and it was that belief that would keep them alive at moments when it all seemed over.

Game 5 was preceded by some off-court drama in Philadelphia. The day before the game Darryl Dawkins had arrived late for the flight to Boston. Many were worried he would not show up at all since he had sat out the previous day's practice with a mysterious ailment he would not discuss publicly. After much probing he revealed he had a virus that had forced him to spend the day in a clinic in New Jersey. Then it turned out the clinic didn't exist. Maurice Cheeks was then stricken with a far less arcane injury—before the game he suffered a migraine headache, a recurring problem that had also plagued him in the playoffs in 1979 and 1980. Cunningham told him to go out there and see what he could do, but ten minutes into Game 5 he had to go into the lockerroom, an ice bag on his forehead.

But the 1980-81 Sixers had their excellent depth to cover them, and they did not seem to miss their star guard in the first half. After a turnover-filled first quarter gave them a two-point lead, the 76ers ran away from Boston. Erving, Bobby Jones and Cheeks's replacement, Clint Richardson, ran the break and kept their poise as the intensity built. Three searing fast breaks towards the end of the half gave Philly a 59-49 lead at intermission, and Boston's weary players looked ready to clean out their lockers for the season as they filed off the floor.

But not Fitch. The man with a bad back and a clear purpose had put in too many hours to see this season end with another 4-1 smokeout. The last man into the lockerroom, he told the video man to leave the monitor off and went into the bathroom and splashed water on his face. He paced back and forth in front of his distraught players. "I can't believe what I'm seeing out there, guys. I can accept losing...I guess. But what I can't accept is letting yourselves lose without even trying. In this game, nothing other than your best, maximum effort will do. I can't allow you guys to let yourselves merely go through the motions... I'm not ready to end *my* season tonight. We have to go out there and play as hard as we possibly can."

Bill Fitch saying he could accept *losing*? Bill Fitch leaving the monitor off? Whether his eloquence and change of method did it or not, the Celtics came out for the second half a different team, keyed by Archibald's running and Parish's discovery of room to operate underneath. When a team has everything to lose and only a reprieve to gain, the motivation to play its best has to be very deep. The Celtics had it, but the Sixers did as well, and what unfolded in the fourth period of that game (after the Celtics had come back to even the contest in the third period) may well have been the first championship epiphany of the Bird Era, the first of many times the Celtics, faced with an almost certain losing situation, pulled out a victory by pure *will*.

As usual Bird started things off, reentering the game with 5:07 left and the score tied. He fired the ball up the first time he touched it. The shot missed, as did McHale's two-handed follow-up. Then out of nowhere Bird swept in for the rebound and dropped in a bucket that gave the Celts the lead. The Garden's din slowly quieted, however, as the Sixers tightened the defensive screws for the next three minutes. Unable to score much themselves, they kept Boston stifled as, with championship precision, they built the lead back up to six, 109-103, with 1:51 to play. The Celtics called timeout and set up for what looked like a do-or-die basket. Bird inbounded, looking for Parish in the low post. He lobbed the ball in, but Dawkins, anticipating the play, powered through Robert's post-up stance and stole the ball.

No one could forgive even the most diehard fan despairing at this point. Even in the NBA, a six-point lead *and* the ball with less than two minutes looks, as Joe Morgan might say, like six-two-even for victory. But the Celtics couldn't afford any negative thoughts. As Fitch said afterwards, "If we would have thought, for an instant, that we were through, we would have lost the game."

Then came the play that Bob Ryan has referred to as the first big turning point of the Bird Era. Toney sped downcourt with the ball, pausing briefly, and drove to the hoop. At the peak of his jump

Maxwell appeared, blocking the shot. Archibald got the ball and ran upcourt, head up. Reaching the right lane, he reversed his dribble, backed in, and scored, drawing a foul. That three-point play gave the Celtics life, and they contested the inbounds play so fiercely the 76ers had to call two timeouts. Here they desperately missed Cheeks's leadership and inbounding ability. Even after the timeout they couldn't get the ball in: Bird stole a loosely thrown pass and, his face showing what Mark Whicker of the *Bulletin* called "pure savagery," stormed through the lane to cut the lead to one. Carr, in the game for the final two minutes, made another key steal, and in the frantic scramble that followed, drew a foul. He scored both free throws to give Boston a 110-109 lead. Bobby Jones then drove hard to the hoop. Parish jumped out at him and Jones lofted a high, arcing shot. Parish's hand reach up and, as he realized any contact would be goaltending, pulled back at the last instant. Jones's shot skidded off, and Carr recovered and was fouled with a second to play.

Some drama remained. Carr made the first and, after lengthy discussion at the bench, deliberately missed the next two (the three-to-make-two rule was still in effect). Fitch reasoned that making the second would give Philly the ball and a timeout to set up a three-pointer. A deliberately errant shot would certainly run out the clock. But the unexpected happened when the second miss went straight to Bobby Jones, who called timeout. Though the Sixers could now tie the game with a two-point field goal, they were too exhausted—the inbounds pass went awry and the Celtics leapt off the bench at the buzzer. In the lockerroom, amidst the hooting and hollering, Auerbach and Fitch got into a heated exchange over the last-second coaching decision. Auerbach stormed out of the lockerroom, saying, "I don't care who he is..." But few were listening. They were getting ready to give the Spectrum one last shot.

The image that stayed with most people from that do-or-die Game 5 was the look on Larry Bird's face as he powered his way to the hoop for the Celtics' final field goal. His intensity, his total immersion in the business of winning, had never been more evident, and though he hadn't shot well, his performance that day clearly said that *hot* and *cold* affected Bird's contribution only relatively. He had proved himself a money player whose hunger for a championship was even greater than his talent. And yet the hole they had dug for themselves was so deep that even after that bravura exhibition the Celtics had to get the competitive fires yet again—and in a very unfriendly arena. When Bird, Carr and Robey sat down with Red Auerbach in the Boston Garden the next day, talking about the previous game, knowing they had a two-year jinx to break, they were defining the task ahead of themselves and building up their self-confidence.

They would need it. The atmosphere in the Spectrum the next day, May Day, was electric. A long white banner optimistically predicted, NEXT GAME: HOUSTON. (The Houston Rockets and Moses Malone, the dominant player in the West, awaited the winners of this series.) Chris Ford and Terry Duerod played a little pregame one-on-one as the crowd swelled to 18,000 plus. The crowd, confident in its team's strength at home, was priming itself for celebration, and the chants and

13 TIME NBA
WORLD CHAMPIONS

The veteran Ford scoffed at criticism that he was "too old" that year. "I just never cared what the media thought."

catcalls flowed as freely as the beer as the Celtics retreated to the lockerroom for their pregame meeting.

The atmosphere in the lockerroom was rich in anticipation and nervousness. The players had dressed in different lockers in an attempt to change their luck, and Bird kept up a steady stream of patter. A former lover of Billie Jean King had declared that day that the tennis star was a lesbian, and Bird asked a cigar-puffing Auerbach, "Hey Red, you been playing tennis with Billie Jean?" In the meeting they talked about getting off to a quick start, of neutralizing the famous and predictable Sixer opening rush. Would Cheeks be playing? "That little sucker will be out there," Bird said, implying that there was no way a competitor like Cheeks would miss *this* game. Fitch

talked defense. "Max, you have to keep faking at Doctor J when he's on his isolation move." Maxwell nodded. Watch Cheeks and Toney down low, he also cautioned. But the men knew what they had to do, and Fitch's talk was simply part of the ritual.

The Spectrum fans were on their feet and roaring before the opening tap, tossing insults at the Celtics and screaming encouragement for their team. The cheers grew even louder when, after spotting Boston a 6-2 lead, the 76ers went on a ferocious tear, knocking the Celtics on their backs with ferocious dunks by Dawkins, Erving and Bobby Jones. The pattern of the series remained consistent, and by the end of the first quarter, when Steve Mix floated in a left-handed jumper, Philly led, 31-19, a lead they would increase early in the second quarter. "We were doing everything we wanted to in the first sixteen minutes of the game," Cunningham said later. But the Celtics remained patient on offense and cunning on defense, coming up with a steal here and there and scoring slowly until the lead was down to a manageable seven late in the half.

Philadelphia had not come into this contest cowed by the defeat in Boston; they still thought they were the better team. "I believe that very strongly," Cunningham said. Erving offered this assessment: "We're making this game our seventh." As dangerous as such a statement may have seemed in hindsight, it was a measure of the 76ers' confidence before Game 6, and it forced Boston to do what only the Celtics of that time and place *could* have done—pull out a victory as difficult and as enervating and as monumental as the win they had managed in Boston just two days before. Yet how could they overcome yet another halftime deficit? From where would they summon the energy to come from behind again? As the 76ers padded their lead to ten in the opening minutes of the second half, the questions sounded louder. Then, in a way that seemed almost fated, the game's complexion was altered by something that happened *off* the floor, and the second Turning Point in as many games resurrected the Celtics' championship hopes.

In a momentary lull under the Celtics' basket, Dawkins gave Cedric Maxwell a subtle little shove—nothing much, but enough to send the unsuspecting forward stumbling into the crowd. Off balance, Max bumped a few fans as he tried to break his fall. Suddenly he was exchanging words with a fan, who reportedly made a racist comment. A fight broke out, and Max was quickly out of the magical world of the basketball court and in the middle of a mob. The crowd began losing control. They had a chance to *matter*! Someone brandished a knife!

"I'm going to kill you!" "*What's going on?*"

The bench rushed to Max's side; for a frightening, chaotic moment the game disappeared. This contest was for keeps. *We're making this game our seventh.*

M. L. Carr has claimed that this game was the most intense he ever played in, and that intensity emanated most from Cedric Maxwell. When Max emerged from that scuffle to a cascade of taunts and boos, he started playing defense that was inspired, fundamental and aggressive. His game moved to a level that was dreamlike and poetic. And his spirit spread to his teammates. Erving, in isolation and off the switch with Dawkins, had taken it to the hoop consistently in the first half. Now, as the Celtics rallied, Max intimi-

dated the Doc so successfully the 76ers suddenly looked leaderless. Anticipating the switch, challenging him in isolation, denying him the ball, Max became the center of a Celtics defense that made the Sixers look like "blunderers." The flow that is so essential to the game, that the 76ers had so beautifully achieved so many times that season, was so effectively denied them that each move seemed discrete and stoppable. And with the clarity that comes from playing beyond themselves, the Celtics saw superstition drop its mantle and float like a ghost into the world beyond the Spectrum. We can win this thing! *We can do it!*

Underneath the basket the tension was taking form in hard, physical play, Dawkins and Parish duking it out, Bird, in one unforgettable sequence, pounding the offensive boards, shooting three times until, tumbling over three bodies, he made the shot as a foul was called. Fully in control of the action, managing *time* in an eerie way, the Celtics fought back with an offense that was as coordinated in its weaves, picks and improvisations as the Sixers' was disjointed. Slowly Philly's advantage melted; slowly the Celtics saw their simple, clean, hard basketball defeating the Spectrum jinx. With Fitch's guidelines on offense, K. C.'s on defense, and their own superb individual talents clicking wonderfully, the Celtics played eighties, Bird Era basketball at its best...

Caught on the sideline with the ball and time running out, Archibald surveyed the court. Chris Ford, on the Celtics' bench directly behind him, saw the defensive formation and said instinctively, "One on one, Tiny!" With a New York-playground flash of the hips, Tiny was by Clint Richardson, flying down the baseline for a layup...

Classic Celtics basketball—that is, textbook ball. Here, McHale blocks out Mike Mitchell and Robey positions himself against Bill Laimbeer, then of Cleveland, allowing Bird the freedom to get the rebound.

Under pressure from the defensive master Mo Cheeks, Archibald forced up a lefty jumper—the ball skidded off, but in the split second when the other players stood still, Tiny observed the basic rule, *follow your shot*, snagged the ball and laid it in...

On the boards Larry Bird, with drive as relentless as a Hoosier winter is cold, used his strength and mastery of position to dominate. Then, the bruising 6-9 body suddenly elegant and precise, he stepped outside for his patented sets, sending the ball through cleanly. Defensively he was everywhere. In one dramatic sequence Erving moved past Max and a switching Parish when Bird swept in, blocked the shot and recovered the ball. On the bench

McHale turned to Duerod and said, "That's it. That's the break we needed. We're gonna win it." Another turning point...

It came down, as it always did against the Sixers, to another frantic ending, the kind that ages the true fan and makes him wonder why he takes it all so seriously his stomach flutters. When Parish stepped back to hit an in-your-face jumper over Dawkins—and was fouled—the Celts were up, 94-93, and the home cooking and the glow of Boston Garden suddenly beckoned. Dawkins answered with a crashing tomahawk dunk that again tilted the scales, and when Parish fouled out setting an illegal pick, the fates seemed to be favoring Philly. But Dawkins botched a chance to go ahead by three and Bird got the lead back for Boston. The final minute arrived—plenty of time for more heroics and some fabled, mystical Celtics luck.

After Philadelphia failed to convert, Bird found himself trapped on the right sideline with the shot clock down to five seconds. Ford, ever the player-coach, shouted, "*Laaaaarrreeeeeee*, shoot it!" Twenty-two feet from the basket, Erving blanketing his vision, Bird send the ball skyward. The rotation looked good, but the shot looked short. It hit the rim, bounced dreamily up and—as Don Nelson's shot had in the last game of the 1969 Finals; as John Havlicek's had to eliminate the Knicks that same year—fell through the hoop: 98-95, Boston. But then Andrew Toney took command, scorching a 17-footer and then stealing the ball from Bird to give Philadelphia a chance to win the game. With less than 20 seconds left, Toney split the court, moving into the lane, stopping for the jump shot that would win the game. McHale, who had come in for Parish, stretched and swatted the ball to Maxwell. The radios of New England reverberated with the rasping euphoria of Johnny Most: "*McHale blocks the shot!*"

Fittingly, Max clinched the game with two free throws after being fouled. He fell into Carr's embrace and paraded with his teammates into the lockerroom. Auerbach, the proud patriarch, glided in with a victory smile. A peak experience, a triumph that ranks with the greatest of Celtics wins, it was nevertheless incomplete—they had to play another game two days later. Bird, knowing they had to transform this euphoria into momentum, spoke to his teammates just before the press spilled in. "We have to play it cool, you guys. Pay them respect and say everything you can to pump our fans up for Sunday. Let's not give them anything out of our lockerroom to respond to." The media entered and looked for words to describe the obvious championship maturity of this young team.

The images that remain from that series are not confined to the basketball court. When the Celtics' charter returned from Philadelphia at three o'clock in the morning, it could not land on the designated runway because 3,000 fans had come out to Logan Airport to greet their heroes. The plane landed at an alternative runway as the fans converged. Leaving the plane, Bird was engulfed.

Later that day, after a loose practice, Bird went home to rest and mow his lawn. The skies above Brookline were bright and innocent. A friend joined him for lunch and commented on Game 6. "What a game." Bird shook his head slowly. If the season were to end the next day there would be enough good memories, enough great performances, to last almost anyone a lifetime. But Bird's demeanor admitted no pleasure. "Yeah," he said. "But it'll be tougher tomorrow."

How many times could the same drama unfold? How many times could the Celtics come from behind (19, 19 and 17 points in the three previous games) against what many thought was the best team in basketball? After three games decided by two points it was time for another nail-biter, another example of the Celtics' maturity and determination, this time in a game decided by a single point. Deep down the 76ers must have known, when they led by 11 in the first half, 11 again in the second half, that any game at this level against this team, was bound to go to the wire. And knowing what it would come to, the teams were suitably ferocious, angling for every advantage, coming close to blows, delivering the heroic plays at the appropriate times. If so much wasn't at stake it might have seemed pedestrian—this was how it had to be with Philly and Boston; this was what the season would come down to. "We made our destiny," Bird said. Indeed they did.

When Doctor J hit a hesitation lay-up to put the Sixers up, 89-83, with 4:34 remaining in the game, there may have been a few people in the Garden seats who were skeptical; but they were a minority. The action that remained (Philadelphia would score only one point in that time) was clutch basketball at its best: defensive gems from Carr, Maxwell and Parish; standout offense from Archibald and Bird. But the game, series and season was best symbolized by the Celtics' final basket of that wonderful series, a basket that, appropriately, came off a Parish steal from Dawkins with the score tied at 89. As the ball rolled free, and the Sixers center came crashing down on Tiny, Bird picked up the ball and sped down the left sideline. He looked to his right, as if to pass, but he was decoying Cheeks. Bird was on a solitary mission that trip. "There was nobody else in the whole world that I wanted to have the ball but me," he said later. He pulled up at 17 feet and banked it home, a shot that did more than win the game, did more than move the Celtics into the championship series. Reminiscent as it was of the clutch shots of the great Sam Jones, it seemed propelled off the glass and into the net by the force of tradition,

by the invisible lines of team history strung along the rafters high above. With that shot Bird was fashioning a Celtics memory that would live alongside the great plays of Russell, Jones, Cousy and Havlicek.

The last minute spun itself out. The tension sang in the air. With one second left Bobby Jones inbounded an alley-oop to Doctor J that hit the top of the backboard. The greatest playoff series of the Bird Era was over. Boston had come from behind in three straight unbelievable games to win a berth in The Finals of the 1980-81 basketball season. And when fans left the Garden to party into the night, they carried with them the image of Larry Bird hitting his clutch bank shot and then waving his fist through the cheers.

The Finals were notable because they gave championship rings to the Celtics, but as a series it could not be compared with the masterpiece Boston had just concluded. The Celtics had beaten Houston 12 straight times going into The Finals, and though Moses Malone and his support would take two games from Boston, including a two-point win in the Garden, the Celtics were not to be denied. Bird and Maxwell (the championship MVP) led the charge, Max overwhelming the Rockets with 28 points and 19 rebounds in the crucial Game 5, Bird taking over in a close Game 6, the last game of that dream season. As Bill Fitch watched the greatest pro season of his career finish to perfection, he reflected on the young man who had done everything he had asked and more. "I watched Larry during that fourth-quarter stretch. I thought, 'There he is, totally at peace with the game, even though the pressure is at its greatest.' I kept focusing on that singular image: Larry Bird, the basketball, the gym.'' With a minute left and the championship ensured, Fitch took Bird out of the game. Seven years later, Bird had this to say about this moment, the moment of his first championship at any level: ''My heart was pounding so on the bench, I thought it would jump out of my chest. You know what you feel? You just want everything to stop and stay like that forever.''

That's exactly where those great moments stay—frozen in time, secure in the minds of those who watched the Celtics become champions again.

"There was nobody else in the whole world that I wanted to have the ball but me."

The 1981 championship series MVP and star of the title-winning Game 7 in the 1984 Finals. Dan Shaughnessy of the Boston Globe *wrote after Cedric Maxwell's 1984 performance: "Tied, ahead or behind, Maxwell never lost control of the night. He taunted James Worthy mercilessly and kept the Celtics in charge." "I just told him he couldn't guard me," Max said. "I said, 'James, this isn't the 2-A league. This is the big time, and you have to guard me.'"*

Among McHale's impressive list of credentials: Gold Medal at the Pan Am Games, 413 consecutive games played, First-Team NBA and First-Team Defense, Sixth Man of the Year in 1984 and 1985 (the league's only two-time winner). After McHale scored 56 points on 22-for-28 shooting to establish a Celtics single-game scoring record, Bird said: "Any time you only miss six shots and score 56 points, you deserve to get the ball every time down the floor."

Bird once described DJ as "the best player I've ever played with." Johnson, asked about the almost telepathic way he and Bird play together, called it a "sixth sense." After Bird and Johnson teamed up on the most distinctive play of the Era, when Bird stole Isiah Thomas's pass in Game 5 of the 1987 Eastern Conference finals and fed Johnson for a game-winning lay-up, Kevin McHale thought the play symbolized the team: "I'll tell my son in the future that once upon a time I played on a team that never gave up. That is the important thing to remember. That there were guys here who never gave up, and that it paid off for them on this night."

Parish told Tony Cotton of Sports Illustrated *in 1981: "I had heard it all—that I had a bad attitude, I only played when I wanted to. Someone even said I was so lazy I got into foul trouble on purpose so I wouldn't have to play. When I came to Boston I knew I'd be tested to see if I had what it took to be a winner. I always knew I did."*

Bird thought Ainge became a star in the 1985 Finals against the Lakers: "I said before that series that if Danny outplayed Byron Scott, we'd win. Well, Danny won the personal duel, but we still lost." K. C. Jones commented after the victory in the 1986 Finals: "Fans don't realize Danny's contribution, but the coaches do. He's such a tenacious player."

K. C. Jones said of Walton during the Celtics' 1986 championship season: "Without a doubt, we became a championship team with Bill Walton coming off the bench...He's a great player, one of the greatest ever. Who wouldn't want him coming off your bench?"

Dennis Johnson once gave this self-report on how he feels when he's playing at his best: "Playing well is the best feeling there is. It's you at your happiest moment, better in its own way than winning the championship. You're getting paid...It's like there's nothing you can't conquer, even if there are two men guarding you...Even if you were in darkness, you would know where the basket is."

Red Auerbach on Bird: "People have asked me why I drafted Larry when I knew he had a year of eligibility remaining. Because you'd rather have potential great fresh blood than potential good fresh blood coming into your organization. Larry, I felt, had that potential—yet I didn't even dream of the surprises that were to come. I didn't realize how quick he was. I had no knowledge of his rebounding abilities. I knew he had a court presence on offense, but I didn't realize he had one on defense, too. And I had no sense of his leadership qualities, or his ability to motivate other people as well as motivating himself."

5

TRYING TO REPEAT

When Bill Russell retired in 1969, he ended a career distinguished by 11 NBA titles in 13 years, including a phenomenal eight straight championships over the late fifties and early sixties. As player-coach for his final three seasons, he followed a playoff loss to the great 1967 76ers team with back-to-back titles. In the 23-year history of the NBA up to that point, 11 champions had come back to repeat the following year. It would be 19 long years after Russell's retirement before the L. A. Lakers won two championships in a row. The general failure to repeat has been so consistent in the NBA over the last two decades that sportswriters have taken to calling the pattern Russell's Curse, as if the Celtics star jinxed every other team in the league upon retiring.

Of course there are good reasons why winning back-to-back championships has been so difficult. We have already seen how the ABA, free agency and a changing business environment disrupted the league in the seventies, making team stability very hard to maintain. The number of teams and the level of talent continued (and continues) to increase into the eighties, and the expanded playoff structure makes the postseason a grueling test, with more chances of elimination than ever before. And of course Bill Russell is not around anymore. He did curse the league in the sense that when he retired he removed a physical and motivational presence that did more for winning consistency than anything else. Larry Bird and Magic Johnson notwithstanding, no player has had the dominance of a Bill Russell—no player ever will.

There is also a natural human tendency to relax after a big victory. Just as the

Celtics have often lost to New York or Indiana the night after an emotional win over Philly or L. A., so too the year following a championship can lead to a letdown, a psychological loosening that increases the pressure of being champions. Expectations go up—expectations that are difficult to match because as champions you are literally on the defensive, defending your crown every time you play. And no one was more conscious of these pressures than Bill Fitch during the summer of 1981. Heading into the new season, Fitch worried that his team would be soft physically and mentally after a buoyant offseason. Being who he

is, Fitch did not celebrate long before thinking of the season ahead, and his demands for excellence were adamant. "I'm gonna ride their backs," he said privately. He knew that teams would be gunning for the Celts, that a visit by the champs to an alien arena would fire up the fans and make every game of the new season more difficult.

And it was tough. The Celtics would win 63 games that year, the second-highest total in team history up to that point, but they had to contend with injuries, expectations and internal dissensions that made the season very long and very tiring. Bird, secure now as the

The Celtics coaching staff 1980-83: Jimmy Rodgers and K.C. Jones, assistants, flank head coach Bill Fitch. M. L. Carr said about Fitch: "Fitch was an excellent coach for a young team. No coach worked any harder...But as we grew and matured and gained experience, there was less need for his kind of policing. Some of us felt we were experienced enough to police ourselves."

league's premier player (and with *Sports Illustrated*'s sanction as the best in the NBA), learned that life could be tough at the top. He was bounced around a lot in the early season, and he struggled. Fitch and Auerbach maintained that the referees were allowing opponents to go after Bird physically, and Larry was a half-step slow in the opening months. Fitch wondered privately if his superstar was in the worst condition of his career. Bird often joked that when his playing days were over he would drink beer to the end of his days with his friends back home. He was being playful, of course, but he did have a tendency to gain weight, and in the early years of his pro career he was not as scrupulous about keeping in shape during the offseason as he was from 1983 on.

And yet how could you criticize Larry Bird? Even this minor failure was one he rectified with tremendous discipline after four years in the NBA, "punishing" himself during the 1983 offseason and coming to camp (as he would every year from this point on) ready to step onto the court and play at his best. But it is tempting to be critical of the champions, if only to avoid the superlatives of recounting another 60-win season, another litany of brilliant performances, another dramatic regular-season and playoff battle with the hated Sixers. Yet wasn't this the year of the Streak, when Boston won 18 in a row midseason, including three tough wins on the Texas swing when Tiny and Bird were injured? And didn't this team match the 35-6 home record (before sellout crowds on every date) of the previous two years while improving its road record by a game? And didn't Larry Bird, MVP of the All-Star game and All-Defense Second Team for the first time in his career, average more points, assists and blocks while matching his prodigious rebound total of the previous year? Who could possibly criticize?

Success breeds raised expectation, and though few fans were unhappy with the 1981-82 season, some felt that it was a letdown from the previous year. And perhaps too the occasional friction within the team made its way into the atmosphere, like steam from a faulty pipe. Fitch made certain his crew worked as hard as ever to keep winning, but unhappiness was condensing slowly, tiny drops of bitterness that took longer to evaporate than in the past. His style rubbed many the wrong way, and his running cold war with K. C. Jones had only got worse. They had agreed to disagree over the years, but this season would not be an easy one for Case. As Fitch berated the world champs in practice and belittled them in games, Jones fumed. After one tough session he said, "He's blowing it! They don't need to be castigated. They *know* they're good. They need to be supported, not torn down." K. C. worried less about Fitch's attitude towards him than about his attitude towards his players. Coming from a background of racism and poverty, Jones had succeeded because of his own inner strength and the positive help of many teachers and coaches throughout his great career. Fitch's style, in his eyes, was negative, the kind of style that would have intimidated the young K. C., and Jones was extremely sensitive about the effect of Fitch's approach on the players. Years later he would write, "As time went on some players began to be very unhappy with the way they were treated or talked to."

K. C. was there for these men, and on at least one occasion he talked a player out of publicly asking to be traded. He acted as a calming influence when tempers flared and players (who were being paid a lot more than their boss) shouted back. He also took his blows and landed a few. Before a game against the Bullets that season he made some suggestions to the players. Fitch told him thanks for the help but no thanks, and from then on Case decided to keep his mouth shut. The frustration built, and by the end of the season he had a lot of resentment stored away. It spilled out on Draft Day 1982, a Monday. Fitch had made it clear that he didn't want K. C. around for the weekend meetings prior to the draft, and Jones had spent those days golfing in Indiana. When he arrived at the Boards and Blades Club for the event, Fitch crooked his finger and called him over. In a rough tone he demanded to know where K. C. had been over the weekend. Seeing how Fitch was jerking him around, K. C. got mad. The words got tougher and the two men scuffled. Fitch told him he was through.

Anyone who knows K. C. Jones's story knows how much an incident like this must have affected him, and even though the two men patched up their differences and spent another year as associates, the fundamental differences did not disappear. K. C., while sharing in the glory of the first championship and taking satisfaction in the guidance he gave individual players, could not have had the full joy of winning during those years. But he would get his opportunity—and even more of the championship pie than Fitch.

But the Boston assistant coach wasn't the only one having problems with Fitch. Parish's complex relationship with his boss continued. Ironically, he and Fitch shared spots in the shadows—Robert in Bird's, Fitch in Auerbach's—and as

proud and talented men neither liked it. But Parish and Fitch had very different personalities and backgrounds, differences that prevented them from forming any kind of permanent bond. Parish, who would hold out briefly in 1983, had contractual problems with the Celtics in 1981 and did not appreciate Fitch's tactless negotiating style. While talks were at an impasse, Fitch drew the Chief aside one practice and told him the Celtics were considering going after James Edwards, who was then playing out his option with the Indiana Pacers. Bristling at the thought of being compared with a second-rate journeyman center, Parish shook his head afterwards and said, "James Edwards!

Cleveland Cavs scout Dick Helms commented in Forty-Eight Minutes: "Robert is so good in post-up situations. He has such long arms and the ability to catch the ball, turn quickly and shoot it. He is dependable. He is so stoic out there, you tend to forget he is a very intense player."

Well, let 'em get Edwards. Fuck 'em.'' They soon agreed to a contract, but Parish never completely trusted Fitch.

But that did not mean that Fitch was not a good coach for Robert. According to Mike Carey, a writer for the *Boston Herald* at the time and a friend of Parish, Robert had plenty to be grateful for to Fitch. ''He made Robert into a complete center, and I don't think Robert would disagree with that statement. Robert did everything when he came to Boston—ran the floor, played the low post consistently, hit the boards. Robert had his ups and downs with Bill. He might focus on the downs, but there were good moments too.''

That year Fitch had also to contend with balancing the needs of a number of talented players, all of whom were competitive and wanted to play as much as possible. Having a good bench, as the Celtics of six years later would discover, is very important in the NBA, but as the young players gained experience the Celtics had more depth than they sometimes knew what to do with. With four potential starting guards in Tiny, Carr, Ford and Henderson, the backcourt situation was further complicated by the arrival of the much-heralded Danny Ainge in November 1981. McHale's offensive development further diminished the offensive role of Maxwell, who had already taken a back seat to Bird. Though Max would continue to start (as McHale turned into the league's most feared sixth man), his scoring average continued to slide downward, as it would for his whole career in Boston. As time went on, Max also worried occasionally about not being in at the end of games; as the Celtics went more and more to McHale, Max must have often remembered Red's famous dictum—''It's not important who starts a game; it's who finishes it.''

Of course Max was refining his role as one of the league's most tenacious defensive stars during this period. When the Sixers or the Knicks or the Bucks came to town, it was Max who guarded Doctor J or Bernard King or Marques Johnson. But in a game where scorers get most of the acclaim (the All-Star roster usually reads almost identically to the list of the league's top scorers), Max was overshadowed, even though his position on the team was as important as it ever was. Members of the media often said that Max ''disappeared,'' implying that he stopped working at his game, an accusation Max fiercely resented. He insisted to his last day as a Celtic that his game hadn't diminished. Fortunately his teammates and coach knew this. Though he might insult him from time to time, Fitch never underestimated Max's value—proven in 1986 when Fitch obtained Max for the Houston Rockets. And Max gave his coach credit too. ''You don't realize what Bill Fitch is doing until later in your career''—and this comment from a man who, with Robert Parish and others, clapped and cheered when Fitch's hated VCR slid from a table at practice one day and smashed on the floor.

But at least Max would get his minutes. Rick Robey, who held out so much promise in '79-80, saw his minutes and scoring average drop considerably as the frontcourt deepened. And the guards on the team had a rough time of it. When Ainge joined the club after a protracted legal battle between the Toronto Blue Jays and the Celtics he did not get a warm reception. Fitch, though he believed from the beginning that Ainge would star in the NBA, treated the rookie exactly as he

Danny Ainge scoring a jumper over Jerry Sichting, then of the Pacers, later a teammate and close friend. Fitch drew a lot of criticism for starting Ainge. Finally, the Celtics coach looked yet another inquisitor in the eye and said, "Look around the league. There aren't any shooting guards better than Danny Ainge, in my view."

treated everyone else—which must have been quite a shock to this young, emotional hotshot who had been at the center of athletic attention and stardom all his life. The veterans also greeted him coldly, and Max didn't even speak to Ainge for five days. In giving Ainge and Henderson their minutes, Fitch cut Ford's drastically and Archibald's slightly (Carr, as a swingman, was used at guard and forward). Charles Bradley, the 1981 first-round draft pick, also had to be fit in. Though Ainge was the ideal replacement for Chris Ford, Archibald clearly saw the whole situation as threatening to his posi-

tion. Race was also perceived as a factor. As the white players increasingly became the offensive stars of the team, some of the black players suspected that the Celtics were trading on that fact (remember—whites are a *minority* in the NBA, the underdogs in a funny sort of way) to attract fans. The scenario was unlikely given Auerbach's record, but the resentment was understandable.

However, the situation was relieved in a negative way that season by a rash of injuries that interrupted the team's smoothness and continuity. Archibald injured his left wrist, a hurt that took longer to heal than his previous injuries (Tiny was now 33 years old). Maxwell strained a knee, Ford his back. But the worst injury occurred during a February 28 game against the Milwaukee Bucks in the Garden, when the physical play that had worried Fitch and Auerbach all year finally caught up with Larry Bird. Reaching around Harvey Catchings in an attempt to steal the ball, Bird took a swinging elbow flush in the face. The whole arena heard the crack, and Bird went to the parquet, out cold. Fitch rushed out onto the floor. "I'm running out there to look at him, and all kinds of things are running through my head. I'm worried about how badly he's hurt. I'm wondering how many timeouts we're going to have to use to get him off the court. And most of all, in the back of my head I'm thinking how many times I've seen him hit with elbows. An elbow is *hard*. Give me the choice of hitting someone with a closed fist or an elbow, and I'll take the elbow every time."

Bird actually came back to play in the second half of that game, a crucial contest for the Celtics that they won with gutsy performances from Maxwell (31 points) and Parish (29). Bird had surgery the next day to repair his crushed cheekbone. Doctors said he would probably be out for ten days. Auerbach was incensed. "What bothers me is that I watch Doctor J and Marques Johnson play, and you go near one of those guys when he's up in the air and you get called for a foul. I see Bird getting knocked on his butt all over the place and nothing is getting called. I don't see why it should be different for Bird." Will McDonough, a friend of Red's and a *Globe* columnist, asked in the paper if the Celtics might consider bringing in an enforcer to protect Bird. "Those days ended when Tomjanovich was crushed," Fitch responded. "I just don't have the type of players on the team to do that."

Nevertheless, the Celtics developed a more physical game during these years, a necessity in the Eastern Conference, where the Bullets, Bucks, 76ers, Pistons and Knicks had big, rough teams. And while the Celtics never had an "enforcer" in the mold of Jim Loscutoff, they did have some players who became known for their physical play, particularly M. L. Carr. A giving, friendly man off the court, Carr was the complete team man once a game started, as aggressive and physical as he needed to be to gain an advantage. "I wanted a guy I was going against to be thinking about M. L. as opposed to fulfilling the task at hand—winning the game for his team," M. L. said in his autobiography, *Don't Be Denied*. "I was willing to give and take my bumps and bruises. Players in the NBA were big, and they could take it."

As friendly a man as he was, Carr had never been afraid to jump into the fray. As a schoolboy in preintegration South he

Bird shooting over Milwaukee's Sidney Moncrief, Game 1, 1983 playoffs. After fracturing a cheekbone following a collision with Harvey Catchings's elbow, he became the greatest sixth man in the history of the game.

had caused talk when he walked through the whites-only entrance to the local doctor's office and drank from the "white" water fountain. His meandering path to the NBA had reinforced his ethic of hard work and belief in himself—the Celtics ethic. Even though he had benefited as much as anyone from the free-agent environment of the seventies and received a handsome financial reward for his journeyman years when he signed with the Celtics for $1.6 million in 1979, he never sat on his laurels and never questioned the roles he was asked to play. His energy and emotional game were invaluable to the Celtics, even in the waning years of his career when Red asked him to "be a morale-builder."

He did, however, have more and more problems with Fitch as time went on. An outspoken supporter of the coach during the turnaround season, Carr's relations with him declined steadily in the eighties. In the 1982-83 season they fought regularly as Fitch's lack of compassion and his treatment of Jones irked Carr. In an exhibition game against San Antonio Carr jammed his thumb while going for a steal against George Gervin. When Fitch told him he hoped that M. L. had hurt his finger because it was a dumb play, Carr blew up, telling him that a coach should *never* wish an injury on a player. Carr lost all respect for Fitch after that comment. But by then the decline was clear; in 1981-82 it was still latent, and most of Carr's aggression was displayed on the court—to the Celtics' advantage.

Bird's injury came at what looked like a very bad time. Predictably, the Celtics and 76ers had been neck and neck for the Atlantic Division lead all year, the Celtics holding a slight advantage at the All-Star break to give Fitch the head coaching job for the midseason classic (Bird was the MVP of that game, scoring 12 points in the final six and a half minutes). After the break, Boston swung through the West for a respectable 3-3 February trip, including a victory in the Los Angeles Forum for the second straight year. Boston was doing well, but the last two months of the season would be crucial, and Fitch was especially worried about the three-game Texas trip and the two March dates against the 76ers. Last season's wars had proved the value of the home-court advantage, and Fitch was determined to secure it.

When the Celtics defeated Milwaukee and Larry Bird went down, the team had three wins in a row. But Fitch was worried. With Bird gone and Tiny still out with his injured wrist, the Celtics were heading down to Texas without their two most creative offensive weapons. A losing streak now could punch a hole in the season and give the Sixers the break they needed going into the playoffs. "Avoid a sweep," Fitch was saying to himself. Even a single win in Texas would have satisfied him. But he was to find out that this group was building towards a rhythm that would become eerily successful, as the starting unit of McHale, Maxwell, Parish, Henderson and Carr came to understand each other's pace, moves and tendencies. That is why the Streak took place.

The first game was in Dallas, against a much-improved Mavericks team with two young stars in Mark Aguirre and Jay Vincent. Head coach Dick Motta had never been a favorite of the Celtics. "I don't like him," Bird said then. "He's always riding you. Sarcastic. How can you like a guy like that?" With Larry watching the game on television in Boston, the Celtics played a tight contest. Vincent broke out for 20 points in the third period, but the Celtics tightened up defensively and got unexpected offense from Ainge. For one of the few times that season—a tough one for the rookie—Ainge displayed the ability that Auerbach and Fitch knew he had, scoring 17 points in the second half, including four straight jump shots down the stretch. Parish, who was averaging 26 points a game since the All-Star break, scored 27. He also had 14 rebounds and six blocks as he stopped the Mavericks inside. Fitch breathed a sigh of relief, and the team headed to San Antonio.

The HemisFair Arena is one of the most raucous in sports, and in the early eighties the Spurs still had the magnificent Ice Man, George Gervin, to go to for automatic offense (San Antonio would win the Midwest Division crown that year). This game was a challenge for the depleted Celts, and they responded with an excellent game from a starting five of Henderson, Carr, Parish, McHale and Maxwell that countered Gervin's 48. Picking up the slack created by Bird's absence, Cedric played the low post like the offensive star of old, twisting, wriggling and jump-hooking his way to 25 points and five assists as he played for 48 minutes. "Give credit to our team," Fitch said, "but give it especially to Max. He was our inspiration out there." Already the Texas trip was a success, and the Streak stood at five.

But it was the game against Houston that was the most inspirational, one of those games that any Bird Era fan will always remember. Boston went into the Summit with confidence, knowing that they had risen to the challenge of their superstars' absence and played excellent team basketball. Moses Malone and the Rockets wanted to show the Celtics that they were still a championship-caliber team, and the game turned into a battle, with Moses scoring 38 points and taking it strong to the Chief. Parish fouled out as Malone, according to Bob Ryan, "bulled, bullied, banged, bashed and bamboozled" him to a premature exit. But again Max came through, scoring 24 in 44 minutes, including ten from the charity stripe. Carr and Ford were in top motivational form, and the team was rarely as unified. In a critical offensive possession, Maxwell penetrated, dishing off to the seldom-used Eric Fernsten. Fernsten went strong to the hoop, scoring and drawing a foul on Elvin Hayes. His three-point

play won the game for Boston, 100-98, and the lockerroom afterwards sounded as if the team had won The Finals. As the media pressed in, the players told them to be sure to include Fernsten's name in the headlines. Fernsten said, "That's what's beautiful about this team. We lose the best player in the league and the best playmaker, and it means we've got some pretty good people behind them." Fitch said, "This was the type of game over an 82-game schedule that the guys can say, 'I've earned my salary.'"

This game was as good as proof as any that the Celtics had become a team distinguished by its controlled egos. As Mike Carey said in the *Herald* on a different occasion, "Larry was fortunate he had teammates like Tiny Archibald, who relieved him of playmaking responsibilities early in his career. And also a player like Robert Parish. Because Parish doesn't care about his own offense. Only about winning." The same could be said for Max. With the Chief, he was playing superstar basketball, averaging over 20 points a game, playing the same consistent defense against the opposition's toughest forward, doing his yeoman work on the boards. Above all he was displaying the kind of leadership that would help turn this season of injuries and hard feelings into an almost complete success.

When Bird returned two games later Fitch faced a dilemma: How could he break up a starting team that was riding an eight-game winning streak and playing outstanding basketball? But how could he not start the best player in the NBA? On any other team this situation would have led to problems. On the Celtics it became a positive force. When Fitch asked Bird to temporarily become the best sixth man in NBA history, he knew that Bird would do whatever he was asked to help the team keep winning. He had that kind of attitude. Bird desperately wanted to play 48 minutes, but he disciplined himself to remain within the team scheme and gave the Celtics a wonderful psychological weapon (a weapon they would continue to have with McHale in the years ahead). Just at the point when the starters needed a break and an opponent was taking its best players off the court, who came in as a sub but Larry Bird! What could have been more demoralizing?

The strategy worked as Boston kept on winning. Ainge made seven steals and sparked a 107-106 win over New York. In the Detroit Silverdome, on a night when Fitch was ejected because referee Jim Capers thought that insults coming from the NBA's most famous fan, Leon "The Barber" Bradley, were in fact coming from the Celtics coach, Max rallied the Celts to a 111-101 win. After Max and Bird paced Boston to wins over Indiana and New Jersey, the guards took over. Carr shut down Dennis Johnson as the Streak rolled to 11 with a win over Phoenix in the Garden. Ainge forced an overtime against the Bullets by nailing a jump shot in the closing seconds. Bird, who had entered at the seven-minute mark and played the rest of the game, scored 31 and had 21 rebounds. But increasingly the talk was of Ainge, who was playing consistent ball and working his way into a sure spot in the rotation. Ford was fading from the scene. In what was proving to be his last season, he saw his minutes plummet. Characteristically, he accepted the change, motivating and contributing in whatever way he could. Not

only did his team spirit help the team at the time, it also laid the groundwork for his later role as assistant coach. Carr, Henderson and Ainge, meanwhile, were functioning very effectively, giving the Celtics a backcourt with some depth and an aesthetic very different from Tiny's flamboyant style.

Henderson's story, which did not have the best of endings, had become a classic success tale. His movement from Virginia Commonwealth to the Western League to the best team in the NBA seemed appropriate for a gym rat who worked as hard as anyone at the game. But his apprenticeship was stressful. Fitch, always hardest on the players he thought had potential, put a lot of pressure on him. Also, as the heir apparent to Tiny, Gerald had to deal with the proud Archibald's brooding as his playing time was reduced. But Henderson responded well, developing mental strength and intensity and a fighting attitude. Though he'll be remembered more for his great steal in Game 2 of the 1984 Finals and his unfortunate and star-crossed trade to Seattle for the rights to the draft pick that would become Len Bias, his contribution in 1981-82 was noteworthy.

Wins number 13 and 14 came in the Garden against the Hawks and Spurs. By this time Boston had pulled out to a three-and-a-half-game lead over Philadelphia, and the team flew to Philly for their first March contest with the Sixers full of confidence. With Dawkins out with an injured knee and Bobby Jones's diabetes acting up, the 76ers were short-handed, but they still had the Doc and Andrew Toney, who had become even more effective his second year in the league. Many people were comparing Toney to the Brooklyn legend and former Sixer World B. Free

Robert Parish pulling in a rebound over Julius Erving and Andrew Toney. In the second half of the '81-82 season, Parish was arguably the league MVP, averaging over 25 points and 15 rebounds a game.

(Free had legally changed his name from "Lloyd"). But Sixer assistant Jack McMahon was rightly insisting that he was a more complete player. "As fine a passer as Maurice Cheeks is, no one on our team makes the lob pass to Doctor J as well as Andrew. Call him a 'World' who also sees all of the floor." When K. C. Jones was asked if the 76ers went to Toney too often, he raised his eyebrows. "*Too* often? Hell, they don't go to him often enough." Three weeks before the March game at the Spectrum, Toney had amazed a national audience with 46 points against the Lakers, including 20 during a clutch fourth quarter. He had become a star.

But not even Toney could not help the Sixers today. The Streak continued as

Boston blew out the Sixers easily. This was a game that delivered a message the Celtics wanted Philly to remember into the playoffs: *We can take you out anytime and anywhere.* But against the 76ers messages can be dangerous, and when Toney, in spite of the Celtics' dominance, nearly got the Sixers back in it a few times during that game with some incredible play, Philadelphia was sending a few signals of its own. Boston, flying high as it was, would see Philly not only end the Streak three games later, but end the Celtics' season as well.

But with 15 wins in a row, the Celtics were now looking to break the franchise record of 17, set by the 1959 club at the height of the dynasty. On the road in Chicago they won number 16 behind Maxwell's 29. The record-tying and -breaking wins came easily: a 136-115 rout of the Pistons and a 125-104 victory over Cleveland. The season and the '81-82 club's place in history were now both secure. The Streak was the longest in the NBA since the 1971-72 Lakers won 33 straight, and the early-season pattern of injuries was over. But all good things come to an end, even in Boston, and when Philly came to the Garden for the second March game they took the tired Celtics easily. It was a loss fans could concede without too much pain. They had come to expect parity. From 1979 to 1985 the two clubs were 18-18 in the regular season and 12-12 in the playoffs. The Celtics brought out the best in Philly, and vice versa. Virtually assured of the best record in the NBA and the home court advantage right through the playoffs, Boston was looking forward to the postseason.

Going into the playoffs, the Celtics were the clear favorites. They had finished five games ahead of the 76ers and six ahead of the Lakers. Ironically, the injuries that had so concerned the club earlier had allowed the games of the younger players, particularly McHale and Ainge, to develop. McHale's intensity had been questioned the previous year, especially after he reportedly said late in the 1981 playoffs that he "wished it were all over already." His playing time had been drastically reduced in The Finals, but a year later he had won the respect of everyone with his play: stronger defense, continued shot-blocking brilliance and an increasingly impressive array of post-up moves. His defensive prowess was tested in the first playoff series of 1982, against the Washington Bullets.

On paper the Celtics should have taken this series easily. All six regular-season meetings between the clubs had been Celtics wins, and the Bullets' odd assortment of veterans (Greg Ballard, Spencer Haywood, Jim Chones) and young players (Jeff Ruland, Ricky Mahorn, Frank Johnson) did not match up well with Boston. But the series was a battle. With Bird and Tiny starting for the first time since coming back from their injuries, the Celtics opened with a 109-91 win in the Garden, but dropped Game 2 as Frank Johnson (who seemed to shoot better the farther away he was from the basket) hit a clutch three-pointer to give the Bullets a one-point win. The Washington frontcourt was extremely physical as Ruland and Mahorn—whom Johnny Most had memorably dubbed "McFilthy and McNasty"—threw their considerable weight around underneath. The series moved to Washington with a lot of intensity, as the Bullets now had the home-court advantage.

But Boston played two very good games in Landover, using a controlled passing

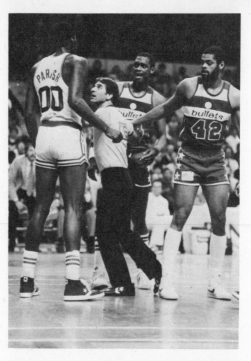

Parish renews hostilities with then-Bullet Rick Mahorn, as Bennett Salvatore intervenes and Greg Ballard looks on. In the fight-filled miniseries, which Boston won 3-1, the challengers pummeled the Celtics constantly. Kevin McHale commented after it was over, "It was our toughest series."

game to take advantage of the Bullets' inexperience in the frontcourt. Parish and McHale starred, the latter posting a playoff personal best of 25 in the Game 4 overtime win. Back in Boston the Celtics closed the series out with a thrilling double overtime win. With only four minutes left in their season and down by 13, the Bullets let Frank Johnson go wild from three-point land. He hit three big shots, each farther out than the previous, to get Washington within two. Ruland drew a foul and sunk both free throws to tie the game and send it into overtime. Then it was the Celtics' turn to rally. Down by five with 40 seconds left in the first overtime, they came back to force a second extra period as Max and McHale hit big shots. A 10-1 run closed the game out, and the players went home to lick their wounds and, for the third straight season, wait for Philadelphia to beat Milwaukee so that the archrivals could slug it out yet again for the Eastern Conference championship.

The distinct feeling of deja vu that permeated the 1982 playoff confrontation between Boston and Philadelphia was misleading. Yes, the personnel were much the same; yes, the Celtics blew the home-court advantage and fell behind, 3-1; yes, Boston came back, winning a monster game in the Spectrum and forcing a seventh-game showdown in the Garden. But that series proved entirely different, in tone and outcome. The previous year five of the seven games, including the final four, were decided by one or two points; in 1982 only one game was decided by less than eight points, and there were three bona fide blowouts. In 1981 the Celtics' play was consistent and injury-free; the following year their performance was up and down and Tiny Archibald was lost in Game 3 with a separated shoulder. Most importantly, when Billy Cunningham entered Boston Garden on May 23, 1982, to confront ghosts literal and symbolic, he brought with him the best doctor in the business. This time the Doc's house call saved the patient—at least for another couple of weeks.

K. C. Jones, who understands such things, pointed out how the schedule-makers unwittingly helped the 76ers in this series. After the Celtics opened the series with a near-perfect game, blowing out the Sixers by 40 points and showing little respect for their opponents in the process, there were three long days between Games 1 and 2—Sunday to Thursday. As Jones sipped a beer at a local bar he thought about the overconfident way the Celtics subs had padded the big lead in Game 1. With a twinge he remembered a tomahawk dunk Charles Bradley had slammed home in front of an angered Sixers bench. "I just don't like the way we did it," Jones said about the win. "With three days off, they'll be *ready*." He also remembered a timeout Billy Cunningham had taken in the final minutes of the game—a seemingly useless timeout in a game long since decided. Had he heard the CBS announcer's comment at the time, K. C. would have agreed: "That's the first timeout of Game 2."

The Sixers proved Jones a prophet in Game 2, responding to their coach's belief in them with a 121-113 win that took away the home-court advantage from the Celtics and spat in the eyes of the media, who had predicted a quick exit for Philly after Game 1. Toney scored 30 and Caldwell Jones also starred, and the series had already taken on the character it would have to the bitter end—one of big shifts in momentum and lopsided victories. But even more important than this victory was Archibald's injury in the opening minutes of Game 3. After losing the ball to Mo Cheeks, Tiny dove across the floor to prevent a fast break and landed heavily on his left shoulder. He was in a lot of pain. Before the half was over he had been diagnosed—a separated shoulder that would keep him out of the remainder of the series. As if responding to Tiny's accident, the Celtics played a tough game, battling back from nine- and 14-point deficits, emotionally trying to regain the home-court advantage. But the rally fell

Tiny Archibald driving past Frank Johnson in 1982 playoff series against the Bullets. When Archibald suffered a shoulder separation in the Eastern Conference final against Philadelphia, the Celtics lost a key player.

short; somnolent all day, Maxwell missed three chances underneath in the closing seconds, and the 76ers won the only close game of the series, 99-97.

As if emotionally drained, the Celtics lost the next day by 25 points—Philly's delayed answer to the Game 1 blowout. Behind 3-1, the Celtics did not look good. Bird was not shooting well and the team in general was inconsistent, lacking Tiny's leadership on the court. Now the media swung against the Celtics, writing them off as if the previous year's comeback had been a fluke. Back in Boston observers were mystified when the Celtics gathered for practice and acted as if nothing were

wrong: Max joked with Tiny; McHale and Robey talked about their golf games; Parish laughed. Had they quit? Did they forget what was at stake? The truth was, this team knew how to win, and they were conserving their energy for a final thrust. They won Game 5 at home, Parish consistently hitting the turnaround over Caldwell Jones and Bird taking his game down low for 20 points and 20 rebounds.

Bird, infuriated with his poor shooting, had done what he always did—adjust. Playing a determined, physical game, he gave confidence to those around him, and the Celtics went down to the Spectrum fully confident that history was repeating itself. Taking their cue from their captain, Carr, Ainge, Robey and Parish had excellent games. The Sixers looked snakebit, and in a game where defense and cold shooting dominated, they lost, 88-75. The home-court advantage was back. *There's no way we'll lose in Boston* was heard more than once in the lockerroom. Billy Cunningham looked like a man without a country as the media shifted predictions yet again. It was back to the Garden, where the Celtics had never lost a seventh game.

More deja vu. Fans dressed as ghosts filing behind the Sixers bench. Outside it was cold and rainy. Cunningham looked over his left shoulder and saw Doctor J, his eyes narrowed and his jaw set. Four minutes before the opening tap the coach took his troops back to the lockerroom. Ever the pragmatist, he told them that ghosts and yesterdays don't win basketball games. Men do. They returned to the floor single file, Cunningham leading, a clear statement of their determination that day. Against the odds they had purpose and belief in themselves.

In the broad scheme of things, it was perhaps inevitable that Philadelphia should win this game, this series. The rivalry was such during those years that neither team was allowed by the hoop god to be too dominant. Certainly Toney scored his 30; certainly Doc led his team. But something was fitting about the overconfident Boston fans having to call off their witch hunt. And they did so by displaying a touch of class and a gesture of respect. As the end drew near and the Sixers emerged as victors, the crowd rose above disappointment and shouted advice and encouragement: "*Beat L. A.! Beat L. A.!*" The Celtics' turn at the Lakers would have to wait another two years. Perhaps it is just 20-20 hindsight, but there seemed to be a distinct awareness in the Garden that day that the crowd had long since seen the Fitch-led Celtics peak.

M ention the 1982-83 season to a Celtics fan and he or she shudders. Plenty of good things happened in the world that year; all sorts of people reached personal milestones. But in Boston the Celtics had the worst season of the Bird Era as the Fitch regimen closed itself out with confusion, sloppiness and acrimony. Sure, by most NBA team standards the Celtics did fine—a 37-12 first half; a 56-win season. But such was the consistency and strength of the Boston club by Larry Bird's fourth year that in the general feeling of failure that followed the season Bill Fitch felt himself forced to resign. Consider this: In the nine years of Larry Bird's career through 1988, 1982-83 was the only season in which the Celts did not win the Atlantic Division crown. It was the only season in which they did not win more games than any

other Eastern Conference rival. And it was the only year in which they did not advance beyond the conference semifinals. Furthermore, it was the only time in Celtics *history* that the club was swept in a best-of-seven series. And as embarrassing as the sight of Milwaukee fans brandishing brooms in the Mecca in early May was to Boston fans, they felt nothing compared with Larry Joe Bird.

Ironically, 1982-83 was Bird's best year as a basketball player up to that point. At 27, he was approaching his physical peak. His weight, given to fluctuation in the off-season, was more stable. His approach to the game, which had always been excellent, was even better. Experience taught him to keep his cool without losing intensity, and he rarely lost his temper. No longer feeling obliged to prove himself to every opponent, he knew that satisfying his own demanding standards was enough to bring out the best in himself. And the improvement showed in the stats. After a personally unsatisfactory playoff performance in 1982 (a career-low 17.8 points per game), he came back to play his best individual offense, with career highs in scoring average and field goal percentage.

Off the court he was also maturing. Though the grace and sense of humor he would consistently display to the public in the late eighties were only latent then, Bird had learned how to handle the media with competence and civility. Even though he had many reasons to resent the press, he was moving towards the realization that dealing with reporters was part of his professional responsibilty. He did not compromise on his privacy, but he was moving closer to the man who would challenge the whole city of Cleveland in the 1985 playoffs ("They want me? I'm gonna throw both barrels at 'em tomorrow night'').

But as Larry would quickly point out, one man (or two or three) does not make a team, and even while he was excelling the team was declining around him. As the players grew older and more certain of their skills, Fitch's Captain Video approach and martinet style grew less to their liking. Bird would always admire Fitch—their personalities and work habits were so similar it was almost inevitable—but many of the other Celtics had moved past the point where Fitch could motivate them. And when you reach the level these men had after three seasons together you *have* to be motivated. In basketball, as in life, personalities and not statistics are the true measure of success. As K. C. Jones understood intuitively, the Celtics players knew only too well what Fitch kept drilling into them over and over again—what they needed was someone to give them the incentive to do it, night in and night out, over the long regular season and the grueling playoffs. After five years in the NBA Cedric Maxwell knew how to box out; as a player he needed someone to convince him that he *wanted* to box out over and over again.

But Fitch would not be able to manage the complexities of personality, ego and experience on the club that year, particularly as the team continued to change. Chris Ford, who had always acted as a unifying force on the team, was cut during training camp. During the offseason, the Celtics had traded the rights to Dave Cowens (who would try an unsuccessful comeback) to the guard-rich Milwaukee Bucks for Quinn Buckner. A 1976 Olympian and a brilliant all-round athlete, Buckner was a good ball-handler and an excellent defensive player. At 6-2 and 190 pounds, he looked like a smaller Oscar Robertson as he shifted his solid body with great quickness, riding an opponent all the way up the court. Never a threat to score big, he nevertheless had very good court sense and a decent move to the hoop.

Quinn Buckner as the outstanding point guard for the Indiana Hoosiers in 1976. Buckner was traded to the Celtics in 1983 in compensation for the Bucks signing Dave Cowens. Buckner played seven years with Milwaukee, three with Boston and a half-season with Indiana, but confided that his professional loyalties would always remain with the Celtics.

The acquisition of Buckner and the flowering of Gerald Henderson and Danny Ainge (whose minutes would quadruple in 1982-83) did not bode well for Tiny, and the veteran star did not react well to the changing of the guard. More injury prone than ever, he continued to miss games, and he worsened his situation by sulking, unable to admit that his career, which meant everything to him, was near an end. His inconsistent performance disrupted the team, which never knew if Tiny was going to play his best, cooperate or play at all. Fitch, who had done so much to bring Henderson and Ainge along, agonized over Tiny's attitude, showing patience as he tried to convince Archibald that he could still be a productive player coming off the bench. On the floor Tiny would sometimes sabotage the team, holding the ball too long on play options, forcing Maxwell and Bird to make cuts on designed plays even if they were open.

The complexities of Tiny's and Buckner's roles on the club would develop as the season went on. The situation with Rick Robey, however, was fairly simple. Coming off a season when his productivity had declined in every single offensive and defensive category, Robey hit a wall with Fitch that was not going to budge. Robey had been a key contributor to the early eighties turnaround, mentally and physically strong behind Parish. But he was always on the cusp in his performance: in good times he was dedicated and aggressive; when he slumped, or had his minutes cut, he lost his drive, his conditioning and his effectiveness. As Fitch lost faith in his backup center that year, Robey reached a career turning point. Virtually benched for two months, he never performed to the level of his potential, and he was destined to leave (in the playoffs he played a total of 29 minutes over five games). Adding to the problem was his relationship with Bird. Still good friends, they presented management with another possibility of "negative influence." The uncertainty of Robey's influence on his

friend was a factor in his being traded to Phoenix for Dennis Johnson at the end of the season.

Observant fans could see for themselves how the team was not what it once was, particularly during the second half of the season, when it was clear the Sixers were having their season of the decade and that Boston was bound to finish second. But the team's image was affected further by the appearance of *Boston Globe* beat writer Dan Shaughnessy on the scene that year. Shaughnessy replaced Bob Ryan (Ryan would return), bringing a younger, more critical perspective to bear on his paper's analyses of the Celtics. In a year when there was frank talk by players (including McHale and Carr) of leaving, when Fitch had running battles with his players at practice, when there was occasional and hurtful animosity between men on the team, Shaughnessy took a deliberately investigative stance that did not always sit well with Celtics brass. From the beginning he had a combative relationship with Fitch. Shaughnessy, of course, had the public forum; Fitch was left to freeze the young reporter out of press conferences. At times his criticism of Fitch seemed personal, and it was clear that the two had a mutual dislike.

But Shaughnessy would report faithfully the decline of this team—and contribute to it in the sense that the media does have an active role in creating a team image. Most players read the papers. Being human, they react. When Shaughnessy saw Parish hobble onto the court with a severely sprained ankle in a December game against the Pistons, he reported the incident as he saw it. In his eyes the Chief had been coerced, however subtly, into playing when he should have been staying off the ankle. The play of expectations

The Boston Globe*'s Dan Shaughnessy interviewing Kevin McHale. Shaughnessy went after one of the most potentially damaging stories concerning the brilliant Bird, a fight in a bar during the 1985 playoffs. "I just grew weary of hearing common people talking about the incident at barbecues," Shaughnessy said in 1988, "and nothing had ever been reported in the newspaper. I felt it was my job [to research and report it]."*

on a player's psyche—from the fans, the doctors, the coaches, himself—turns a notion like "responsibility" into an ambiguous rationale. Certainly no one *told* Robert to play; but the pressure was there, and seeing the defiance in Parish's face Shaughnessy drew his own conclusions.

To a certain extent Shaughnessy's reports of dissension that year were symbiotic with the team's decline. He wrote about cynicism and defiance, reinforcing it in players' minds as the bad feeling grew. Fitch's orders, which had brought Boston three superb years, were now echoing vacantly through the Hellenic College gym. Max and McHale joked while Fitch was giving instructions.

Henderson often blatantly ignored the coach. One morning Fitch and Carr argued openly while Max, a few yards away, mimicked his coach with waving arms. Fitch told Carr he was about to be traded. Carr said he would retire first. McHale was threatening to leave, though he later said quietly that if K. C. Jones became coach, he would remain in Boston. The scene was bad.

Auerbach, meanwhile, Fitch's staunchest ally not long ago, was absent that season more than ever before. He scouted and spent a lot of time with his family in Washington. He seemed to have lost interest in the day-to-day proceedings of the club. Knowing that owner Harry Mangurian was deciding to sell the team, Auerbach was thinking of how the team would be run under new ownership. At one time, in the flush days following the championship, it was assumed that Fitch might some day take over from Red and run the team. No more. Even before the disaster in the Mecca there was change in the air.

Not all of the Bird Era changes were on the court. The Celtics' organization was a model of effectiveness in the eighties not only as a team but as a business. Adapting to the evolving forces of a complex salary structure and increased player power, using new media technology and marketing techniques to expand the club's commercial potential, the Boston Celtics had developed a corporate structure that had a direct and positive bearing on the court. If your business makes money, you can afford to pay your players; you have the freedom to negotiate (within the salary cap) and the reserves to absorb a loss. Ironically, as the Celtics were unraveling under Fitch, the front office was solidifying, and the team was moving towards a new ownership that contributed to the success of the next five years by providing much-needed stability.

Harry Mangurian's ownership had been steady and responsible since John Y. Brown's departure in 1979. Mangurian let Red run the ballclub—a move Brown had not had the wisdom to make. But without the will or the funds to adapt to a changing corporate environment, Mangurian looked to sell the team in 1983. After one bid failed he sold the club to the team of Don Gaston, Paul Dupee and Alan Cohen. Gaston and Dupee, both former vice presidents of Gulf and Western Industries, brought extensive corporate experience to the organization. Cohen had a background in sports and communications that was ideal for the new NBA. Former director of Warner Communications and CEO of the Madison Square Garden Corporation, Cohen knew the intricacies of cable televison and the business of marketing a basketball team. Together these men transformed the team into a major stockholding corporation and, under Cohen's guidance, established the most substantial cable television and radio contract in the NBA. By the mideighties the club would be grossing over $50 million. They would also pick up $50 million in the stockholding deal, giving Auerbach the freedom he needed to negotiate with Bird prior to the 1983-84 season. None of the rancor of the original signing marred the negotiations, and Bird came to camp as one of the highest paid players in the league. Of course, Bird's prowess gave the Celtics a marketing tool of unparalleled strength, a tool the owners shrewdly used in their own negotiations. As always Red had been the common denominator, the man who orchestrated the harmony of basketball and business.

The Celtics' front office had also developed into one of the brightest and best in the league. Taking its cue from Red Auerbach, its personnel knew that the

Red Auerbach with the new Celtics ownership: Don Gaston, Alan Cohen and Paul Dupee. Through brilliant management techniques, the Celtics maintained one of the most fiscally sound sports teams in the country.

best way to run a basketball team was to know the game and its players. Jan Volk, who was to assume the general managerial duties in 1984, set the tone. Starting in 1971 as director of ticket sales, Volk worked his way through the organization, slowly expanding his expertise and responsibility. "He's paid his dues," Auerbach has said. Volk, a graduate of Columbia Law School, had refined his knowledge of sports law so thoroughly he gave the Celtics an indispensable tool in the age of salary cap and free agency. Volk's staff of sales and promotion experts also increased in importance under the new ownership. As the club became a multimillion dollar entertainment business, the front office's constant work at marketing, community relations, advertising and radio and television contracts became essential to the team's success on the floor, with Tod Rosensweig, Stephen Riley, Joe DiLorenzo, Duane Johnson, Jeff Twiss and David Zuccaro providing the expertise.

Volk's baptism came in 1983, when the prospect of a players' strike shadowed the season. Throughout the winter and early spring fans feared a stoppage similar to the strike that had so severely disrupted the 1981 baseball season. The Celtics were fortunate in having Volk, perhaps the league's expert in the salary cap, to negotiate. But they were also lucky in their player representation. The trade that brought Quinn Buckner that year brought more than a highly skilled defensive guard—it also brought a key member of the Players' Association, a man whose integrity and leadership helped resolve the differences between players and management without the damage of an actual strike, something major league baseball and pro football were not able to avoid

in the eighties. Just as Bob Cousy and Tommy Heinsohn had spearheaded the first players' union in the fifties without compromising their winning attitude, so too Buckner had the tact and intelligence to stand up for his teammates and their needs without violating his integrity or dedication as a Boston Celtics player.

Buckner was a winner. A member of Indiana's national champions and co-captain of the 1976 Olympic team, he knew instinctively how to contribute and lead. From his first day in Boston he refused to be drawn into the guard difficulties created by the emotional Archibald and the ambitious Henderson. He remained loyal to his coach, teammates and Players' Association throughout the threatened strike, earning a respect that was never to leave him, even when his own position as a player became questionable.

In the midst of all this change stood Fitch, a man losing his grip, a man who needed a strong hold on his team in order to function. Just as he was losing control of his players, so too he was drifting away from what two years ago had seemed a solid career path within the organization. Mangurian had always been a middleman in the decision-making group he formed with Fitch and Auerbach. When he decided to sell the team, Fitch effectively lost an ally. Also, as the first outsider to coach the Celtics, Fitch had never communicated well with the front office. But the most important rift was between the coach and Red. Auerbach had always been Fitch's strongest supporter, and in the early years he gave credit for Boston's success to Fitch above anyone else. "Never have I seen a man work harder or be more prepared," he said in 1980. "I think most of the credit *has* to go to him.'' Knowing how much Red had thought of Fitch, knowing how he had even planned to have Fitch take over the reins of the team as Red grew older, observers, including Shaughnessy, couldn't help but note the distance Red had put between himself and his coach that season. It was as if the team's patriarch had sensed dissension and passed judgement with his actions. But could he have foreseen the club's complete fall from grace that year?

When Tiny Archibald left practice at Hellenic College that year, more often than not he got into his Jeep and headed for another, more informal session of hoop. Making his way out of one of the wealthiest suburbs of Greater Boston, he drove down Route 1 to the tough neighborhoods of Roxbury and Mattapan, where the landscaped gardens and fine homes of Brookline gave way to concrete yards and walls layered with graffiti. The tension of a diminished NBA career and long bench minutes eased slightly as the black faces of the neighborhood flowered into smiles of recognition. Here, at Bob the Chef's eatery or the Roxbury YMCA, Tiny was at home. The man who had traveled through the Midwest and NBA glory had never really left the inner city, and as the painful season continued, the last full season of his career, he turned more and more to his roots. When he left the Celtics' two-hour practice his basketball day was just beginning. Another three or four hours of playground ball followed, a universe away from the NBA and its politics. Here he tested kids and rapped with an audience sympathetic to his predicament. He was their hero, always

would be. He wasn't there to intimidate; he was there to play *with* them. At 34 he still had all his moves; his game hadn't altered. Why was Fitch not playing him? He needed more *time*.

Tiny knew he still had it. Hadn't he controlled the L. A. Lakers in a big game that year, steering the ball effortlessly, commanding the rhythm of the game, setting up his teammates with the precision everyone was implying he'd lost? Hadn't he shown these young guards the *right* way to run an offense, the way no one could but himself? After that game Magic Johnson had said, his voice buoyant with admiration, ''Oh, there's no doubt Tiny's the master. Shoot, I used to watch him and Oscar Robertson for hours.'' The *master*. Now he was playing little more than half the game. *Half*. He needed more time, he'd say to his friends in the inner city, and they'd nod. They understood.

That Laker game was Tiny's high point that year, his last in Boston. Ainge and Henderson were the guards of the future, and Quinn Buckner was being groomed as the first guard off the bench. And though Tiny did have enough left to contribute meaningfully, he was caught between a proud disposition and the numbers game. The Celtics had arrived at an awkward point—in some people's eyes they had *too* much talent. In the frontcourt there were Bird, McHale, Parish, Maxwell, Robey, Carr and Scott Wedman (who had been acquired from Cleveland in January), every one a quality NBA player. The backcourt was equally impressive: Archibald, Ainge, Henderson, Buckner and the lone rookie on the club, Charles Bradley. With this kind of talent the Celtics should have been building on the success of the last three years. Instead they were drawing apart. ''What you

Bird was ejected from this March 1983 game after throwing the ball at referee Hubie Evans. The following day in the Boston Herald, *Mike Carey supported the referee's decision. At practice, after he had read Carey's article, Bird agreed with Carey's assessment. "Otherwise," Bird told the writer, "I'd never have any respect for him and word would spread around the league that he could be pushed around."*

want," one player hypothesized, "are eight really good players and four mediocre ones. Before, guys like Terry Duerod and Eric Fernsten really had no aspirations of being great players and didn't demand playing time. Now, with so many good players on the team, it's easy to be disgruntled."

But this analysis did not ring true. Great teams have their down times, and 1982-83 was the lowest the Celts would get during the Bird Era, in spite of their talent. But it is natural to look for explanations. Well behind the blazing 76ers, McHale offered another form of false reasoning as the team entered the playoffs: "The problem with our season is we became an average team. Philadelphia was too far ahead of us, and Milwaukee too far

behind...If we won five games in a row it didn't matter; if we lost five in a row it didn't matter. So what was the point?" The point was that the Celtics sensed failure and were looking for ways of accounting for it. McHale had talked frankly throughout the second half of the season about leaving the team. He was in the final year of his contract, and he did not like the atmosphere. Though Bird thought McHale's public airing of his attitude had hurt the team, the captain must have sensed the malaise himself.

The Celtics' troubles were compounded by the Sixers' success. Philly's new owner, Harold Katz, had moved aggressively in the free agent market and acquired Moses Malone, signing him to a multiyear $13.2 million contract. He

Robert Parish defends Moses Malone in the 1982-83 season, the Sixers' year. "It's Julius's team; I'm just here to work hard," Malone said after signing a multiyear $13.2 million dollar contract before that season. But as Tony Cotton of Sports Illustrated *wrote, "It soon became apparent that Malone was Philly's most important player."*

adjusted to the newly instituted salary cap by trading Dawkins to the Nets and sending Caldwell Jones to Houston as compensation for the MVP center. With a quality veteran team around him, Malone became an even tougher opponent, and the Sixers blew away the league with a 50-8 record two-thirds of the way through the season. Moses had a lot more than the Petersburg high school team to support him that year—Erving, Cheeks and Toney joined him on the All-Star team, and together they led the team to a 65-17 final record.

Out West the Lakers were rebounding from their complacent '81-82 season, but

their playoff chances were dealt a blow when their great rookie James Worthy broke his leg. The Lakers would make it to The Finals, but this year belonged to Philadelphia; this year the Doctor would finally get his ring.

So there was a sense of foreboding as the Celtics entered the postseason. For the first time in the eighties they had to play the dangerous best-of-three miniseries, against the Atlanta Hawks and rookie Dominique Wilkins. All three games were tough, physical contests, but even in a bad year the Celts were too much of a match for the Hawks, who would have to wait a few more years before they could challenge Boston. The highlight—or lowlight—of the Celtics' 2-1 series victory was a brawl in Game 3 in which longtime Celtics nemesis Tree Rollins bit Danny Ainge's finger as the bodies rolled on the floor. In a way, that comic touch and the headlines it prompted in Boston newspapers were a fitting symbol of the year of Fitch's exit. There was certainly little to laugh at in the games with Milwaukee that followed. Nothing at all, in fact.

In his autobiography, M. L. Carr recalled that after the 116-95 Game 1 loss to the Bucks, the Celtics had filed into the Garden lockerroom as if they didn't care anymore. In effect, the season ended with that game. Outplayed and outhustled all night long, the Celtics exhibited an extreme form of the malaise that had been snapping at their shorts all season. Fitch groped all game long for a combination that would stop the Bucks' persistent attack, an attack that, unlike the Celtics' discontinuity, had a purpose and a plan every trip down floor. Bob Lanier's post-up prowess was the first option. If Parish stopped him, the Bucks shifted to a one-four set, with Marques Johnson working on Maxwell. From the perimeter, Brian Winters, one of the best spot shooters in the game, kept the Celtics' guards away from the inside, and Sidney Moncrief, as usual, did it all. This offense came together smoothly, and the Bucks' tight, almost zone defense throttled the Celts at the other end.

As if losing the home court advantage wasn't bad enough, the Celtics' suffered another blow when Bird—the only player untouched by the general lack of intensi-

Wilt Chamberlain, Moses Malone's predecessor in Philadelphia's championship legacy. M. L. Carr wrote, "Wilt Chamberlain made basketball come alive in my neighborhood. He always struck me with his dominating play and staggering numbers. I was awed by the way he was able to combine speed, size and grace."

ty that season—woke the morning of Game 2 with a debilitating case of the flu. Out for the contest, he watched Ainge and Wedman shoot the Celtics into a 44-26 lead; but Milwaukee, patiently executing and defending, came back slowly and won going away, 95-91. For the first time in the history of the franchise, Boston had lost consecutive playoff games at home, and the team headed to Milwaukee in the worst of condition—down, 0-2; their star player ill; the opposing team riding a wave of adrenalin expertly directed by Don Nelson, who was on the threshold of achieving his coaching fantasy of sweeping his old team.

Nelson's intensity that series matched Fitch's. Prowling the sidelines, his clothes rumpled and his face lengthened by an open-mouthed scowl, he battled the team he had done so much for over 11 seasons as a player. Beating Red Auerbach's club meant more to him than anything else because he knew how much Red had done for him, how much Red knew about the game. Nelson had learned a lot from his mentor: strategy, psychology, motivation. And in a series marked by bad feeling, he created one of the biggest off-court stories of the postseason in a deliberate attempt to distract a key Celtics player.

Danny Ainge had had an excellent Game 2, hitting nine of ten from the field and giving Boston a lead that in any other year would have assured victory. During the game Nelson took exception to what he thought was an undercutting of his players by Ainge. He got off the bench and shouted at the Boston guard, who did not respond. After the game Nelson saw a tape of the Ainge-Rollins brawl, which was shown at halftime of the CBS telecast of a Lakers-Trail Blazers playoff game. This was enough to set the tempermental coach off, and he complained loudly to the Milwaukee press, saying that "Ainge has gained the reputation in the league as being a cheap-shot artist...He hips [our players] while they're in the air. I don't mind a hard foul, but it's another kind of foul to get a man in a bad position and use your leverage to injure a player...The films of the incident with Rollins showed that...Ainge went for Rollins's eyes under the pack before he was bitten...Innocent Danny Ainge isn't so innocent."

The personal tone of that final remark underscored the seriousness of the accusations, and the Celtics reacted with appropriate indignation. Nelson had attacked Ainge's professionalism just as the Celtics were about to play a pair of games in the Mecca, a move that exposed Danny to all kinds of fan abuse. His most serious remarks were made on the basis of viewing a film clip on television, divorced from its context. Jan Volk pinpointed Nelson's strategy. "He's doing something right out of Red's informal strategy book—distract the player. Nellie's no fool. He's seen how well Danny's playing. He's just giving Danny something extra to think about." But Red did not like the move and refused to talk to Nelson for months after the incident. Ainge, who was in the midst of a difficult fight for a starting spot on the Celtics, had always been a competitor, but never a dirty player. Nelson's remarks (and Ainge's own boyish pout, the natural expression of his intensity) would give him a reputation, however, that would hang around the league for years to come.

The immediate problem, though, was the impending sweep. Though Bird returned for Game 3, he was still bothered by the flu, and the Bucks took the game, with Moncrief overpowering Henderson

"He doesn't say much, but he plays the game hard with both his mind and his body. In the playoffs he is a marvel with the big rebounds, the big blocks and the big shots. Robert Parish knows when the game is on the line. He can be unappreciated all through a game—especially a big game—and then bang! He turns things around." K. C. Jones on the Chief.

and Marques Johnson taking Wedman inside for several important late baskets. Smelling blood, the Mecca fans arrived at Game 4 with raucous voices and all kinds of props, from brooms (*sweep, sweep,sweep!* they cried) to a stuffed toy bird, its neck squeezed pencil-thin (*This is you, Larry!*). The game wasn't even close. In his finest hour, Nelson led his charges to a 107-93 win and the first sweep of the Celtics in their history.

The Mecca's visiting lockerroom is an old vaudeville dressing room. The walls are all mirrored, and tiny light bulbs border the reflected images. As the players filed in after the game, the series, the season, their failure expanded infinitely in the facing mirrors. There was nothing to say. Bird, the last man to leave, answered the press's questions with a voice distanced by disbelief. He was certain the team would bounce back next year...He honestly didn't understand how the team had played this poorly...He would work long hours this summer to make sure it wouldn't happen again. His eyes were trained at a time and place beyond his immediate embarrassment.

Fitch would also conduct the endless interviews over the next few days. The pain in his face was also unmistakeable, but there was also a hint of relief. The long season was at an end. Too much talent, too little control. He would never have another year like this—at least not with the Celtics. It was time for a changing of the guard.

6

CHANGING
OF THE GUARD

Serious, purposeful, he walked into the press conference knowing his decision was the one the press wanted to hear. As was his practice, he had thought long and hard about what he would say. It had not been easy. Happy about his tenure in Boston, secure in his achievements over four seasons, he was resigned about his decision but still reluctant to leave. The 1981 championship had been the highlight of his career—probably always would be—and the good memories far outweighed the bad. But though the arguments for staying were strong, too many ghosts haunted his office on 150 Causeway Street, too many impossible expectations filled the stands. It was time for a change. So he told the assembled reporters that he was resigning as head coach of the Boston Celtics, that the change would be right for everyone—the organization, the team, the players,

himself. Those in the know said that Red Auerbach had not and would not have asked him to resign. But neither did he stand in his way.

Sadly, thoroughly, William C. Fitch cleaned out his desk drawers, pausing over scraps of paper and minor mementoes that gained new meaning on this early summer morning. Perhaps he thought of happier days, of how he had built a young team from scratch and taken it to the peak of his profession. Perhaps he reviewed the other teams in the league that might need a head coach with an impressive resume. As the confrontations that were the inevitable offshoot of his aggressive style came back to him, perhaps, too, he thought about who would succeed him, whom Red would choose to breathe life back into this moribund team. At an important crossroads himself, he must have considered what was to come and what had gone before.

His legacy was secure. From the Eastern Conference finals in 1976, when his overachieving Cleveland Cavaliers had taken the Boston Celtics to six games (and Red Auerbach had come down from the stands to sit on the end of the Celtics' bench after Tom Heinsohn was ejected in Game 5), to his 242-86 record over four seasons in Boston, he had earned the occasionally begrudging but always steady respect of Auerbach and the clannish Celtics organization. And yet Fitch was leaving in 1983 without the plaudits, without even the simple wishes of good luck. The fact was that Fitch would *never* have fit comfortably into the Celtics' line of succession, and the long-term hopes bred by his first two seasons had been unrealistic. As in any sphere of life, in sport personality plays a key role, and Fitch's personality was not right for the Boston Celtics after 1982. He had had his day, and now it was time for him to give way to a man who had deeper roots within the organization, a man whose style was perfect for the second half of the Bird Era, when the team's character would develope beyond Bill Fitch's methods. And as Fitch left the Celtics that day he may well have been thinking of how far he and his rival, K. C. Jones, had come since the very different days seven years ago, when his upstart Cavaliers had beaten Jones's Washington Bullets in the greatest series of Fitch's young coaching life.

The meeting between Washington and Cleveland in the 1976 Eastern Conference semifinals had consequences that were still affecting its principals eight years later. It was a match between a veteran team, coached by the subtle and reserved Jones, and a young group of overachievers, headed by the direct and volatile Fitch. Fitch was at the height of his success at Cleveland; Jones had been under fire in Washington all season long. Fitch knew that a successful playoff would mean expanded opportunity in the NBA; Jones knew that anything less than a championship would result in his ouster and hard times. As a white coach and general manager, Fitch was establishment NBA; as one of the few black coaches in the league, Jones was a clear underdog. In both cases this series had personal and dramatic ramifications well outside the world of basketball, effects that would not be resolved until the ironic reversal of fortune in 1983, when Fitch's regime would give way to the more open rule of the man who had struggled for seven years to vindicate himself as an NBA head coach.

The two Bird Era coaches were as different in 1976 as they were in Boston, and their playoff match-up was, among other things, an exercise in contrasts. A year before, K. C. had directed the Bullets to a 60-22 record, a Central Division crown and a playoff victory over the Boston Celtics that had landed him a berth in the 1975 Finals. He had taken a team of talented but occasionally self-centered individuals—including Elvin Hayes, Wes Unseld, Kevin Porter and Phil Chenier—and gotten them to play aggressive team ball. With a club full of contrasting personalities, Jones had used his own personal skills to get players to rise above moodiness and petty rivalries, a job that elicited the supreme compliment from John Havlicek, who said that playing the Bullets was "like looking in the mirror." It was a year in which he had felt he had arrived as a head coach in the NBA, and he was proud of himself.

Assistant coach Chris Ford pulls K. C. Jones away from Mike Mathis. "M. L. Carr told a friend of mine," Jones wrote in Rebound, *"that he had never seen anyone put as much pressure on himself as I did my first year as head coach."*

But that year of solid play and careful coaching unraveled when the Bullets ran into the white-hot Golden State Warriors, who played inspired ball as they swept Washington in four games behind the play of the great Rick Barry. The Washington press, groomed all year to expect a championship, could not contain its disappointment. Since 1970, the year the Central Division was formed, the Bullets had topped their division every year; yet only once before 1975 had they advanced to The Finals—a similar 4-0 loss to the Lew Alcindor-led Milwaukee Bucks. Frustrated fans and sportswriters looked for a scapegoat but found the wrong man— and the evidence on which they con-

victed K. C. was pathetically thin. Rick Barry interrupted his postchampionship celebrations just long enough to accuse Jones of sending Mike Riordan after Barry on a headhunting mission. The media played on this nonsense as they had jumped on an earlier incident. In an unfortunate example of how television can have a detrimental effect on the game, a CBS camera had taken a national audience into a crucial Bullets' timeout in Game 2, where viewers saw assistant coach Bernie Bickerstaff outlining a play while K. C. looked on silently. In fact, K. C. had just told the team to run a certain play, and Bickerstaff had asked Jones if he should diagram it. But to viewers (aided by some erroneous off-the-cuff remarks by the television commentator), the scene suggested that Jones was not running his team.

This misperception was to have an even worse effect on Jones's career than the loss itself. In the wake of Golden State's victory, the Washington papers would not let go of the notion that Jones was not in control of his team, and the accusation followed K. C. throughout the 1975-76 season, when injuries diminished the team's strength and overconfidence sapped its potential. The Bullets finished behind the Cavaliers by one game in the Central Division, and by the time Washington met Cleveland in the playoffs, K. C. was hanging on to his job by his fingernails. Fitch, meanwhile, was peaking with the Cavs. His five-year plan as coach and GM had yielded, as in Boston in 1981, a team perfectly suited to his style, a predominantly young group with a sprinkling of stabilizing veterans like Nate Thurmond. With Jim Brewer, Bingo Smith, Jim Chones, Jim Cleamons, Dick Snyder and Campy Russell, Fitch had a balanced, deep team that could run the ball or take it inside, and when the Bullets foolishly and publicly declared that they would beat the inexperienced Cavs, Fitch's team had all the inspiration they needed going into the semifinals. "They *never* took us seriously," Chones said. "But we kept going at them, repeatedly, even when we were down."

The series was one of the finest in the annals of the NBA, a thriller in seven games, three of which were decided on the final possession, another of which went to overtime. Reputations were made and lost. There was some great basketball. The Cavs ran Fitch's motion offense superbly; the Bullets played excellent defense when they had to. Elvin Hayes shrugged off an unfair *choke* label by playing brilliantly throughout and leading the Bullets to a must-win Game 6 victory with six blocks. But this year was Fitch's, at least in the Central Division, and when, in the waning moments of Game 7, Dick Snyder lofted a difficult shot over the outstretched hand of Phil Chenier, the ball banked home, taking with it K. C.'s chance at vindication and giving Fitch the push he needed to start on the road to Boston. Fans swarmed onto the floor of the Richfield Coliseum as Fitch approached Jones. The two men shook hands. Fitch followed his celebrating players, barely able to contain his joy. K. C. walked silently to the dark end of the gym.

The walk was a long one. Jones was fired soon afterwards and, in his own words, "began to fall apart as a man." Professionally, he went through a very lean time, when job offers ceased for a long spell (the Washington stories would haunt him, and race was a factor) and those that did come went sour (when he eventually landed an assistant coach's position on the Bucks, Don Nelson released him after a few short months). Personally, it was worse. His marriage fell apart, and he started drinking more than was good for him. Though he came back to the Celtics in 1978 (as an assistant under Satch Sanders), he endured along with everyone else through the late stages of John Y. Brown's crazy ownership. He and his first wife suffered through a divorce. Then, when the Celtics experienced the resurgence of the Fitch years (a period in which Jones had made a significant contribution), he had to endure the acrimony with Fitch and the occasional humiliations.

For a man who had won 155 games in three years with the Bullets, it was a lengthy and frustrating sabbatical. Though he had paid his dues far more than was necessary, he had still not been given the second chance he deserved. If anybody was ready for another shot at success, K. C. Jones was.

"Sometimes a change is best for everybody." So Fitch had said on leaving Boston, and once again his instincts proved right. With the appropriate cooling off period, Fitch's accomplishments would be appreciated and remembered. But now it was K. C.'s turn in the sun, and it was fitting that the man whose darkest days in life followed a loss to Fitch should rebound as his old rival departed, as if life were imitating sport. A proud man, a man who had only known success before his failure with the Bullets, Jones had learned to temper ambition and accept what life gave him. In doing so he was given a great opportunity—and he made the most of it. As Jones said in his autobiography, "M. L. Carr said he never saw anyone put as much pressure on himself as I did my first year as head coach. I felt that Red Auerbach had gone out on a long, bending limb for me, and I was convinced that the limb would break if the team didn't win the championship." Red certainly knew what he was doing.

Change at the top was paralleled by changes on the team itself that summer, and the middle seasons of the Bird Era were marked by mature team play, at times brazen self-confidence and a horizontal rather than vertical leadership style. Larry Bird, more than ever the center of the team, brought a more focused and more articulate sense of purpose to the club. Bird had grown into a pro player under Fitch's tutelage, serving an apprenticeship that brought his game to an MVP level. With that father figure gone from the bench, Bird was now forced to rely more on his own instincts, and the freedom opened up his game and enhanced the creative dimension to his play. Jones was the perfect coach for Bird at this stage of his career. He encouraged Bird to take more of a leadership role and follow his instincts on the court. Naming Bird team captain, Jones spread out responsibility in a way that was crucial for a veteran club. K. C. saw that the key to the Celtics' success was motivation, and from his first day as head coach he worked at the subtle psychological process of getting the team to motivate itself.

Red Auerbach had followed his choice of Jones with his most productive summer in years. As well as overseeing the delicate and complicated change of ownership, he engineered the trade that was to give the Celtics' backcourt the same solidity and leadership the frontcourt enjoyed, acquiring Dennis Johnson from the Phoenix Suns in exchange for Rick Robey. Ever a student of the game, Auerbach had followed closely the league's tendency towards larger guards, observing how, in the Western Conference particularly, the classic point guard/off guard pairing was giving way to a tandem of tall, muscular players who could pass, shoot, rebound and defend with the quickness of a small guard and the size and strength of a small forward. Though there would always be a place in the league for a Gus Williams or a Tiny Archibald, the league and the Celtics looked for someone who could run the offense *and* guard the Andrew Toneys and Magic Johnsons of the NBA.

DJ fit the bill. From his early days with Seattle, where he had led the Sonics to the

Dennis Johnson as a Western Conference All-Star in 1981, when he was also First Team NBA. John Papanek wrote of his 1979 playoff MVP performance, "Dennis Johnson was operating far above the baskets, where 6-4 guards are seldom seen. He did everything but change the light bulbs in the 24-second clocks. He scored, rebounded, blocked shots and broke up three-man fast breaks— singlehandedly. As he said, 'I did just about whatever I thought needed to be done.'"

world championship in 1979, to his time at Phoenix, where he had helped the Suns become one of the premier teams in the Western Conference, Johnson had been a solid All-Star and a defensive specialist. Coming to the Suns in 1980 in exchange for Paul Westphal, he had a standout season, averaging 18.8 points per game and earning First Team All-Pro honors as the Suns topped the Lakers by three games for the Pacific Division crown. Paired with the incredibly quick Walter Davis (a transformed forward) in the backcourt, DJ

led an experimental attack that seemed unstoppable, and going into the playoffs, most writers expected the Suns to sweep to The Finals, especially after the Lakers lost to Houston in the miniseries. But the Kansas City Kings upset Phoenix as Scott Wedman and Ernie Grunfeld matched the Suns' big guards effectively, and Houston went on to win the Western Conference championship before losing to Boston.

That year was DJ's high point at Phoenix. Over the next two seasons he became unhappy with coach John McLeod's substitution pattern, which limited all players, regardless of ability, to approximately 33 minutes a game. Johnson debated the wisdom of that strategy, and also McLeod's insistence on constant practice. After the team had been forced to practice following a difficult road trip (more demanding in the Western Conference because of the distance between cities), DJ voiced his complaints to the press, and the suggestions that he was a "problem player," a stigma that had plagued him in Seattle, surfaced again. Phoenix GM Gerry Colangelo started shopping Johnson around, and Red expressed interest.

Though Auerbach had never wavered in his commitment to discipline and team play, he was never reluctant to bring a "problem" case into the organization if the situation called for it. He knew that NBA reputations were formed for a variety of reasons, and experience taught him that so-called problem players could, when surrounded by team-dedicated men, subscribe to the work ethic and fit in. He had discussed DJ with Bill Russell, who had coached Dennis as a rookie and been impressed with the way the young man had handled the pressure of his first year in the NBA. Auerbach also knew that

DJ's background had given him the will to succeed. The eldest of 17 children, Dennis had starred at Dominguez High School in the Los Angeles area. After graduation he had opted not to attend college and worked construction for a year. Long conversations with his parents helped him decide to attend Harbor Junior College in Wilmington, California, where he had two outstanding seasons and earned a scholarship to Pepperdine. His game there (where he occasionally played the center position) attracted the interest of professional scouts, and his summer scrimmages in L. A. impressed Jerry West, who still liked to play against Southern California's best during the off-season. West told DJ he was an NBA caliber player and that the Lakers wanted to draft him. But the Sonics got to DJ first, selecting him in the second round, the 29th pick in the 1976 draft.

DJ's rise to prominence was quick, sometimes problematical. His college experience in the low post, his excellent leaping ability and his exceptional quickness made him an all-around threat. By his second year in the league he was a star, and his defensive ability was obvious to everyone when, in the 1978 conference finals, he rose to the challenge of guarding Denver's David Thompson, said by many to be the best player in the game. Thanks in great part to Johnson's containment of Thompson, Seattle moved past Denver and took the Bullets to seven games in the 1978 finals. DJ was standout, but with the series and the MVP award for the taking, he suffered through an 0-for-12 seventh game. "I *prayed* I would hit just one shot," he said, "but I knew I wouldn't. It was a horrible experience. Especially for a 23-year-old." DJ worked hard on his game and conditioning that summer and returned to camp even better. That season, 1978-79, he led the Sonics to their sole franchise championship, winning MVP honors in a sweet-revenge victory over the Bullets in five games. DJ hit the clinching field goal in the final game, a 17-footer from the wing that exorcised the memory of the horrible game the year before and was a slap in the face of Washington coach Dick Motta, who had been insulting DJ in the media all series long.

But the next year Dennis faced criticism from within. After holding out for a new contract, he demanded an increased role in the Seattle offense, a need that upset the team's balance and bothered coach Lenny Wilkens. Suffering from Russell's Curse, the Sonics could not match their success of the previous two seasons. According to David Halberstam, the tension between player and coach worsened as the season wore on, culminating in Wilkens's statement that DJ was "a cancer to the team." The trade to Phoenix soon followed, and the cycle started all over again.

But Dennis was maturing. On the plane from Seattle to Phoenix, he said later, he realized that NBA basketball was a business, and he vowed he would play so hard he would never be bartered again. Three days after his trade to the Suns his son Dwayne was born, and Dennis began identifying himself as a man playing basketball rather than simply a ballplayer. He became a better, more measured professional in Phoenix, in spite of his confrontations with McLeod, and the individual honors poured in. As the disappointing '82-83 season came to an end, DJ and his agent, Fred Slaughter, prepared to sign a new contract with the Suns. Colangelo never mentioned that a trade was brewing, and when DJ's phone rang in late June he thought the GM was calling to discuss terms. Instead he found out he was now a Boston Celtic. A West Coast player all his life, DJ was heading East.

Many people were sorry to see Robey go, especially Jones, who had a strong personal relationship with the young man and liked his skills. K. C. broke the news to Rick, explaining the business nature of the decision. Auerbach would make Robey virtually superfluous that summer by consolidating the core of the team, in the front office and on the court. He and Jones met with individual players, discussing the future and defining roles. His biggest piece of business was re-signing McHale, who had publicly spoken of leaving and whose agent had been shopping him around. Red made the negotiations very interesting by playing a few mind games with the New York Knicks, an emerging rival in the Atlantic Division. The Knicks, who had developed a young team around superstar Bernard King, were trying to sign McHale as a free agent. Acting on the advice of Jan Volk, Auerbach signed Marvin Webster, Rory Sparrow and Sly

Red Auerbach wrote in his autobiography, "Our pride was never rooted in statistics. Our pride was in our identity as the Boston Celtics. Being a Celtic meant you were someone special. The Celtics represent a philosophy which, in its simplest form, maintains that the victory belongs to the team."

Williams—three key players in the Knicks' rebuilding program—to offer sheets. Forced to match the offers, the Knicks ended up paying their three players more than they probably would have *and*, under the newly instituted rules of the salary cap, did not have enough left in the kitty to make a decent offer to McHale. Shortly afterwards, Auerbach signed McHale to a handsome long-term deal.

All of Auerbach's behind-the-scenes work that summer, from hiring K. C. to sparring with the Knicks, was aimed at restoring the fire the Celtics had lost in the turmoil of the '82-83 season. He wanted his team thinking only of winning; he wanted all conflict directed at the opposing team, not the coach or fellow players or management. He had brought the competitive instincts of Dennis Johnson and K. C. Jones to the club and given Bird the freedom he needed to lead by example. He had solved the contractual problems of the league's best sixth man and talked to the league's best twelfth man, M. L. Carr, about restoring his aggressiveness. ("What's going on, M. L.? I see you collide with someone on the floor and you bend down to pick him up. This isn't like you.") Finally, he had signed a resentful Parish to an extension of his contract, with a substantial bonus for signing, after Robert had seen the generous size of McHale's salary. Within the minefield of the eighties NBA, laden with delicate egos, complicated rules and monstrous salaries, Auerbach had maneuvered with skill and determination, proving once again he had the most protean and intelligent mind in the game and directing his team into the new season with renewed aggression and determination to win.

The first two years of K. C. Jones's reign saw the re-emergence of the oldest and most intense rivalry in the National Basketball Association. During the Bill Russell era the Boston Celtics and Minneapolis/Los Angeles Lakers met in seven championship finals, all of which the Celtics won. Between 1969 and 1983—a period longer than the Russell era—the Lakers and Celtics each won three NBA titles and appeared in championship finals a collective nine times. Coincidentally, however, they did not play each other in even one of those championships. It was as if each of the two best teams of the era took its turn winning while the other rested. But with the arrival of K. C. in the East, and the emergence of Pat Riley as the finest coach in the West, the rivalry returned with renewed intensity, giving NBA fans two of the most exciting and well-played championship series in decades.

The great Lakers teams of the eighties have been characterized by intelligence, durability and incredible athletic prowess. Though less knowledgeable Celtics fans have enjoyed accusing the Lakers of being glitzy and without substance (as if the team were an extension of the Forum fans, who arrive fashionably late and often evince little interest in the game), in fact the Lakers have succeeded because of hard work, excellent coaching and shrewd front office management—in other words, in much the same way the Celtics have succeeded. Anything more than a superficial examination of the club reveals that Los Angeles has a winning tradition because it does what the Celtics do—maintain a tradition of teamwork; choose personnel carefully; plan long-term rather than short-term; and build a front office

Bird drives past Bob McAdoo in the Celtics' midseason 111-109 1984 defeat of the Lakers. "I'm not sure fans appreciate the energy Larry expends in every minute of every game that he is on the court," K. C. Jones said, "expending all that energy shooting, driving, passing and rebounding. He stays ahead of every play."

of people who know basketball. It is no accident that the two men most responsible for the decision-making in the Lakers organization in this decade have been Jerry West, the definitive Lakers player of the fifties and sixties, and Bill Sharman, the great Celtics guard who also coached L. A. to a championship in 1972. K. C. Jones, it should be added, was an assistant coach on the Lakers that year, yet more evidence that the ties between the clubs extend well beyond the on-court rivalry.

Together, West and Sharman made the trades that landed key draft choices (Magic Johnson, James Worthy, Byron Scott, A. C. Green) and brought important role players to the club (Michael

Cooper, Mychal Thompson). Molding their team around the great Kareem Abdul-Jabbar and using the fast-breaking Russell Celtics as a model, they combined old-fashioned fundamental basketball with state-of-the-art eighties athleticism, fused within the discipline of the tough head coach, Pat Riley. Along the way, West and Sharman made the hard decisions that needed to be made, and they always seemed to be right. By allowing Magic to win a power struggle with Paul Westhead in 1981, they stabilized on-court leadership (not an easy decision—Westhead had led the Lakers to the championship in 1980). In trading Norm Nixon for the rights to Byron Scott, they took a lot of heat from fans and the media. (Nixon was a popular player, and Scott took some time to flower.) Phasing out Jamaal Wilkes in favor of James Worthy continued the movement towards youth and speed (though Magic was a friend and supporter of Wilkes), and redirecting the offense from Abdul-Jabbar to Magic completed what was the most successful structuring of an NBA team in the eighties—with the possible exception of the Celtics. The Lakers did all this in an environment of expanding salaries and difficult egos, and their record speaks for itself.

Frank Dell'Apa, the *Boston Herald* writer who covered L. A. during the 1984 Western Conference playoffs, observed coolly that the Lakers were a team of "nine starters." "Put the first five together with the second five and you have the most impressive collection of talent in the NBA. They have won ten MVP awards, five scoring championships and four Rookie of the Year awards. They figure the sixth-man strategy is so effective they have quadrupled it, with Jamaal Wilkes, James Worthy, Bob McAdoo and rookie Byron Scott taking turns filling the role.'' On paper L. A. was superior to any team in the league, and the Celtics knew from the moment they gathered for training camp that the Lakers would be their biggest obstacle to another championship.

The Lakers' rise coincided with the slow decline of the Philadelphia 76ers. Philly continued to be a force after 1983, but never again would it capture the chemistry of that magic season. The aging of Doctor J, the disaffection of Moses Malone and the physical decline of Andrew Toney were more than the arrival of the phenomenal Charles Barkley could compensate for. Unlike the other two NBA powers, Philadelphia management made all the wrong choices, and the Sixers would not advance to The Finals for the remainder of the era. But bad news for the Sixers was good news for league management, who were delighted with an extended showdown between the physical, blue-collar Celtics and the lean greyhounds of L. A.: the clubs' contrasting styles and dynamic superstars did more for fan interest than any million-dollar Madison Avenue strategy could have, and the debate over the relative merits of Larry Bird and Magic Johnson went back and forth until Bird temporarily settled it with three consecutive MVP years (Magic's play from 1986 on would reopen the issue). But marketing and NBA executives aside, there was no doubt about the intensity and excitement of that rivalry.

The Celtics' renewed aggressiveness came through on the court in their play and their talk. ''That team,'' Carr said of the '83-84 team, ''talked more junk than any team in the history of the game.'' And the talk worked because the players had the ability to back up the bravado.

Kareem Abdul-Jabbar is blocked by Robert Parish, 1985. Abdul-Jabbar suffered through a miserable Game 1 in that season's finals. He himself said he was ''embarrassed.'' He sat in the front row during film sessions after that game to motivate himself and then went on to win the playoff MVP.

''They'd *always* be talking trash,'' Michael Cooper said. ''Calling us 'fakers,' they'd go out and try to intimidate us. It was a serious obstacle for us.'' Cedric Maxwell had always been free with words, and he was joined in loquaciousness by McHale, Carr and Bird, who had talked to opponents from his first NBA exhibition game. Rivals were intimidated because these Celtics did what they said they would, attacking with defense, playing tough, physical ball and running the break. They predicted victory and then followed through. They were waging war on the basketball court, prepared to challenge all-comers for the title they felt was theirs. They were, in Carr's memorable phrase, ''not to be denied.'' Becoming virtually unbeatable in the Garden, where fans celebrated the return of K. C. and the brash style of their heroes, they won 62 games in '83-84 and 63 in '84-85, tops in the league both seasons. Though the Sixers were the defending champions that first year, the Celtics played as if *they* were, and the attitude was so convincing they had a natural psychological advantage in every game they played.

The 1983-84 exhibition season set the tone. With DJ quickly earning a starting role (after a confrontation in practice with K. C. that both men learned from) and Bird playing with more confidence than ever before, the team quickly made clear that it was serious. That preseason featured back-to-back games against the Lakers in Hartford, Connecticut, and Worcester, Massachusetts, spots where the Celtics are revered but seldom seen. The Celts whipped L. A. soundly in

Hartford, with K. C. jawing with the refs and barking constantly at his players. Anyone who thought that the new coach's reserved demeanor off the court would extend to the sideline quickly learned otherwise. The following night the Celtics came from 13 behind to win, with Bird starring and Parish playing overwhelming defense. Those two games convinced Boston it could play with the best, and the malaise of the previous season vanished as if it had never been there. A game against the Sixers later in the preseason featured three explosive confrontations: Bird squared off with Marc Iavaroni; Max challenged Moses; and Henderson took on the rookie Sedale Threatt. The last fight brought both benches to the floor, and with both teams rumbling, Red Auerbach descending from the stands, and Billy Cunningham ripping his sports coat down the back, the whole scene looked like a cross between vaudeville and

 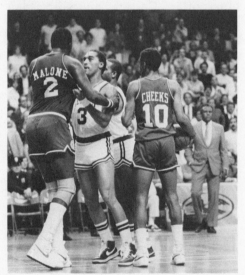

Bird fighting with Marc Iavaroni, preseason 1983, and Johnson holding off Moses Malone, 1985. In the 1983 preseason brawl, Red Auerbach, aged 66, came out on the floor to engage in the hostilities. The competitiveness between the franchises still lingered in the late eighties, but the 1985 Eastern Conference final, which the Celtics won convincingly, was a turning point. Alex Wolff in Sports Illustrated *noted that in that series, ''The Celtics had control.''*

Wrestlemania. But the Celtics organization's commitment to victory was clear, the confusion of Fitch's last stand was over.

The Celtics' regular-season play over those two seasons proved many things: K. C. was a top-class coach; Larry Bird was at the height of his game; Kevin McHale was an All-Star force at both ends of the court; Dennis Johnson was not a problem player. Unlike many NBA teams, the Celtics took the regular season very seriously and responded to the challenge of landing the best record in the league and securing the home-court advantage throughout the playoffs. They were the model of consistency: in '83-84 they had losing records against only the Lakers and the 76ers; in '84-85, against only the Milwaukee Bucks. Without Tiny Archibald, Bird had more control of the offense and responded with increased point and assist totals (he averaged a career-high 28.7 points per game in '84-85). He also redesigned the texture of the team. Maxwell and Parish were now more defense-oriented, and McHale assumed his sixth-man status with renewed team spirit. As DJ learned his new teammates' style, he adjusted his own game to theirs. He was always a lion on defense, but he adapted to his increasingly important role of ballhandler and gradually became a master at hitting Bird (so adroit at moving without the ball) beneath the basket.

But there were also important changes over those two years, changes that affected two of the most important players of the first half of the Bird Era. Ironically, these two men—Cedric Maxwell and Gerald Henderson—were the heroes of the 1984 championship: Max for the inspired way he carried Boston to a victory in Game 7; Henderson for the steal in Game 2 that would rank with Havlicek's (and later Bird's) on the Johnny Most apoplectic meter. The manner of their departure saddened many fans, but in the business environment of the modern-day NBA (and on a team with incredible depth in both the front- and backcourt) it was inevitable.

In a season when Bird was raising his offensive game to another level, one-time offensive force Cedric Maxwell spent much of the 1984-85 campaign away from the court. The problems started in the preseason, when Max held out during a contract dispute. He hadn't expected to be late reporting; his agent, Ron Grinker, had met with Auerbach at summer camp in early August and anticipated no problem. Based on a comparison with other forwards in the league, Max was asking for $800,000, but the delay occurred when the Celtics stuck fast to their offer of a half million.

Max ended up getting his money, but the club's intransigence did not sit well with him, particularly since the late start hampered his early-season performance. He had come off a magnificent Game 7 of the 1984 championship; he had gotten married during the summer. In his eyes, he should have been rewarded without question for his years of service to club. Instead, he got delay, and it hurt. The internal pain was soon matched by physical. As the season went on, his knee started aching, and he had to undergo exploratory arthroscopic surgery in February. McHale stepped into the starting role brilliantly, shooting over 57 percent from the floor and averaging over 24 points a game from that point on. His year peaked with a 56-point performance against Detroit on March 3, a team record that would last of all nine days (Bird would score 60 against the Atlanta Hawks in New Orleans

March 2, 1985. Kevin McHale connects on a free throw en route to his 56-point performance against Detroit. "McHale is a bright person," K. C. Jones said. "He loves to read. He loves basketball and loves to play the game. He likes to put the ball in the hoop, get an offensive rebound, work down low. He'll do everything required of him."

on March 12, moving even further into legend by fulfilling his prophecy after McHale's record: "That record might not last too long.") Max, meanwhile, was joking that he might be watching the playoffs from Charlotte. Perhaps he had realized that McHale's moment had arrived; perhaps he was making a point. K. C. Jones, asked if he would consider putting Max back in the starting lineup, said, "The man [Maxwell] said he [McHale] should be playing. I can't take McHale out." As it turned out, Max would not contribute meaningfully to the Celtics again. After a subpar postseason in which he averaged less than four points a game, he became the subject of trade rumors. Auerbach reportedly was upset because Max, in Red's eyes, had reportedly not worked hard enough on rehabilitation. In September he was traded, sent to the L. A. Clippers (from "the penthouse to the doghouse" the headlines read) for Bill Walton. It was a sad ending, the close of an era within an era, but Max left many good memories, not the least of which was his 1984 playoff performance.

Henderson, however, left earlier and with more rancor. Slowly, steadily, he had ascended from his days as a young Bill Fitch project to the point where he was a starting guard on the best team in basketball. The summer after the '84 championship many people retained the image of the Game 2 hero spitting champagne into the air, a photo that had celebrated the Celtics' victory on the front pages of the *Globe*'s sports section. He had weathered the mood swings of Tiny Archibald. He had survived the arrivals of the highly touted Ainge and the veteran Buckner. He had proven himself under Fitch and maintained his role under K. C. And though many people were saying that

Ainge was the guard of the future, the fact was Gerald was playing and Danny was reportedly upset at K. C. for not giving him more minutes.

The numbers backed him up. In 1983-84 Henderson had career highs in scoring average, assists, steals, field goal percentage (.524, excellent for a guard) and three-point field goal percentage. Buckner, though he continued playing excellent defense off the bench, struggled more and more offensively. Ainge had flashes of brilliance but suffered through an erratic, frustrating season. Coming off a postseason in which he had averaged over 12 points a game and made the heroic steal, Henderson, whose self-confidence had paralleled his development as a player, felt very good about his position on the team. Yet he must nevertheless have known that Ainge was, as he had once been, a project. He knew Danny's determination and ability, and he must have wondered occasionally about the number of good guards on the club.

As with Maxwell, trouble came in the form of contract negotiations. After five steady years with the organization, Henderson felt he was due big money. In an attempt to cash in on his starring role in the playoffs (and feeling the responsibility of family after the birth of his first child), Henderson asked for a sum the Celtics were not prepared to pay him. When negotiations stalled, as they did with Maxwell, Henderson's agent, Scott Lang, went public with the figures, a move the organization did not appreciate. Never keen to open dealings to the public, the Celtics usually only did so in the case of superstars. Henderson did not merit *that* consideration. As the days drifted by and the talks went nowhere, Ainge's situation also changed. Danny had been pressing Jones about playing time, asking what he could do to earn more minutes. Typically, K. C. told him to keep practicing hard and work on his game over the summer. Joining the Los Angeles summer league, Ainge played brilliantly, impressing everybody and winning the MVP. His confidence renewed, he came back determined to cash in on Henderson's contractual difficulties. The Celtics liked Ainge's attitude and thought he had proved that more minutes would give his game the stability it lacked. Suddenly Henderson was expendable. With Ainge and DJ starting, and Buckner, Carlos Clark and the rookie-camp surprise Rick Carlisle coming off the bench, Boston had sufficient depth at the guard spot. Henderson's behavior—hardly unique in the eighties NBA—gave the organization the excuse it needed to trade a veteran player. When Seattle offered Boston cash and a 1987 number-one draft pick for Henderson, Jan Volk saw an opening. He held out for the 1986 number-one pick, nearly blowing the deal in the process, but the Sonics, in need of a point guard, eventually agreed. Henderson was hurt and angry at the trade (when Seattle played the Celtics in the Garden that season, Henderson played very well in a Sonics victory and spiked the ball hard in front of the full house—a delayed statement of his displeasure). Many people thought it foolish to break up a championship unit, which the team's sometimes uneven play in 1984-85 sometimes seemed to confirm, but as Ainge developed into an All-Star starter, Henderson was soon forgotten (at least until the summer party when Len Bias, that 1986 pick, died).

It was easy to forget about the team's changes in the '84-85 season. Bird's individual game was never sharper, and the

Bird backs in against Kelly Tripucka in 1985. Before the first game of the 1985 playoff series between the Celtics and the Pistons, Bird was asked about Tripucka. He had lauded him when he was a rookie star in 1981, but four years later Bird growled, "You know what I'm gonna do? I'm gonna take his competitive heart right out of him." Bird scored a playoff career high of 43 in that series.

presence of DJ in the backcourt continued to help enrich his offensive game. It was also during this season that Bird refined his mastery of the double team. By then he commanded enough respect from the league referees to get away with floating away from his man in a way that had opposing coaches like Hubie Brown accusing the Celtics of playing an illegal zone defense. With his quick hands, great anticipation and superb court sense, Bird always seemed to be around the ball (he had a career-high 98 blocks that season). And yet he rarely fouled: for the fourth consecutive year he played a full season without fouling out of a game.

But it was Bird's offense that amazed. Every year fans said to themselves that Bird couldn't possibly play any better; every year Bird proved them wrong. As well as hitting for 60 against Atlanta that season, he put together a string of great offensive displays from December on that clinched his second straight MVP award. In another game against Atlanta he outdueled Dominique Wilkins, 48-47, as the Celtics won on a McHale tip-in at the buzzer. He also scored 48 against

Portland, including a game-winning corner floater. The following night, against Isiah Thomas and the Detroit Pistons at Hartford, he won another game at the horn with a drive through the lane. In January he scored his 10,000th regular-season point, and a month later, in a game against Utah, he registered double figures in assists, points and rebounds and also had a team-record nine steals. In a gesture that proved his disdain for statistics alone, he refused to reenter the game and go for the rare quadruple double. Ten times that season he hit for over 40, yet he also had over ten rebounds a game and a then career-high 531 assists.

There were some lowlights as well. In November, in a game that seemed symbolic of the Sixers' decline, Bird lit up Dr. J for 42 points through three quarters. It was a physical game, made all the rougher when official Jack Madden was injured and Dick Bavetta had to officiate alone. Late in the third quarter Bird slid through the lane, put up a soft shot and was fouled. Nothing was called, and on the transition Bird and Erving exchanged ugly remarks. Suddenly the competitiveness of the two men crossed a dangerous boundary, and they began punching. The crowd and the players were stunned. Afterwards Cunningham said that the Sixers would "get somebody to take care of Bird" the next time they played, but after a fine and a warning nothing came of it except bad feeling. Philadelphia was clearly frustrated at Boston's dominance (conclusively proven in the playoffs, when the Celtics handled the Sixers easily, 4-1). Though the Sixers won 13 games in a row midseason, the Celtics had two ten-game streaks and a second straight 60-win season as they continued to play well for Jones in their quest for back-to-back championships.

In many ways the postseasons of the first two years of K. C.'s tenure were similar. In both the Celtics had the home-court advantage throughout the playoffs; in both they advanced through tough early rounds (Washington and New York in 1984; Cleveland and Detroit in 1985) before relatively easy Eastern Conference championships (over Milwaukee, 4-1, and Philadelphia, 4-1); and in both they met the Lakers in The Finals. The differences, however, were more dramatic. The 1984 championship was not to be repeated, and there was a tangible feeling of relief among fans when the long ordeal of the 1985 playoffs was over. The rhetoric of back-to-back championships was there, but the 1984 intensity was missing. Perhaps it was the disaffection of the bench: Maxwell was ineffective, Buckner

Bird's elbow injury sharply reduced his shooting effectiveness in the 1985 playoffs, after 28.7 points-per-game shooting during the regular season. K. C. Jones commented, "I don't know if it's his bad finger or bad elbow. He never says."

was seldom used, and Carr, a key role player in the '84 championship, was not a factor. (He's going to have to play *one* of us, they said to each other.) None of these players would be on the team the following season. Perhaps it was the power of the Lakers themselves, who played the championship series as if on a mission, who were determined to prove that the Celtics did not own L. A. in the eighties as they had in the sixties. There can be no doubt that their proud unit (pride emanating from Riley and Abdul-Jabbar) earned the respect of Boston that year. Or perhaps it was the injuries: late in the season Parish, Buckner and Bird were nagged by minor aches that diminished their effectiveness during the long postseason. Against Cleveland Bird twisted his elbow, forcing him to miss Game 3, which Cleveland won. (Watching the game from his hotel room, Bird heard the cocky Cavalier fans yelling "We want Bird!" The next day he told the assembled media, "These people don't want me. They don't want no part of me." He proceeded to put away the Cavs with 34 points, 14 rebounds and seven assists as Boston won the game, 115-114, and the series, 3-1. "I loved every minute of it," he said.) During the Eastern Conference finals against Philadelphia, Bird got involved in a celebrated fight in a North End bar, twisting his finger and introducing doubt into his performance from that point on.

The 1985 finals had some high points for the Celts, especially Scott Wedman's 11-for-11 shooting performance in Boston's Game 1 blowout and DJ's game-winning jump shot in Game 4 that tied the series at two and seemed to promise a thrilling finish. But it was the Lakers' year, and they won the remaining two

Scott Wedman versus Julius Erving in 1977, when Wedman was with the Kansas City Kings. Wedman hit the game-winning shot in Game 2 of the 1984 Finals against the Lakers. Asked afterwards if he were nervous attempting that shot, he quickly answered, "No. You've got to want it."

games easily. Their championship (the biggest in the history of the franchise) balanced out those midyears of the Bird Era and cemented the renewal of this outstanding rivalry. The tone of the Celtics team after that loss was twilit and somber. The day after the final loss to the Lakers the players assembled for a team portrait at the Garden. Afterwards Maxwell and Kite met each other in the parking lot. Max was with a friend and turned to Kite, a man he liked, a man who knew better than anyone on the team what it was like to sit on the bench, what it meant not to matter on the court in the playoffs. The backup center had seen Maxwell's decline and felt for the star. He said as much, tactfully, respectfully. Max thanked him and turned back to his friend, who expressed the same thought. "Hey, don't worry about me," Max said. "I've got my contract." They parted, knowing, it seemed, that the following year would be different.

Celtics fans are much more likely to remember the long, intense 1984 postseason, when everyone was healthy and everyone contributed. That postseason gave fans two of the most exciting seven-game series of the Bird Era. The first came against the New York Knicks, who came into the Eastern Conference semifinals at their peak. They had played the Celtics well all year, splitting the season series, 3-3, and beating Boston in two early-season games, part of a four-game Celtics slump, the first time Boston lost that many in a row since Bird's arrival. New York's Bernard King was incredible that year, providing Bird's chief competition for the MVP award. The Knicks came to Boston after beating Detroit in the miniseries, a victory that included an electrifying shootout between King and Isiah Thomas in the final game, Isiah scoring 20 in the final three minutes, but King hitting 50 to lead New York to the win.

The Boston-New York series featured more than a Bird-King match-up. It also contrasted DJ and Ray Williams (later a Celtic), Parish and Bill Cartwright, Jones and Hubie Brown (there was no love lost between those coaches). It was a series that evoked memories of Cousy against Richie Guerin, Russell against Willis Reed, Havlicek against Bill Bradley. It was a series that saw two proud cities stage a classic battle as the home team won all seven games and the team's superstars, Bird and King, each averaged 30 points a game. The games were high scoring and physical. Ainge and Darrell

Walker engaged in a free-swinging fistfight ("The white guy loses again," Hubie Brown said), and Rory Sparrow floored Bird on a breakaway. The cockiness that the Celtics had shown all season reached new heights after Boston took the first two games. McHale said that the Knicks were in the grave and the Celtics were shoveling dirt on them. Max, charged with guarding King, said he was "going to stop the bitch" (a private remark overheard by a reporter). Those words came back to haunt those men as the Knicks won a pair in Gotham. After the Celts took Game 5, King scored 44 in a Game 6 New York victory. It was a series, Dan Shaughnessy said, of "duelling insults, raucous crowds, national television, a bench-clearing brawl, three ejections and obscene chants at both Gardens." And so the series proceeded back to Boston and one of the greatest games of the Bird Era.

Bird had been tired the Saturday before that Sunday game, his arm aching from the whacks he had taken throughout the series, but he was rested by gametime. "Nobody can say he will have a good day before he has it," he said later, but this was a game Bird was not going to let get away. Just as he had appealed to his teammates midseason to make an extra effort to give Jones the coaching position in the All-Star game; just as he had stood on the plane towards the end of the year and asked them to "win it for Case"; so too he was not going to let Jones's first season as head coach of the Celtics end this early. With 39 points, 12 rebounds, ten assists, three steals and two blocks in 42 minutes, he gave an MVP performance. It was the game he must have dreamed about practicing in the gym at Springs Valley, the perfect game when everything was on the line and everything was under his control. In a game full of big shots the biggest was a three-pointer late in the third period, a shot he took without hesitation that gave the Celtics a 21-point lead. "It was the same type of shot I took in the final game against Houston when we won the title," Bird said. "I knew if I made the shot the game would be over." K. C. looked forward to Milwaukee. After the game he and Brown avoided each other.

Bird's reference to 1981 was not accidental. Three long years had passed since that championship, and he and the other Celtics were hungry. They prepared for Milwaukee, bent on revenge for the previous season's sweep. "We're just going to play our game," Jones said, though everyone knew differently. The Bucks offered only token opposition. With Lanier and Moncrief injured and Marques Johnson said to be fighting a drug problem, the team that Nelson had carefully brought along was falling apart. They managed only one win in the series and Boston got ready to face the Lakers.

Going into The Finals, the Lakers certainly looked stronger, in spite of the Celtics owning the home-court advantage. After a slow start that year (Magic missed

Maxwell, Bird, Parish, Johnson and Henderson, pregame, January 1984. This unit won the 1984 NBA title, creating many important plays with aggressiveness, none more meaningful than Henderson's steal of a James Worthy pass in Game 2 of The Finals. "What will I remember most from this series?" Pat Riley asked. "Simple. Game 2. Worthy's pass to Scott. I could see the seams of the ball, like it was spinning in slow motion, but I couldn't do anything about it."

13 games with an injured finger and Abdul-Jabbar slumped), L. A. won 56 of 61 upon Johnson's return and swept easily through the Western Conference playoffs. Along the way Abdul-Jabbar broke Wilt Chamberlain's record for field goals converted (that game was in Boston, and the Garden fans gave him a standing ovation). In April, against the Jazz, he broke Chamberlain's scoring record when he hit his 36,420th NBA point. But individual honors meant less to him than beating the Celtics, and the Lakers arrived in Boston as the determined favorites.

That championship series, the first of three between these two clubs over four years, was certainly the most exciting. The player contrasts were intriguing: Bird and Magic were meeting in a championship for the first time since the 1979 NCAA final, and in those intervening five years they had established themselves as the best in the sport; in Dennis Johnson the Celtics had a big guard who could guard Magic, and in Michael Cooper the Lakers had Bird's toughest defensive foe; Kareem and Parish were the best centers in the NBA that year; Cedric Maxwell, the big-game player *par excellence*, matched up with James Worthy, who probably would have won the series MVP award had the Lakers prevailed (he had a championship series record .638 field goal percentage); the rough-and-tumble Kurt Rambis saw his physical style imitated by Kevin McHale and M. L. Carr. Unlike later years, the Celtics had a superior bench that year (in The Finals the Boston bench scored 220 points, the Lakers' bench 197), but the overall matchup was so balanced and the two teams played so evenly that the series had to go down as a certified classic (as Bob Ryan said before Game 7, "Each team has

demonstrated that it has the heart and intelligence to match its talent. The runnerup will be disappointed, but surely not embarrassed'').

The media made much of the superficial trappings. On the court the Lakers were flashy and athletic, and their brilliance extended to their arena, the glamorous Forum, where Jack Nicholson, Michael Douglas, John McEnroe and Dyan Cannon came to see and be seen. The building's plush seats, modern decor and clean lines couldn't be more different from the Garden's antiquated angles and blue-collar feel. The Celtics played on the difference, casting themselves as the hardworking underdogs against the more talented but less physical Lakers. In truth the Lakers probably worked just as hard, but the Celtics' stance gave them a subtle psychological edge that just might have tipped the series.

"The Lakers are more talented than we are," K. C. said, but he never said they were the better team. As if to demonstrate their talent, L. A. came out smoking in Game 1, robbing the Celtics immediately of the home-court advantage with what Maxwell said was "the best fast break I've ever seen." L. A. had finished their conference championship series with Phoenix only 36 hours before, but they showed no signs of fatigue as Magic, Cooper and Worthy blew by the flatfooted Celtics. In Game 2 Boston came out determined not to be blown away again, and they led most of the way. But the Lakers, behind Worthy's play, came from behind to lead 113-111 with 15 seconds remaining. When McHale missed two free throws at that point the Garden went very quiet as fans pondered the prospect of going out to California two games down— an almost certain end to the series. All the

Lakers had to do was hold onto the ball and run out the clock—or hit the free throws after the inevitable foul.

The echo of Johnny Most describing what happened next still echoes in the Garden rafters. L. A. called a timeout, and Boston pressured the inbounds pass relentlessly. Worthy panicked at the worst moment and heaved an ill-advised crosscourt pass to Byron Scott, disastrous for L. A., historic for Boston. Henderson had watched the play develop and zoned in on the weak side, waiting for just such a move. He flew in for the steal, raced to the basket and laid the ball in. As Most and New England celebrated the Lakers looked stunned as Boston received another life. In overtime Wedman hit a pressure baseline jumper and the Celtics moved on to a 124-121 win. After the game the Lakers' lockerroom was a deathwatch: Riley was completely overwhelmed as he pondered the loss of near-certain victory.

But to their credit the Lakers came swarming back in Game 3, letting loose a torrent of transition baskets (Magic had 21 assists) that had fans wondering how the Celtics could ever win. Three games had yielded two L. A. wins and a game they should have won, and in the lockerroom afterwards Bird said, "We played like a bunch of sissies." A group of Celtics fans who had gone out to California with Saugus Travel canceled their Game 4 reservations and flew home. "The Lakers are too good"—that refrain was heard all over as reporters on both coasts said the Celtics didn't have a chance. But Johnny Most, angry at those who were already saying Worthy would be the MVP of the series, camped in the lobby of the Marriott Hotel the night before Game 4 and presented his version

of organizational loyalty. "You know, everybody always writes us off. Everybody. But I remember they did the same thing in 1969. They had balloons hanging from the rafters, and they were all ready to celebrate before the game had even started." That season had been a comeback season for Most as well, who had suffered a stroke before a team flight to Washington, and he wanted to win with as much intensity as any of the players.

In this context, Game 4 may have been the most inspirational win of the series for Boston. This was the game where the Celtics decided that they would have to fight speed with muscle. Bird, frustrated outside early in the game, took it inside repeatedly (he finished 9 for 24 from the field and 10 for 10 from the free throw line). DJ and Henderson also delivered key baskets as Boston came from nine points down to send the game into overtime (Magic inexplicably let the clock run down in regulation). In a pivotal defensive decision, Jones took Henderson off Magic and put DJ on him, a match-up that would stay for the rest of the series. Carr, meanwhile, was politicking on the bench for a more physical response from the Celtics, nudging McHale as the Lakers built an early lead and saying, "*I* wouldn't let them do that." In the game a few minutes later, McHale clotheslined Rambis on a breakaway, provoking a confrontation that breathed life into the Celtics as they won their second overtime game. (Max, who gave the most loquacious performance of his career that series, said, "Before Kevin McHale hit Kurt Rambis, the Lakers were just running across the street whenever they wanted. Now, they stop at the corner, push the button, wait for the light and look both ways." Riley had a terser summary: "They're a bunch of thugs.")

148

Magic Johnson defends Dennis Johnson. A key development of the Celtics' 1984 triumph over Los Angeles was DJ's move onto Earvin beginning in Game 4. After he had scored but four points in Game 3, he scored 22, 22, 20 and 22 in the next four. "I thought I was into the game, but Game 3 convinced me I wasn't," DJ said at the time. "Even K. C. had to come over and ask what was wrong. I told him that whatever it was, it wouldn't be there again. It was a case of getting mentally and physically aggressive."

Game 5 will be remembered for 97-degree heat, oxygen on the Lakers' bench and a transcendent, searing performance by Larry Bird. Sweat streaming from his face, Bird hit 15 of 20 from the field as he scored 34 points and gathered in 17 rebounds in spite of constant double-teaming. "I *love* to play in the heat," he said with a smile. "I just run faster, create my own wind." Not the Lakers. "How hot was it?" Abdul-Jabbar asked rhetorically. "Take a hundred laps around the court with a winter coat on and then go take a sauna. That's how hot it was." With CBS cameras trained gamelong on the Garden thermometer, the Celtics romped to a 121-103 win. Celtics fans celebrated the team's rebirth and aggressive play. One group carried pieces of clothesline, complete with wooden

pins. ("It's OK, Kevin," one of them said. "That play looked like a charge by Rambis to us.") But Jones was cautious. "We're not letting up," he said after the game. "We're approaching the sixth game as our championship game."

But the Lakers summoned reserves of their own to stave off elimination and force a seventh game. Abdul-Jabbar, plagued by migraine headaches all series long, made a quiet speech beforehand. "We are better," he concluded. "We should win it." Angry at what he saw as the arrogance of the Celtics organization, he wanted desperately to beat Red Auerbach and exorcise the Celtics ghost from the L. A. past once and for all. With Byron Scott, he led a furious late game charge to clinch a come-from-behind win. The action was intense. Answering

McHale's rough play in Game 4, Worthy dropped Maxwell hard on a breakaway. As the Celtics filed into the lockerroom someone dumped liquid into Carr's eyes. It was back to Boston.

M. L. got his revenge. In a coaches' meeting in the hotel after Game 6, it was decided that M. L. should be the first man off the bench in Game 7. From the moment the Lakers entered the Garden he taunted them. "You're not coming out of here with a win," he said as they passed the Celtics' lockerroom. "In the Garden? Forget it." Wearing goggles to protect his eyes (and to mock Kareem), he kept up the patter. But the hero that night was Maxwell. Bird gave an MVP performance throughout the series, but Cedric was the man in Game 7. And he knew it from the moment he arrived in the lockerroom. "Hop on my back, boys," he said. "I'm ready to carry you." His performance was vintage low-post basketball, the kind of offensive dominance that had distinguished his early career, and the Lakers didn't know what hit them. He was a terror off the offensive glass, sneaking in between the double-teams, putting up those twisting shots, drawing fouls, passing when he needed to (he had eight assists). By halftime he had hit 11 of 13 free throws, and the Lakers never did figure out how to stop him. With Parish getting big rebounds, the whole team playing great defense and the trio of guards—DJ, Ainge and Henderson—hitting for 41 points, the Celtics built an early lead and then withstood any L. A. attempt at a comeback. The 15th championship was secure.

The celebrations were an event in themselves. In the lockerroom K. C. was near tears. The long trip that had begun when he left the Bullets seven years before was over—he had a head coach's ring for his finger and pride back in his heart. As his players and friends embraced him he rejoiced. Ever the master of understatement, he said, "I like this. I've got to say I like this." In another corner Auerbach, the architect of it all, was holding the championship trophy with a smile on his face and a cigar in his mouth. Bird was fielding questions from the media with aplomb. Champagne was everywhere. News came that President Reagan wanted to meet the players in the Rose Garden the next day. Most of the players would go (and have the privilege of hearing Reagan mispronounce the name of almost every Celtics hero through the years in the process).

It had been an inspirational show, a perfect conclusion to K. C.'s wonderful year. Looking back, it was made all the more meaningful by being Maxwell's swan song, the last game in which he performed the magic that entertained us so much on and off the court over the years. And if there is one scene that captures the feeling of that championship most completely, it has to be Maxwell chattering away to the assembled media, buoyant in victory, squarely on the throne. He is passed the championship trophy, holds it impishly, kisses it, and then says in that playful voice of his to anyone who can hear: "How sweet it is, boys."

Maxwell at his peak as a Celtic, 1984. Tony Cotton wrote in Sports Illustrated *that Maxwell was "spectacular" in the 111-102 Game 7 1984 victory over the Lakers. "He made this series, perhaps his last as a Celtic since he is a free agent, a memorable one." He also hit his verbal stride in this series.*

7

THE RETURN
OF BIG BILL

Like beautiful, hand-carved bookends, the years 1977 and 1986 bracket the long basketball comeback of William Theodore Walton. Celtics fans, graced already through the years by the greatest players in the game, had the good fortune of seeing another legend of the sport end nine years of frustration with a season full of the two things the big redhead values more than anything—health and winning. The 1986 NBA championship closed the book on Walton's quest for excellence left open since 1977. Between came the blank pages of frustration, injury and sour relations with teams as distant from the winning tradition of the Celtics as a Valley girl is from Harvard. Knowing the pain of those years—and knowing how much Walton likes to win—is the only way of understanding what the 1986 crown meant to the man who helped so much to bring it back to Boston.

By 1977 the young, intense Bill Walton had a distinguished career behind him and the world of professional basketball before him. Twenty-four years old, he had just led the Portland Trail Blazers to their first and only NBA championship. The league leader in blocks and rebounds, owner of an 18-plus points-per-game scoring average, and the best passing big man in the game, Walton had, after a three-year professional apprenticeship, become perhaps the most complete center in the history of NBA, a man (so like Larry Bird) with tremendous individual skills who always thought *team* first. With a series of incredible performances (including 20 points, 23 rebounds, seven assists and eight blocked shots in the deciding game), Walton had led the Blazers, down 2-0 to the 76ers, to a dramatic comeback victory. Afterwards Dr. Jack Ramsay had this to say about his center: "Bill Walton is the best player,

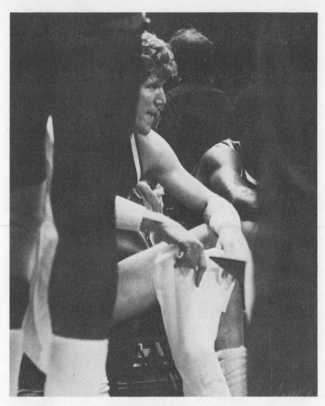

Bill Walton, 1977, Portland Trail Blazers. "I've never coached a better player, a better competitor or a better person than Bill Walton," Jack Ramsay said after Walton led the Blazers to NBA championship in 1977. Later, the relationship between Walton and Ramsay would change, specifically because Walton felt he was coerced in medical decisions surrounding his taking pain-killing shots during the 1978 playoffs. Walton played on what turned out to be a badly broken foot and was never really the same. David Halberstam wrote: "The worst had happened: he had played and been hurt; he had gone against his own precepts on injections; at the crucial moment, when the pressure was greatest, he, like everyone else, had given in, violating his principles."

best competitor, best person I have ever coached.'' Postchampionship hyperbole perhaps, but the kind of all-encompassing praise that had already been following Walton around for a long time.

Walton was certainly used to praise by the time he strode into John Wooden's office at the beginning of the 1971-72 season, a gangly kid with long red hair, sharp elbows and even sharper opinions. After leading Helix High in La Mesa, California, to 49 consecutive wins, he had come to UCLA highly recruited by the greatest college coach ever. As a freshman he had led his teammates to a perfect season, but his first year was only a prelude to a career that was to establish him as the finest college center to play the game, his sky-hooking predecessor with the Bruins notwithstanding. Three days after that initial meeting with Wooden the team assembled for their first practice. Walton's long locks were shorn and his face showed the determined look that was to bring himself and his team such accolades that year. While Daniel Ellsberg published the *Pentagon Papers* and 200,000 antiwar protestors marched on Washington, the 1971-72 Bruins won all 30 of their games by a major-college record average of 33 points a game. Not even Lew Alcindor's dynasty had had such a successful season.

A shot blocker who had opponent coaches comparing him to Bill Russell, a brilliant rebounder who knew his fundamentals perfectly, and a passer with touch no other big man could lay claim to, Walton dominated the college game completely. Teams that tried to play him one on one watched him eat up the boards and score at will. Teams that doubled down or smothered him with a zone saw him toss crisp, well-timed passes to Keith Wilkes or Henry Bibby or Greg Lee. And for Bill, stats did not matter; winning did. Against Denver University, which used a 1-3-1 zone collapsed around him, Walton scored only eight points. But UCLA won, 108-61, and John Wooden said, "Walton is the type of player who wouldn't have to score at all—yet he'll dominate the game. And the pleasant thing is, he enjoys not scoring."

But as Walton's college career continued he made as much news off the court as he did on. Coming of age at a crucial point in American history, a time when old stereotypes were being questioned and old policies turned around, he was very much part of a college culture that did its best to change America for the better. Like Bird, Walton was very much the product of his background, the time and place of his upbringing. The son of a welfare official from suburban San Diego, he was compassionate and spirited and determined. Like many of his contemporaries, particularly those on the college campuses of California, he spoke out on behalf of the oppressed and against the war in Vietnam. Unlike his fellow protestors, he was seven feet tall and the best basketball player in the country. When he interrupted a class and shouted, "Shut this school down!" or got himself arrested for barricading UCLA's Murphy Hall, he may have been a small part of a large movement, but being who he was he made headlines and caused controversy. He had an "image crisis." And yet through it all this shy young man, not at all comfortable with publicity, ignored the attention and continued doing what he thought was right.

It was a difficult period for a lot of people (most of all for those who decided to go to war), but an athlete in Walton's position had a particularly tough time of it. America's ambiguous love affair with sports had, as one of its rules of affection, the peculiar notion that the best athletes are cleancut men who follow authority blindly and love their country without question. Jocks did not grow their hair long, groove to the Grateful Dead and argue that government defense policies are misguided and immoral—at least not before the late sixties. Walton did, and drew fire from unthinking people because of it. The image of Tommy Smith and John Carlos raising their black-gloved fists to the sky as the national anthem celebrated their Olympic medals in 1968 was still fresh in people's minds in the early seventies, and they didn't like it any better when Walton did not pay proper deference to the American flag or when he refused to try out for the Olympic team. Wasn't this guy supposed to be the Great White Hope? Who did he think he was, and what did he think he was doing?

Though occasionally pushed by the zealousness of youth into overstatement, Walton knew exactly what he was doing. Ironically, in his political gestures he was exhibiting the same virtues that helped him excel on the basketball court—selflessness, idealism and intelligence. He always put the team before himself, always played his role to help the cause. And in his campus and court life he was doubly fortunate in having John Wooden as a coach. On the surface Wooden was poles apart from Walton—a Midwestern conservative who preached strict discipline and clean living and took pride in his communications with Richard Nixon. But Wooden was a man everyone respected because he respected everyone. He might have disagreed with Walton or Greg Lee or Keith Wilkes, but he always respected their right to their opinion and never held it against them, on or off the court. He was a man who stuck by the rules and expected others to do the same, but he admired no one more than the person who broke a rule out of principle. Bill Walton learned more than the fundamentals of basketball from the Wizard of Westwood: he learned that the commitment and discipline of a game can be a learning tool in life. He learned that when it is not a front for hypocrisy or a substitute for life, sports can indeed help build character.

When Walton moved on to the NBA many things changed. His politics became

Bill Walton, Sixth Man of the Year, 1986. David Halberstam used Bill as the key figure in his classic, The Breaks of the Game. *Halberstam wrote, "His high school coach realized Bill knew there was a lot of big time basketball ahead of him. Walton didn't lack ego, even though he shot infrequently (his ego was immense): it was that he was more in control of his ego and knew how to funnel it into the game itself, the better to help his teammates and in the process the better to exhibit his own unusual talents. At Helix High, there were glory days...the team undefeated, basketball a complete and wonderful universe, everyone was in the right place and the right things happened."*

less confrontational, his game even more dominant. Like Larry Bird he had trouble relating with the press—a tough problem when you are the number-one draft pick in the country and carry a reputation of being a radical. He did his talking on the court, pulling down 28 rebounds and scoring 26 points in his pro debut against the Lakers. The man who had led UCLA to two national championships and an 86-4 record was just as hungry for success in the pros. Walton became a master of the outlet pass and the most ferocious rebounder in the game. He took high percentage shots on offense and passed beautifully. Most of all he wanted to *win*.

Unfortunately his body was not as strong as his principles or his desire. He had always had weak knees and ankles, and his first two seasons were marred by injury. Playing for an expansion team that expected the world of him, he played hurt most of the time as he adjusted to the bone-crunching style and schedule of the NBA. "For two years I wasn't able to run up and down the court freely without making a conscious effort out of it. Without *thinking* about it. That's no way to play basketball."

Walton also suffered in other ways. With a lot of dissension on the team and a guard-oriented coach in Lenny Wilkens, who failed to use Walton as well as he could have, the Trail Blazers were in disarray. Stars Geoff Petrie and Sidney Wicks were constantly fueding. In his first year as coach, Wilkens was finding his feet. The team struggled and, predictably, the criticism fell like Oregon rain on Walton's head. The Portland press had expected him to do what would have been unreasonable even if he were healthy. He withdrew. He brooded (partly because of the incessant bad weather). His stats were respectable, but he played in less than half the regular-season games during those two years as his joints ached.

Then came 1976 and Jack Ramsay. In the softspoken doctor Walton had a mentor who, like Wooden, was a stickler for detail, a motivator and a team man all the way. Ramsay would teach Walton a lot about individual defense. He would also construct a team tailored to Walton's strengths, a team with speed and intelligence that ran the fast break off Bill's quick outlet passes and played pesky, pressing defense around the center's commanding presence underneath. With Maurice Lucas to help enforce the boards, the outstanding Bobby Gross moving well without the ball and passing brilliantly, and Lionel Hollins and Dave Twardzik running the offense, the Blazers had a tightly knit group that only got better as the season went on, culminating in the victory over Philly that had the entire Pacific Northwest celebrating.

With Walton finally fulfilling his potential and Ramsay deftly bringing out the best in his new players, the Blazers seemed to have a minidynasty in the making. The following season they looked certain to repeat as they overwhelmed the competition. Walton was at his rebounding and passing best, averaging five assists a game and fueling the most potent offense in the league. Then, as Portland's record stood at a Celticlike 50-10, disaster struck. Walton broke the tarsal navicular bone below his left ankle and was lost for the rest of the regular season. Without their mainstay, the Trail Blazers lost 14 of their remaining 22 games—still good for the best record in the NBA. But with Walton hobbling in the playoffs they were beaten in the first round, and the promise of a repeat championship was gone.

The frustration only deepened. Over the next four years—when he should have been in the prime of his career—Walton played a grand total of 14 games. In 1978 he asked the Blazers to trade him. He was angry over what he said were irresponsible medical practices in Portland (on one occasion, Walton said, team doctors injected a sore leg with Xylocaine at halftime; after the game he couldn't walk, went to the hospital and discovered he had a stress fracture). At the end of the season, during which he hadn't played one game, he signed a seven-year, $5 million contract as a free agent with the San Diego Clippers. But though Southern California was a congenial place to live, the injuries continued. Walton missed the entire '80-81 and '81-82 seasons as he had his left foot surgically reshaped to alleviate stress on the navicular bone, and ex-Clipper owner Irv Levin, charging that Walton has misled the team about his physical condition, filed a $17 million lawsuit. Walton enrolled in Stanford Law School. His basketball career looked over.

In 1982 his reconstructed foot felt better, and he started another comeback. He began by playing weekends (as Elgin Baylor and Lenny Wilkens had done in the early sixties while serving in the army) and gradually worked his minutes back to the level he had played in the midseventies. But the injuries kept coming. He had surgery for a bone spur in his right foot in 1983 and broke a bone in his hand during the 1983-84 season. The Clippers tried to keep him under 30 minutes a game and avoided playing him in back-to-back games. In 1984-85 he played in 67 games, a career high, even though he averaged less than 25 minutes a game.

By now Walton, 32 years old, knew he was never going to have the health to dominate the NBA as he once had. But he knew he could play pro basketball and contribute to a winning club if given the chance. The Clippers had slipped and slid into what seemed like a permanent cellar-dwelling role, and Walton, who knew what it was like to win, who knew how much he *liked* to win, said publicly that he wanted to finish his team with a winner—and by the mideighties the winners in the NBA were the Lakers and the Celtics. Walton's home was in California, but his heart was in Boston. "When I was a kid," he said in 1979, "my favorite team was the Boston Celtics—Russell, Sam and K. C. Jones, Satch Sanders, Bailey Howell, John Havlicek and Don Nelson. I liked them because they won all the time and I liked the way they won. Dedication, hustle and defense." The thought of playing for K. C. and with Larry Bird would be like stepping into a time machine for Walton. It would be a dream come true.

At the beginning of the 1985-86 season the Celtics were interested in Walton for two reasons. First, they needed a backup for Parish. In 1984-85 Robert had had his typically All-Star season, solid, consistent and workmanlike. He had hit his 54 percent from the field, pulled in his ten rebounds a game and scored his 18 points a contest. But there were also signs of wear and tear. At 31 years of age, Parish had averaged the highest number of minutes of his nine-year pro career. Backup center Greg Kite, while he possessed a classic Celtics attitude and a big body, simply did not have the tools to spell Robert for more than a couple of minutes a game in a Jim Loscutoff role. With Maxwell injured for much of the season, the Chief had been called upon for yeoman duty, and the strain had shown in the championship loss to the Lakers. Having one of the best centers in the game coming off the bench could make Parish

General Manager Jan Volk, Bill Walton and Coach K. C. Jones at a news conference announcing Walton's acquisition in exchange for Cedric Maxwell in 1986.

more effective and give Walton the role he was suited for at this stage of his career.

Second, the Celtics front office had reluctantly come to the conclusion that Cedric Maxwell, after eight seasons as a Celtic, was expendable. With MVP credentials and proven ability at both ends of the court, Max was perfect trade material for Walton, whom the Clippers were certainly not going to give up for a draft pick. For a number of reasons, there was a perception among many of the Celtics brass that the veteran did not have the drive he once had. Bad feeling had existed since Max's holdout in 1984, when the Celtics drew out what Max thought should have been a straightforward negotiation—and the fact that the Celtics ended up giving Cedric what he asked for seemed to prove his point. Off to a bad

start, Max struggled for the first three months of the season. Later came his surgery and the rumors that the front office felt he did not bounce back as quickly as he could have. McHale in the meantime had come into his own. How would Cedric, a starter all his career, accept coming off the bench? His poor playoff performance was a also sore point, and though Cedric would argue the point vociferously, he had lost the confidence of many of his associates.

Yet Cedric Maxwell was still extremely popular among his teammates and the fans. Any knowledgeable observer had seen how he had swallowed his offensive pride and turned into a defensive stopper. The fans had laughed with him, celebrated with him, marveled at his elegant play and low post bag of tricks. How could *Max* go? How could you trade the man who had carried the Celtics to the throne room in two championship series?

Also, as attractive as the trade sounded, many observers had serious reservations. Walton's health was an obvious concern; though he had passed a physical in Boston there was word from L. A. that the Lakers weren't interested because they saw serious physical problems. Then there was the question of how Robert would respond to Big Bill's presence. Always sensitive about his better-paid teammates, the Chief's ego might have a counterproductive effect. After all, *he* had never complained about playing too much. (Walton later visited Parish at his home, a move the Chief appreciated.) And if Maxwell were to depart, who would be the Celtics' small forward? Who would guard the Bernard Kings and Adrian Dantleys of the league? When Max was at his best he was the perfect offensive and defensive complement to the Celtics' frontcourt.

Of course the trade happened. On September 6, 1985, Big Bill came to Boston in exchange for Maxwell, Boston's 1986 first-round draft choice and an undisclosed amount of cash. Max moved on to different pastures with the blessings of his teammates and the memories of great moments. Walton suited up as if he were in high school and looked forward to what he hoped would be his finest year in a decade. He would not be disappointed; neither would the Celts.

Everyone welcomed Bill—who could not be in awe of the man?—but Larry Bird was particularly pleased. During the summer Walton had called Red Auerbach from California, making a pitch, doing his best to land a spot on his dream team. Bird was in Red's office when the call went

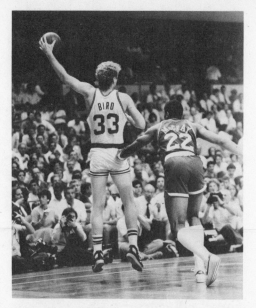

Larry Bird catches a pass on the left side against Rodney McCray. The isolation of Bird on one side against one defender was the most preferred Celtics offensive play in their 1986 championship year.

through, and Red put Walton on hold for ten minutes while he discussed the possibility of aquiring him with the team captain. Bird knew a soulmate when he saw one and counseled trade. Bird himself was to spend a lot of time with Walton that season—at practice, on the phone, in the lockerroom. These two men shared more than great reputations—they both had a magical combination of court vision, wondrous ability and focused intensity that put them on a level of their own. Two players of their caliber in the same league was a phenomenon. On the same *team*? That was a treat even Celtics fans didn't have a right to. If Walton stayed healthy.

He did, and in doing so put together a season as personally satisfying as the 1977 championship in Portland. Spelling Parish off the bench, he averaged less than 20 minutes a game—minutes he made count.

He had career highs in games played (80) and field goal percentage (.562). His 165 assists were his second-best total since leaving Portland, and he hauled in 17 rebounds for every 48 minutes played. His tenacity and performance earned him the NBA Sixth Man award, signifying the league's best reserve player. But stats and awards meant nothing compared to the championship and the rapport he achieved on the court with his new teammates, particularly Larry Bird. The timing of his acquisition was perfect, as his skills and attitude fit the Celtics' needs of that season like a Chuck Daly suit.

No doubt Celtics fans have been spoiled over the years. By 1985 the Bird Era alone had given them two championships and two rivalries that fans of other clubs spend a lifetime waiting for. In K. C. Jones they had the ideal coach for a veteran team, and every starter was a potential All-Star. With the 76er front office in disarray, the divisional rivalry with Philadelphia was becoming a thing of the past (Boston would win the Atlantic Division by 13 games in 1985-86). By this season a Boston-L. A. final was almost a given, and fans and the media could not be blamed for expecting everything. The players too, as hard as they drove themselves, were human and open to slacking off against the less-than-stimulating competition of most NBA clubs.

Into this environment of potential complacency came Walton, acting as if he were trying out for his high school team. His gung-ho attitude and back-slapping, let's-go-for-it-guys style had people wondering if this could be the same guy who, 15 years ago, was Mr. Counterculture. Wasn't this *corny*? Uncool? Not at all. Walton's enthusiasm was such that when he had a basketball in his hands he became extremely singleminded and competitive. Nothing was put on. Remember, this was the man who played intramural ball at Stanford as if the world championship were on the line. He loved basketball more than anything else, and he had just been handed the opportunity of playing with the best team and the best player in the world. How could he *not* be gung-ho? And as it happened, his enthusiasm was just what this veteran team needed. In practice and in games Walton became the driving force behind the green team, the Celtics' second team, motivating, encouraging, pushing them to push the

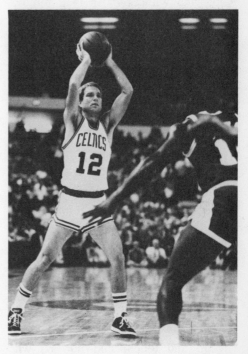

Jerry Sichting, a key reserve on the 1986 title team. After he was traded for Jim Paxson, Larry Bird's fiance, Dinah Mattingly, described the feeling among members of the Celtics family about the popular Sichting and his family's departure: "I know there have been trades, and they're part of the business. But no trade has affected me as much as this one."

starters. He raised the intensity of the practices and gave K. C. a cohesive unit that could spell the first string as smoothly as starters and keep Boston fresh throughout the regular season. And some of those green/white scrimmages were *very* intense. The second unit was better than many NBA teams—Walton, Sichting, Wedman, Rick Carlisle, David Thirdkill—and Walton led by example. And team confidence was at such a level that year that the starters welcomed the competition off the bench. Parish proved that worries about his starting ego were nebulous. He and Walton worked together a lot, and without those long minutes wearing him out, the Chief played with fresher legs than he'd had in years.

But perhaps the biggest beneficiary of Walton's presence was Bird. Larry had already taken his individual game to the limit. Fans knew by now that Bird would always work to maintain his Olympian level of play, would always come up with a pass or save or shot that had never been seen before. But by 1985, after six professional seasons, Larry was playing at his peak. The time was right for a player of Walton's intelligence and style to give Bird an added dimension, a level that he could not achieve alone. After the championship of that season, the most memorable moments for Celtics fans came between January and April of 1986. By the new year Walton had found his rhythm and touch, and no one who followed Boston's progress will forget a handful of plays that should be recorded on videotape and buried in a vault for the edification of future hoopologists. Usually Bird would begin the process by feeding Walton in the post. Using his 240-pound body as a shield and extending the ball away from his defender with his long arms, Bill would feint slightly and edge towards the basket. While the opposing team prepared for one of Walton's patented rolls to the hoop, Bird was doing another of the things he does better than anyone else—moving without the ball, sliding his defender off a pick or faking to an open spot and cutting to the hoop. Just when the defense thought it had shut off all the lanes; just when it seemed that Walton had held onto the ball a *little* too long—suddenly Bird was under the hoop with a millimeter to spare and Walton, *without looking*, was whisking a deft over-the-shoulder pass that Bird kissed into the basket. How did they *do* that? How did Bird know where to be and how did Walton know he would be there? Basketball at its best provokes those kinds of questions, and Celtics fans had the chance to ask them quite a few times that season.

But with or without Walton Bird was magnificent that season. Player of the Week four times and Player of the Month twice, he played every game of the season for the first time since '80-81 and never put in less than a first-rate performance. He became the second person in NBA history (after Cliff Hagan of the 1960 St. Louis Hawks) to finish the season in the top ten in five different statistical categories (scoring, rebounding, free throw percentage, three-point field goal percentage and steals). He became the third player and first noncenter in NBA history to win the season MVP award three straight times. He had ten triple doubles and a second consecutive 2,000-point season. He was also passing the ball brilliantly and notched a career-high number of assists. At the All-Star game in February, held in Dallas, he moved into the realm of legend. In the

"Picture this: Indiana State is playing, and Larry is being double- and triple-teamed every time he gets the ball. On a fast break, he fires the ball off the backboard at an angle, simultaneously dodging two defenders. They think it's a crazy shot, but Larry goes right to where he knows the ball will come off the board and in the air he takes the pass he just made to himself and dunks the ball." K. C. Jones in Rebound.

game itself he scored 23 points and had seven steals, five assists and eight rebounds in 35 minutes of play. But fans remember his victory in the NBA's first three-point shootout more. After a week of woofing Bird went out with icewater in his veins and outshot the best in the league for what should have been an insignificant trophy. But not for Larry. "I'm the three-point king," he shouted, arms raised, "I'm the three-point king!" The man's competitiveness knew no bounds, and he finished the miracle season with an MVP performance in The Finals and another ring for his misshapened hand.

Not that Bird didn't have support. Kevin McHale responded to his first full year as a starter with an All-Star year. In spite of missing 14 midseason games with a sore Achilles' tendon, McHale had the finest season of his career, averaging over 21 points a game and leading the team with 134 blocked shots. Whatever misgivings fans had about Max's defensive absence were lost in McHale's performance: he made the league's All-Defense First Team and had 43 blocks in the postseason. His long arms and great timing—which he had always had—were now strengthened by a surer sense of positioning and an avoidance of bad fouls (he had the fewest number of fouls that season of his six-year career). And in spite of his increased offensive production, he was passing better than ever. His 181 assists, the highest he had recorded, were 40 better than the previous year, when he had played in 21 more games. With a low-post game he had refined into the most potent in the league, McHale was also developing into a master of the inside-out pass. As opponents doubled down on him, he would rifle a pass around the hip of the outside defender to a waiting DJ or Ainge who, averaging 26 points a game between them, were becoming increasingly responsible for hitting the outside jumper and keeping Boston's fabled frontcourt free to operate inside.

Boston's passing game that season was the key to its dominance. Everyone was playing focused, unselfish basketball; everyone was following Bird and Walton's example and looking for the open man. It was not uncommon to see a a basket off a play covering the full length of the court in which every man on the team touched the ball and the ball did not touch the floor. They ran the break with precision when they needed to and moved the ball with control in a half-court offense that was the most effective in the league. Their options were myriad: Bird complemented his outside shot and power game with a series of refined one-on-one moves that (unlike so many isolation moves in the NBA) more often than not ended up with a pass to a teammate cutting to the hoop. McHale added a jump hook to his repertoire of wriggle moves and fadeaways that had garnered his 56 points against Detroit the year before. Parish, revitalized with Walton to back him up, also had a career-high number of assists, though he played the fewest minutes since '82-83. With the guard tandem of Ainge and Johnson secure and the newly acquired Jerry Sichting, who also complemented Walton's style by moving well without the ball and provided quality minutes off the bench, fans

Kevin McHale posts up Moses Malone. McHale's confidence was established for good during the 1984-85 regular season when he replaced the injured Cedric Maxwell in the starting lineup.

witnessed the most efficient and successful team of the Bird Era—if not of Celtics history.

The team never let up. It had a winning record against every club in the Eastern Conference and a losing record against no team in the league. It had winning streaks of eight (twice), nine, 13 and 14 games. It moved into first place on November 2 and did not relinquish it for the remainder of the season. After the All-Star break Boston was never ahead of second-place Philadelphia by less than seven games, and it cruised to a club record 67 victories, which included a 40-1 record at home. They made nearly 51 percent of their shots and won by an average margin of 9.4 points, the best in the NBA. While the Lakers were self-destructing out West after an excellent start themselves, Boston was aiming at the playoffs, intent on getting the championship back where it belonged.

The cohesiveness of this team was probably best represented by the play of the bench. Unlike more recent campaigns, when K. C., reluctant to use a weak bench, ran his starters to exhaustion by the playoffs, the '85-86 season was marked the best all-around team effort of the Bird Era. Scott Wedman, who had adjusted to a limited role in Boston after a long and stellar career with the Kings and Cavaliers, proved his flexibility by filling in superbly for McHale when Kevin went down with a foot injury. With Wedman as a starter, the Celtics went 15-3, and Scott scored in double figures 14 times, including a team-high 24 in a 97-88 win over the Bullets in late January. Walton was consistent throughout, and Jerry Sichting proved the wisdom of his acquisition by playing in all 82 games and choosing his shots so carefully that he ended the season with a .570 shooting percentage, amazing for a guard. With these solid reserves at center, forward and guard, the Celtics were covered.

The bench also gave Jones the flexibility to experiment, and some of the most intriguing player combinations of the Bird Era appeared that year. Opponents, faced with the incredible frontcourt of Bird, Parish and McHale (all All-Stars that year), suddenly had to adjust to the twin towers of Walton and Parish, or the *triple* towers of Walton, Parish and McHale. Against slower teams Bird or Wedman would occasionally play guard, and the Celtics fielded what must have been one of the tallest teams in history. K. C. could also go with the small, quick combination of Ainge, Sichting, Bird, Wedman and McHale. And as the wins mounted, Jones

Parish powers in for a score against World B. Free and Phil Hubbard of the Cavs, 1986. Bill Walton: "There's so much emphasis on Larry and DJ and Kevin McHale, as well there should be. But there wouldn't be the Boston Celtics without Robert. Everyone is well aware of that."

McHale. And as the wins mounted, Jones took delight in creative lineups and the frequent *en masse* appearance of the green team—usually in critical situations. Walton, taking pride in his green team leadership, was disappointed if the second unit did not hand the game back to the starters with a bigger lead than it inherited. Pride was a hallmark of this club.

There were remarkably few dips in the year's cycle, but this team had the ability to turn the few disappointments there were into positive lessons. After ripping off winning streaks of eight and nine (separated by a single loss to Indiana) at the beginning of the season, the Celtics became a little sluggish in December. The last three games of the nine-game streak came on the road, including an impressive 130-111 win over New Jersey in which Ainge had led the club with 26 points and Walton had his first team high with 13 rebounds. But Boston came home flat and lost for the only time that year in the Garden on December 6, as Jack Ramsay's Trail Blazers glided to a 121-103 win. Though the Celts bounced back with home wins over Atlanta and Sacramento, they suddenly seemed snakebit on the road, losing all three road games out of the next five they played. Hoping to break out of this minislump, they headed down to Madison Square Garden for a Christmas Day game with the Knicks that was nationally televised.

While the rest of the country woke up to holiday preparations and presents, the Celtics crawled out of their hotel beds and traveled through the empty streets of Manhattan to the Garden. They mightn't be having any home cooking, but they were prepared to feast on the hapless Knicks (New York would finish with the worst record in basketball that year, losing

59 games). And for much of the game they did just that, with McHale scoring at will underneath and Parish dominating Patrick Ewing on the boards. But with a 25-point lead in the third quarter the Celts let sugarplum fairies dance in their heads, and suddenly the Knicks were coming back, slicing into that fat lead as if it were plum pudding. Ewing became unstoppable, and the young Knicks got all pumped up as they roared back to tie the game. K. C. tried every combination off the bench (though he only played Walton for three minutes) and also played McHale for 50 minutes, but nothing worked as the Celts lost in double overtime and were humiliated before a nationwide audience. Boston had lost two in a row for the first time that year, and with four of its next five games on the road the team's dream season was quickly facing its first crisis.

"The team that makes the *most* mistakes probably will win." Piggie Lambert, another Indiana basketball genius, made that cryptic remark a long time ago. What he meant, of course, was that the team that makes mistakes and *learns* from its mistakes will develop into a winner. Losses are never easy—especially when they embarrass a team completely—but that loss in the Big Apple was a good thing for the Celts in the long run. It made them question their intensity at just the right point in the season. It forced them to regroup and bear down heading into the long months of January and February, when divisional crowns are won or lost. K. C. did not shy away from criticizing his troops to the press, but he wouldn't have had to say a word. The players knew what they had to do.

They started by curing their road woes at once, beating the Jazz, Clippers and Pacers in a wide New Year swing. After

Ralph Sampson against Larry Bird, 1986. Before The Finals that year, Bob Ryan wrote, "Sampson has been Mr. Enigma since entering the University of Virginia. He is proud of his skills and doesn't want to be restricted to posting up, a life he was saved from by the advent of Akeem Olajuwon." Sampson was booed unmercifully at the Boston Garden after fighting with Jerry Sichting, and shooting 1 for 12. About being hit by Sampson, Sichting said, "My sister has hit me harder."

a home win over the Nets they lost to the Pistons in the Silverdome as Isiah Thomas scored 39, but then they went on a 13-game tear, during which the average margin of victory was over 14 points against the likes of the Hawks, Lakers, Sixers and Bucks. Bird led the team in scoring in eight of those 13 wins, including a 41-point performance in a thrilling overtime over the Hawks in the Omni. The Hawks had talked a lot of trash in the first half of that game, and at intermission K. C. knew he didn't have to say anything. Playing the finest ball of the year, Bird and the Celts went into the All-

Star break with the streak intact, a 38-8 record and an eight and a half game lead over second-place Philadelphia.

Sacramento stopped the streak on the first game of the West Coast swing immediately following the break, but the Celts continued playing well, beating the Lakers in the Forum and avenging their earlier loss to Portland with a 120-119 Valentine's Day win in which Bird scored 47 points (in January 1985 Bird had lit up the Blazers for 48 in the Garden). Larry was doing it all: 36 points against Golden State, 31 against Seattle; 18 rebounds

Kevin McHale against Charles Barkley. The New York Post's Lyle Spencer wrote in the 1986-87 season, "For your dream team, you start with Larry Bird and Magic Johnson. Then add Akeem Olajuwon to rebound, reject and dunk, and Michael Jordan to take flight, say hello to the folks in the upper deck, and jam on his way down. For a power forward: Kevin McHale. He's not spectacular like his teammate Bird, just spectacularly effective with his subtle array of post-up jump-hooks, fadeaway Js and drives. He kills you softly, but surely."

against the Lakers, 16 against the Nuggets. After finishing the swing 4-3, the Celts returned home and started another win streak of eight games. After two road losses, there was *another* streak—their longest of the season, 14. The genie the loss in New York had let out of the bottle kept the Celtics working and complacency at bay. The Celtics went into each game knowing they would win, sure that their individual skills and team play could overwhelm any opponent. It was during this stretch that Bird put a lock on his third straight MVP year with a series of offensive shows that was even impressive for him. In six games over the course of eight days, Bird scored 50 (a tough one-point loss in Dallas), 31, 33, 26, 36 and 43. Three days later he was back on another run, with 32, 36, 35, 27 and 40, all wins for Boston. By the time the Sixers stopped the streak on April 4, Boston was four games away from its best regular season ever, and K. C. was planning for the playoffs. Larry Bird would finish the season as the team leader in scoring average, assists, rebounds, steals and minutes played, but he had his eye solely on the championship.

The 16th Celtics championship came in the same way the regular-season crown did—with systematic yet passionate play by everyone on the team, an MVP performance throughout by Larry Bird, and critical help off the bench by Walton and the green team. Besting Chicago, 3-0, Atlanta, 4-1, and Milwaukee, 4-0 (sweet revenge for the infamous sweep of '83), the Celtics had as easy a time in the early rounds as Moses Malone and the Sixers did during their "fo', fo', fo'" playoff domination in 1983. This was a championship that the Celtics felt "predestined" to win, one that talent and determination assured, and the players made sure that they dispensed with the Eastern Conference teams as efficiently as possible.

But the preliminary series were not without drama. Against the Bulls, Boston had to contend with the amazing Michael Jordan, who showed the form that would make him the league's most potent offensive force the following year. Activated late in the season after recovering from a foot injury, Jordan came flying at the Celts, putting on a one-man show in Game 1 that amazed the Garden crowd and netted him 49 points. But with no other guns to go to, the Bulls lost, 123-104. The Celtics, in awe of Jordan's moves, plotted a defensive strategy for Game 2 aimed at keeping him at bay. DJ's usual tight man-to-man would funnel Jordan into the center, where the Boston big men would swallow him up. After Game 1, DJ, who had had a great game himself, answered media questions with this statement: "I'd better not talk too much or next game Michael'll go out and score 52." Jordan would make Dennis a prophet. The Celtics executed, but Jordan was too much. Blowing past Dennis, slamming home fierce dunks over Parish and Walton, the young guard had what was probably the finest offensive game in Garden history, scoring 63 points and propelling an otherwise limp Chicago team into a double-overtime playoff classic. The Celtics won, 135-131, with Bird scoring 36 and Walton and McHale both grabbing 15 rebounds. But much of the credit for the win has to go to Ainge, who took command of his own destiny at a crucial point in the game. Midway through the third period he was cruising downcourt when he saw K. C. summon Sichting off the bench. Rightly surmising that he was

Before the 1980 playoff series between the Celtics and the Bulls, the Boston Herald*'s Mike Carey wrote a story about the matchup between Dennis Johnson and Michael Jordan. Both men, knowing their remarks would be published, flattered each other. Johnson, told of Jordan's kind remarks, finally countered, "George Gervin used to tell people, 'It's really tough playing against Dennis'—yet all the time he was scoring 30 points a game against me. You gotta like guys like that."*

about to be taken out of the game, Danny threw up a shot and hit it—his first points of the game. The next trip down he hit another. By the time there was a break in the action, DJ was tired, and Sichting replaced him instead. Ainge ended up scoring 24 points in the last 18 minutes, including the shot that forced the overtime. Boston fans went home with the double thrill of a great playoff victory and a historic performance by Jordan.

Michael was out of gas by the third game, which the Celts took easily. The Atlanta and Milwaukee series were equally perfunctory, as Boston lost only a single game and won the remaining eight by an average margin of 16 points. The Celtics swept the Bucks with such devastating precision that the Milwaukee media (still in the Celtics' bad books over the treatment of Ainge three years prior) could find nothing more exciting to write about than the ridiculous accusation that Celtics players were taking drugs on the bench. What they should have been reporting was the importance of Walton. After missing two of the Atlanta games with a sprained knee, Bill came back against Milwaukee to give Boston 19 minutes a game, 59 percent shooting from the field, and an intensity that was contagious. Everyone on this team wanted to win.

Out West the Lakers, who had been struggling with the defending champs' disease of complacency all year, finally bowed out to Houston, where Bill Fitch's current version of the twin towers was doing its best to win Fitch a second ring. The Finals would be a homecoming of sorts for Fitch, and he wanted to shoot down his old team with such fervor you could see the tension etched on his face throughout the series. He certainly had the artillery. The 1986 Rockets may have been a ragtag bunch, but Fitch had done his usual overachieving job with the people he had. Akeem Olajuwon had proven that season that he was the NBA's center of the future. He finished eighth in the league in scoring average and third in blocked shots, and was named to the All-NBA Second Team. Ralph Sampson, the second of Fitch's towers, had the potential to be even better than his Nigerian teammate. A 7-4 center with a deft outside shot and excellent speed for his size, he was unstoppable when he was on. He could also rebound—his 11.1 per game was good for fifth in the league. Along

with Olajuwon, Jim Petersen gave Houston the muscle any team needed to successfully challenge the Celtics, and in Robert Reid and Rodney McCray, Fitch had two solid small forwards who could run the break and play excellent defense (particularly against Bird). Finally, the backcourt, which many argued was the Rockets' weak spot, nevertheless had three very serviceable guards in Lewis Lloyd, Mitchell Wiggins and Allan Leavall, who knew enough to get the ball inside and could hit enough outside shots to keep a defense honest. The Celtics had to respect Houston—after all, they had beaten the mighty Lakers. And no one knew better than the Celtics' veterans

The classic matchup: Abdul-Jabbar against Walton, January 1986, both UCLA champions, both superstars, players who made their teammates better. Walton, growing up in Southern California, modeled his game after Abdul-Jabbar, then known as Lew Alcindor, then with the Bruins. Later in his career, desparate to play again, Walton again found himself trying to emulate Kareem: to play until he's 40 years old.

what Bill Fitch could do with a young team.

The youthful vigor that Walton had contributed season-long to the club continued into the championship finals. Late in the season, he, Bird and McHale had agreed to give up drinking beer until the postseason was over. The actual abstinence was less significant than what it stood for—motivation. Calling each other up constantly, pressing each other to keep their pledge, these three men built up a collective determination that was obvious in their performance, leaving K. C. free to conduct the business of coaching. Jones was not lacking in motivation either. For obvious reasons he was very eager to beat Fitch and win his second ring as a head coach.

Many observers thought that Sampson would be a key factor in the Rockets' game. Notorious for his lapses, he could be alternately brilliant or lackluster, and his presence had a big effect on Olajuwon, who, though always consistent, had his game opened up if Sampson played well. Game 1 was a lesson in this respect: Sampson drew his third foul less than five minutes into the game and had to sit out the rest of the half. When he came back after the break, he missed 12 of 13 shots to finish with two points and a lot more Garden jeers (which would only get worse as the series went on). Akeem played well (33 points, 12 rebounds) but had to contend with constant double-teams and the full weight of Boston's formidable frontcourt (McHale and Parish had 44 points between them). Bird, meanwhile, entered the first of six MVP performances in the ledger—21 points, eight rebounds, 13 assists and four steals. More often than not it was Bird who dropped down on Akeem, sniping at the ball, forcing him

to give it up to Houston's lesser lights. With DJ and Ainge scoring 22 in the third period and the team as a whole shooting 66 percent for the game, the Celts won easily, 112-100.

Bird goes up between Robert Reid, Mitchell Wiggins and Akeem Olajuwon, of the Houston Rockets, Game 3, The Finals. Bird's figures in Game 3: 25 points, 15 rebounds, 11 assists, four steals. But the Rockets held him to 3-for-12 shooting in the second half and won, 106-104. Houston Chronicle *columnist Ed Fowler wrote, "Now that the Rockets have discovered the answer to Larry Bird, maybe they can cure communism."*

Game 2 was all Larry, one of those complete Bird performances that even the superhuman stat line doesn't do justice to. With 31 points, eight rebounds, seven assists, four steals, two blocks and *no* fouls, the captain played a complete game that kept the Rockets at bay all afternoon. He continued his pesky defensive doubling, using his quick hands and superb court sense to disrupt the Rockets' inside game. On offense he isolated himself a lot on McCray, backing in slowly and then driving to the hoop or hitting the open man. On one play, deep in the corner and covered by Olajuwon on a switch, Bird faked a two-handed pass that had the Rockets center wheeling into the middle. Pulling the ball back, Bird hit a jump shot as the fans went crazy. Inspired, intense, Bird was extending the brilliance of his regular-season play like an arrow aimed at the championship. Though Sampson's play improved in Game 2 (18 points, eight rebounds), he still did not do enough to free up Akeem's game, and Bird and the Celtics used a 34-19 third quarter to blow the game open.

Those two games were sandwiched around Bird's reception of his third straight MVP award on May 28. The event was significant for a number of reasons. Only two other players have won three straight—Russell and Chamberlain. Bird had joined some very select company. As the only noncenter to achieve the feat, Bird showed how much he had come to dominate the game, and he did it in an era when there was more NBA talent and competition than ever before. In accepting the award, Bird also displayed some of the humor and self-confidence that marked how far he had come since the awkward days of his first press conferences. Handling the media horde with skill and intelligence, he passed on some memorable and controversial remarks. "I'm proud to be in a group with Bill Russell," he said, "but Wilt Chamberlain talks a little bit too much for me." But Bird showed he could talk too. This year, he said, "I just felt there was no one in the league who could stop me if I was playing hard...For the first time every team tried to double me. Trying to beat two guys was a lot more

fun...What makes me tough to guard is that once I'm near the three-point line I can score from anywhere on the court. It's kind of hard to stop a guy who has unlimited range." After Game 2 the following night, Akeem would have agreed. "He's the greatest player I've ever seen." On two continents.

The Celtics headed to Houston with the home-court advantage intact and the momentum clearly on their side. But Olajuwon for one was not about to concede. "I just don't see any way they can beat us here, now that we're at home." The Summit had been good to the Rockets that year (they were 36-5 at home), and with the 2-3-2 format in effect they had an opportunity to claw back into the series. The Celtics were hoping not to have to return to Boston at all—or, at worst, return with a 3-2 advantage. And until the Rockets won a game they were not about to scare Boston's veterans.

But they did just that in Game 3. For a while the Celtics looked as if they would take an insurmountable 3-0 series lead, coming from behind in the third period to go up by 11. The climax of their run (and a play that symbolized the success of the whole season) occurred when Bird, rolling off a pick, hit Walton in the lane with a left-hand pass. Covered himself, Walton hit a wide-open McHale on the other side of the basket for an easy dunk. Boston led, 76-65, and the three players who had given up beer in their quest for victory and solidarity ran back down the court, excited and eager for the flag.

But Ralph Sampson and Robert Reid were waiting for them. Fitch put in Reid to guard Bird, and though Larry insisted that the change made no difference, Reid did seem to do a better job than McCray, jabbing at the ball with his long arms and

Robert Reid defends Larry Bird, 1987. Reid had success defending Bird in two finals, 1981 and 1986, although the Celtics won both championships. Bird insisted Rodney McCray played better defense against him than did the loquacious Reid. After Bird sealed the 1981 set with 27 points against Reid, the Houston swing player said to Jack Gallagher of the Houston Post, *"I tried to keep him from scoring. I think I did a reasonably good job. I never said I was going to stop him from rebounding, assists and steals."*

keeping his body in front of Bird. Sampson, meanwhile, was finally waking up. After three steady quarters, he was overwhelming in the fourth, owning the boards and scoring two key baskets (he finished with 24 points and 22 rebounds). Suddenly lethargic, the Celtics seemed unable to stop a 9-0 Houston run that gave the home team a 103-102 lead with 1:07 remaining. Ainge hit a jumper, then Mitchell Wiggins tapped in an Olajuwon miss to restore the Houston lead. With 31 seconds remaining, Walton watched from the bench as the 24-second clock wound down and Parish missed a desperation rainbow. Jake O'Donnell blew his whistle inadvertantly and, after some confusion, called for a jump ball. Sampson tipped it to Akeem, who was immediately fouled by Bird. He hit one, and Boston called timeout with a chance to tie or win, but on the inbounds play Parish stepped on the sideline as he received the ball from DJ. The game was over and Houston had received a life.

"They got lucky," Bird said afterwards. "I think we're the best team in the league and the best team usually wins." But Boston could not hide its disappointment. It was not like the club to blow a late lead, no matter where they were. Walton sat in the lockerroom afterwards, looking as dejected as he ever had. He had not played in the stretch, and the sight of his team disintegrating while he watched from the bench was devastating to a guy who wanted more than anything to play and win.

There was tremendous drama left. Game 4, perhaps the most tense of the series, saw a Celtics resurgence and a Walton triumph. A tough, physical game, it was marked by tight defense and heavy hitting as the lead see-sawed and K. C. and Fitch played move and countermove.

Sampson and Olajuwon continued their dominance underneath, wearing down Parish (who led the team with 22 points and ten rebounds) and keeping their club on the heels of the Celtics, who used DJ's sniping to stay ahead. But two clutch baskets tipped the balance in favor of Boston. The first came with 2:26 left in the game and the score tied at 101, when Bird hit one of his stake-in-the-heart three-pointers that so demoralizes the opposing team. The second came with :40 remaining. Up by one, the Celtics were controlling the ball. The atmosphere was incredibly tense, and the Summit fans were howling for a turnover. The ball was knocked away from DJ, who ran to the halfcourt line to retrieve it. Looking up, DJ saw Walton pointing to the basket, yelling at him to put it up as the 24-second clock ran down. Johnson threw up a bad shot, which bounded off the rim. Walton—in for the stretch to replace an exhausted Parish, getting the chance he had been denied the game before—ran in from the right corner, grabbed the ball and dunked it home. It was the perfect punctuation to his comeback season—the winning basket in the waning seconds of a crucial championship game. In the lockerroom after the game the media applauded the center, who was as jubilant as he had been dejected two days before. He had come through under pressure. He had been there.

Celtics fans will always remember Game 5 for the Fight. Playing for the privilege of returning to Boston, the Rockets came out strong, playing the Celtics evenly through the first period. With 9:40 left in the first half, Sichting and Sampson became entangled on a Rockets possession. They bumped, and Sampson threw an elbow. Never one to back down, Sichting said, "I'll get you for that." Suddenly Sampson (15 inches taller than his rival) turned and started punching. DJ ran over "to pull Jerry away" and got a Sampson fist near his left eye for his trouble. Both benches emptied, with Akeem and DJ squaring off and Walton tackling Sampson. All the intensity of a physical championship final was momentarily funneled into the brawl, and after the smoke cleared, referee Jack Madden ejected Sampson. But this apparent move towards justice backfired for the Celts. As Sampson was leaving, veteran Robert Reid, the only Rocket who had faced the Celtics in the 1981 finals, ran over to Jim Petersen, Sampson's replacement, and said, "See that guy walking off the court? He was gonna give us 25 points tonight. He's our leader." The speech worked because Petersen, with McCray, Wiggins and Olajuwon, combined to give Houston its finest game of the series, swarming all over the Celtics for a 111-96 victory. Olajuwon finished with 32 points, 14 rebounds and eight blocks.

After the game K. C. called Boston's game "organized chaos," but most of the postgame comments centered around Sampson's attack. Sichting said he didn't know whether "it was a punch or a mosquito bite." Bird had plenty to say about the officiating and the Houston fans but saved his best comment for Sampson *and* Sichting. Why had Sampson picked on little Jerry? "My girlfriend could beat him up." Back in Boston, Johnny Most, never an advocate of understatement, added to his legendary status among Celtics fans with this poetic afterthought: "Ralph Sampson is a gutless big guy who picks on little people, and he showed me a gutless streak. That was a gutless, yellow thing to do." Sampson returned to the Summit floor after the game and waved to the fans like a heavyweight champion. He heard his last cheers of the season.

The Fight may have energized the Rockets, but the loss gave the Celtics the last shot of determination they needed. They returned to Boston intent on finishing the job in Game 6, going straight from the airport to the Garden for an intense practice. On Saturday, the day before the final game, the players practiced so hard K. C. "had to call it off before they beat each other up." McHale left quickly. Bird said, "I'm ready to go. And if I'm ready to go, usually the other guys are, too." And the fans could hardly wait to fill their role as the most effective seventh man in the league. Armed with preprinted posters declaring "Sampson Is a Sissy," they howled and roared and stomped their way through a game of passion and great performance. Sampson, booed roundly every time he touched the ball, had a terrible game, finishing with eight points. But even a dominant Sampson couldn't have stopped the Celtics on that day. Larry Bird made certain of that.

On the day he was named championship series MVP to add to his list of honors for the year, Bird was in no mood to fool around. He took control of this game early and carried the Celtics to a 114-97 victory that hung the 16th banner high above his heroics. The stats were there, of course, including his second triple double of the series, but the real story was in his attitude, which was most dramatically revealed in a few classic plays. Today was a day when he smelled blood early and went in for the kill. Early

in the fourth quarter, with Boston ahead, 84-61, he grabbed the ball off a broken play and, with the shot clock winding down, dribbled *away* from the basket and into the far left corner. Standing in front of Fitch, he threw up the most arrogant three-pointer of his career, a shot that told his ex-coach (a coach for whom he still had the highest respect) *take this!* Fitch knew then that the game was over. Earlier, falling in pursuit of a loose ball, he had screamed at Ainge from his knees, "Come to the ball!" And when McHale, running ahead of Bird, failed to look for a pass, Bird yelled, "Look up, dammit!" "When Larry talks," Jimmy Rodgers said, "we all listen." That day Larry spoke with a clarity and force that befitted the greatest player in the world, at the height of his career, leading his team to the third championship of his era. It was the perfect ending to the perfect season.

But as much as that game meant to Bird, it probably meant even more to Walton, who reached the end of his nine-year comeback on that warm Sunday afternoon in June. His symbolic moment came right after Bird's stake-driving three-pointer, when he sank a 15-foot jump shot, turned to the crowd and raised his fist in a gesture of total triumph as the noise reached its highest decibel level of the season. In that moment, all the pain of foot surgery and lost games, all the despair of losing seasons and bad advice, all the doubt and self-questioning, disappeared into the echoing reaches of the hallowed Garden rafters as he and the fans celebrated the completion of a transcendent, splendid year.

Bill Walton, Game 4, The Finals, 1986. After scoring the game's key basket on an offensive rebound dunk, he was center stage in the postgame interview room. "This time last year," he recalled, "I was watching these games at my house in San Diego wishing I was in them. Now I'm in them and I'm having the time of my life. This is sort of why I play basketball, what I get the most fun out of, playing in key games like this with the crowd all fired up and the refs leaving their whistles in the lockerroom. I'm a basketball player and games like this are what I live for."

8

THE END
OF AN ERA

Through the final days of the 1985-86 season, days K. C. Jones called "sweet," Celtics fans had double reason to celebrate. Just as the team was putting the wraps on its most dominant championship of the Bird Era, so too it was laying the foundation for the future, giving fans the happy feeling that they could look forward with as much pleasure as they looked back. No one could deny that this was a veteran team: at 27, Ainge was the youngest starter; Parish was 33 and Walton 34; Bird would turn 30 in December, but his seven blue-collar seasons in the NBA had given him 20 years worth of bumps and bruises; McHale (28) and DJ (31) rounded out the oldest starting five in basketball, and key sub Scott Wedman would turn 34 in July. Yet there was no reason why the starting unit, with the right kind of support off the bench, couldn't continue performing at

the highest level for the next five years. Walton's year was an inspiration. If he could stay healthy he would give Parish new life (and Kareem Abdul-Jabbar was proving how long a healthy and talented center could last in the NBA). The patient half-court offense the Celtics were settling into was tailored to suit their older team, and with the right amount of rest these men could also run when they needed to. But the biggest factor in the feeling of future success that year was the vision and planning of the front office, which, never content to celebrate the present, was completing the long process, begun with the Henderson trade nearly two years before, of choosing the Celtics' next franchise player.

In the wake of the 1986 championship, many media people asked Jones if this team was the greatest ever. He had played in the dynasty years; he had coached the

1972 Lakers team, winners of 69 games; he had been with the club as a coach throughout Fitch's time. Bigger, Jones answered. More talented. More balanced. But the best? Yes, perhaps they were. After all, this was the team that smoked out Atlanta (and Coach of the Year Mike Fratello) with a 24-0 fourth-quarter run in a key playoff game that had everyone shaking their heads. This was the team that had rolled over regular-season competition and completed an inspired playoff. This was the team that sported a frontcourt of *four* future Hall-of-Famers. And yet K. C. knew as well as anyone that no team is so good that it can't get better; which is why, even at the height of their playoff success, the Celtics paid such close attention to the draft lottery in New York.

Since the lottery's inception (designed to take away the negative incentive to lose games late in the season), the league had turned the event into a spectacle, a prime-time televised show in elegant studio surroundings. Shown at halftime of a nationally televised playoff game, the lottery featured the drawing of enveloped logos of the seven participating teams from a revolving plexiglass drum, while the teams' general managers looked on. The order in which the clubs were drawn determined their place in the draft, so the club with the seventh worst record in the league had the same chance at the number-one pick as the team with the worst. The element of chance certainly added drama to the affair, and if there was a franchise-making player in the draft (a Patrick Ewing, for example) the tension could become intense. But the 1986 lottery was distinguished by a number of excellent prospects, including Brad Daugherty, William Bedford, Len Bias, Kenny Walker, Chuck Person and Ron Harper, who were close in ability and all attractive as number-one picks. Landing in the top three was the goal of the seven clubs participating (the Celtics, 76ers, Suns, Pistons, Knicks, Pacers and Warriors). Boston had earned a spot among the seven by virtue of Seattle's poor showing (an interesting diversion for Celtics fans that season had been gloating over the Sonics' abysmal progress and seeing the Henderson trade grow more inspired daily), and Auerbach sat confidently at the dais, cigar in place, as Commissioner Stern plodded through the proceedings.

Celtics luck appeared again as the cards emerged from the drum and Boston landed the number-two pick (Philadelphia number one). Red said afterwards that landing anywhere in the top three was as good as getting the number one, and Boston looked forward to securing a franchise player who would become the linchpin of the club in the nineties. As he had with Russell in 1956 and Bird in 1979, Auerbach was confident that his dealing and research had made the difference, that Daugherty or Bias would solidify the current bench and emerge as a leader in a few years.

During May and June the Celtics had brought the nation's top college prospects to Boston for physicals and interviews. Georgia Tech's John Salley was in the Hub during the series against the Hawks, but it was said he didn't merit much consideration (he would eventually go to the Pistons). When Bird received his third consecutive MVP award, William Bedford of Memphis State looked on. Bill Russell was in town to present the award, and afterwards he joined Auerbach, Volk, Jones, Rodgers, Ford and Ed Badger for an interview of the young man. Red wanted Russ to talk about the team and its sense of itself, but he was just as eager to see Bedford's reaction to meeting the greatest center in the game. Bedford was suitably impressed, but the Celtics weren't. He didn't *feel* right to the men assembled there, and for Red, for whom chemistry means so much, that in itself was enough to bypass Bedford.

But Auerbach already had a pretty firm notion of whom the club would pick (if it could get him). The previous summer, at the Red Auerbach Basketball Camp, the Celtics had gathered together the rookies eager to try out for the club. It was at that camp that Sam Vincent had impressed the brass, but there was also an underclassman there who had soared through the air and crashed dunks in the hot summer night with an authority not seen this side of Michael Jordan. At 6-8 and 220 pounds, Len Bias had the size, strength and speed to compete in the NBA. But his basketball gifts impressed Auerbach most. He could handle the ball like a guard; he executed his outstanding vertical leap with excellent timing; he practiced the fundamentals precisely. And he loved to play. Red knew he was looking at a player who could be a Celtic.

Auerbach had invited Bias to camp on the strength of a meeting the previous spring, when he had had dinner with Bias, the player's parents and Maryland coach Lefty Driesell. Bias was thinking of leaving college after his junior year to enter the draft, and Driesell wanted Auerbach to talk to him. Red went into the meeting with an open mind; he was prepared to advise the young man to enter the draft

The Celtics traded Gerald Henderson to Seattle, hoping to bridge the Bird Era to a new generation of success. K. C. Jones wrote, "Henderson played great basketball for the Celtics, but we'd had Gerald and Danny Ainge splitting the job at guard, which is like playing football and splitting the job of quarterback. Both players—and the team—suffer." M. L. Carr wrote that when Henderson was traded from the Celtics, he told Henderson, "Even though you loved the Celtics, accept that it is over. Get Seattle back on track."

if his character suggested that route. But Red was so impressed that he told him to remain in school. He had been frank with the Bias family: if Len were to leave now he would probably go in the first 15; if he waited until after his senior year he would almost certainly be a lottery choice. The money would be bigger; his education would be complete.

Red followed Bias's last college season closely, a brilliant season in which he averaged 23.2 points per game. Consensus All-American and ACC Player of the Year, he was, most said, the top player in the country, and observers said that the possibility of playing for the Celtics motivated the man more than anything else. When he came to Boston during the 1986 Finals that observation rang true. He wanted to be there. "Please draft me," he said to Volk after leaving a meeting with Celtics brass. Everyone felt very positive about the player. The *feeling* was right. Bird told Red he would make a rare appearance at rookie camp to work with Bias. As the franchise's future, Bias commanded the attention of everyone in the organization.

So the Celtics were leaning strongly towards Bias as Draft Day neared, though the temptation to take a big man was affecting many of those involved in the decision. Traditional NBA thinking said that a center was always preferable, that the pro game revolved around that position, and the seven-foot Daugherty, a possibility at the number-two pick, merited serious consideration. Auerbach liked Daugherty very much but thought (correctly as it turned out) that the Sixers would take him at number one. Also, the emergence over the last few years of a different kind of dominating player—a Michael Jordan or Clyde Drexler type with all-around gifts

and the ability to control a game—made Bias seem more attractive. David Thompson's emergence in the seventies had challenged conventional thinking (the 6-4 star had routinely outrebounded seven-footers, scored at will and given the game a new dimension). As one of the league's main attractions in the years following the merger and preceding the appearance of Magic and Bird, he had proved that a swingman could control a game as completely as a center. His play presaged that of Michael Jordan's—and his career contrasted Jordan's in a way that relates directly to Len Bias's tragic death.

Much has been said about the pressures on the NBA athlete: the sudden stardom, the big money, the temptation to yield to self-destructive choices. Jordan presents the classic success story. Highly recruited out of high school he starred from his freshman year onward under Dean Smith at the University of North Carolina. An NCAA champion, a member of the Gold-Medal winning Olympic team, College Player of the Year in 1983 and 1984, he came to the NBA with as fine a resume as possible and then proceeded to play *beyond* his potential. Rookie of the Year in 1985, he went on to win back-to-back scoring titles in 1987 and 1988. In the league only four years, he signed a $28 million contract and won the league's MVP award in 1988. Yet from all accounts Jordan is as controlled and responsible off the court as he is brilliant on it. He manages fame and wealth without incident and impresses everyone with his personable character and down-to-earth style. Unlike Thompson's career, which unraveled in a trail of alleged cocaine addiction and an infamous fight in a disco, Jordan's has been conducted without incident.

The differences between these two players (so similar in style on the court, so different off it) is important to note because of the increasingly common tendency to discuss drugs among athletes as a black phenomenon. The well-publicized habits of Micheal Ray Richardson, Marques Johnson, John Lucas, Lewis Lloyd, Mitchell Wiggins and other black NBA players have given rise to a disturbing tendency among observers to consider drugs as a problem plaguing only black players. NBA basketball is a unique profession. With 80 percent of its members black, it follows logically that 80 percent (or so) of the problem players will be black as well. If there are white players who use cocaine they obviously get less publicity. The tendency to yield to drug use is personal and has nothing to do with race—just as the ability to handle the pressures of fame is individual. Those men who know themselves and have the discipline to learn from their position and their mistakes usually become the most successful at dealing with the trappings of stardom. As Larry Bird said when asked if he would submit to a drug test (and soon after his infamous fight in a North End bar), ''I don't use drugs. Hell, I get into enough trouble just drinking beer.'' It is very difficult for a man in the NBA to make a mistake when the press is ready to trumpet every detail. A player dealing with a problem has to deal with the attendant publicity as well, and the ability to do that is entirely individual. How is it John Lucas conquered his habit and Micheal Ray Richardson did not, even when the latter had a $3 million incentive to stay straight? That question cannot be answered along racial lines.

Len Bias, of course, didn't have enough time in his limited experience of cocaine to develop a habit. One shot was all fate gave him, and that was enough to keep him out of a Celtics uniform, or any other uniform, forever. When Draft Day 1986 arrived and Bias was announced as the Celtics' pick, every fan had visions of the following season: Walton hitting Bias backdoor for a soaring slam dunk; Bias aggressively defending against Alex English or Dominique Wilkins; Bias giving confidence to his friend San Vincent; Bias coming off the bench with that intensity, that love of the game, that seemed to be the predominant characteristic of the Maryland film clips that littered the sports news that week. The Celtics brass must have had these visions as well, but officially, of course, they would not announce the expectations of more titles.

Those were hectic and stressful days for Len Bias. Three days before the draft he had been in Washington, D.C., finalizing details with his agents. Then it was out to the West Coast for a battery of physicals with the Golden State Warriors, who owned the third choice in the draft. On the plane back he must have thought about the trials of his development as a player: how he had spent a summer dribbling blindfolded; how he had learned to control his temper; the difficulties of being an outstanding individual player on a mediocre Maryland team his senior year. Sunday he was in New York; Tuesday he was back in Boston, wearing a cap that proclaimed *Celtics, 1986 Champions* and hearing the words of David Stern: ''The Boston Celtics announce the selection of Len Bias.'' ''Praise the Lord!'' the born-again Christian said, and then there were more press conferences, more interviews, more meetings with Celtics players. He found out he would wear 30, M. L. Carr's old number, with Carr's blessing. He negotiated a million-dollar deal with the Reebok sneaker company. The world was in his hand, and he must have felt all-powerful.

The details of his death are familiar. In the dawn of June 19, 1986, he died of cardiorespiratory failure after ingesting a good deal of cocaine as he partied in a Maryland dorm with friends. The high he had been on all week apparently wasn't enough, and in one tragic stroke the dreams and potential and future were canceled. His death stunned the Celtics organization and its fans and thrust the drug issue into even further prominence. But after all the rhetoric, all the talk about what this tragedy would mean to basketball and the Celtics' future and the nation's youth, the final image of his parents at his funeral proclaimed the simple truth: the senseless death of an athlete dying young; the acute pain of those who loved him.

That tragedy colored the Celtics' quest in 1986-87 for back-to-back championships (and their future for much longer). And as if the loss of Bias were not enough, injuries sapped the energy of the team that had swept through the NBA the previous year. Scott Wedman underwent surgery to remove bone spurs from his heel in June and never fully recovered. He would see limited action in the opening weeks of the season and did not play after December 5. Ten days before training camp Walton broke a finger practicing with Parish. Soon after-

wards he scrimmaged lightly without taping his foot and suffered an ankle injury that sidelined him for seven months. Coming off the great previous season, the injury was particularly distressing to Walton, and he tried to come back too soon, running before he could walk. He flew out to California in December, where a bone scan revealed abnormalities in the navicular bone—the same bone that had caused him to miss so many games over the years. He underwent surgery and started on the long, familiar process of rehabilitation. Because Walton had been such a star the year before, and because the media felt it had to feed its readers and viewers stories about him, the speculations about *when* he would return continued *ad nauseum*. When some reporters questioned his desire to play, the situation got ugly. A local television reporter wondered aloud on air if Walton were feigning injury, and Walton's wife, Susan, chased him down the hallway, screaming, "What are you *talking* about?"

But the sportscaster wasn't alone. One veteran player wondered privately if Walton had made the right decision submitting to further surgery. "If he increases his minutes it'll straighten itself out. But that's a personal decision. But there was certainly nothing personal about the other injuries on the club. Danny Ainge fell hard on his back, injuring nerve fibers around his spinal column and missing a month of action; or Bird's strained Achilles' tendon that kept him out for a week; or Sichting's stomach virus that weakened him considerably for three months. Wedman, meanwhile, was talking of retirement as K. C., in a move that was to become a pattern over the next two seasons, turned more and more to his

McHale posts up former University of Minnesota teammate Mychal Thompson, the major acquisition of the Lakers in midseason 1987-88. Thompson's first game as a Laker was against the Celtics, and it represented a turning point. The Los Angeles Times *had run an advance story about the Celtics-Lakers game, asking in a headline, "Is McHale Unstoppable?" In a game that matched teams with identical best records in the league, Thompson helped L.A. win, an important emotional victory in the Lakers' title season.*

starters as the season wore on. McHale and Parish, who were not getting any younger, played more minutes in 1986-87 than they had in any previous season in their careers. With Sam Vincent and Rick Carlisle seeing limited playing time, DJ and Ainge also played as many minutes as they ever had. The media grew progressively critical of the coaching. But it was tough for K. C. to do anything but play his starting five. In 1987-88, when he had three rookies, Reggie Lewis, Mark Acres and Brad Lohaus, coming off the bench, the loss of Bias was felt even more

keenly. The Celtics' consistent success and consequent low draft picks over the years had left them with one of the weakest and most inexperienced benches in the league. The starting unit, on the other hand, was clearly the best, so the long minutes for the stars seemed the only alternative. K. C. also came from a Celtics' tradition that said young men should be able to play 40-plus minutes game in and game out, and that young players had to sit on the pine as they paid their dues.

The Eastern Conference, meanwhile, was growing younger and stronger. Chicago, Cleveland, Detroit and Atlanta had strengthened themselves to the point where, with Milwaukee, they made the Central Division the toughest in the NBA (three Central Division clubs finished the 1986-87 season with 50 wins or better—the other divisions had only one 50-win club each). These youngsters were gunning for the world champions every game, and Boston had to battle. Though they remained virtually invincible at home (39-2), the Celtics had a losing road record for the first time in the Bird Era (20-21). For the first time since 1983, they did not have the best record in the league (the Lakers finished six games ahead of them), and they even had to battle to season's end to ensure the home-court advantage in the Eastern Conference as Atlanta played tough. Both situations had repercussions in the playoffs. Having to fight Atlanta for the best record meant that K. C. could not rest his already weary starters at the end on the season. Abandoning the home-court advantage to L. A. was a factor in The Finals, when the Lakers took the first two games in L. A. with ease and then swept to a 4-2 victory over a tired Celtics team. The 1988 playoffs repeated the pattern. Atlanta and Detroit finally caught up with Boston, using their young legs to push Boston to a tough seven games against the Hawks and an inevitable six-game loss to the fired-up Pistons. In 1988 the Celtics did not reach The Finals for the first time since 1983, and there was a definite feeling that they had reached the end of an era.

But during those two years the Celtics still had one of the best teams in the NBA, and the regular seasons ('86-87 in particular) had all the highlights and great games that fans had enjoyed throughout the decade. The starting five, playing without an uncertain relief corps, developed a group mind that enabled them to run their offense flawlessly—the rhythm was almost always right; they instinctively ran the right options; they conserved their energy for the right moments; they won games by finding the right man for the right shot. How many times over those two years did Boston bolt to a lead, let the opposition crawl back in, and then win with a gutsy performance at the end? All too often, according to Jones, but in retrospect this pattern was a direct result of long minutes the starters had to put in. By 1988 criticism of K. C.'s rotation was public: Bird complained of tiredness in the playoffs, and Bob Ryan questioned substitution patterns in the *Globe*. Yet expectations of success were so high by now that it was almost impossible to please with anything less than a championship.

But these were the years when the Lakers became the first back-to-back champions since the days of Bill Russell, a feat they achieved with excellent coaching, a brilliant starting five, a deep bench and teamwide determination. Magic Johnson, who had emerged as leader of the Celtics' biggest rival in much

Larry Bird knifes in for a lay-up against the Lakers. Tom Heinsohn wrote of the rivalry between Bird and Magic Johnson: "They are the Chamberlain versus Russell of today— although, because they play different positions, they never really face each other...They're two historic players, two fierce egos pushing each other harder and harder, bringing out the best in each other while bringing out the best in themselves."

the same way Bird had in Boston, had never forgotten the tag of *goat* he had been given after the '84 Finals. "That's one championship I don't have, and I want every one I have a chance to get." After the 1985-86 season of injury and internal dissension, the Lakers came at the opposition as if on a mission. L. A. was the only '86-87 team in the NBA to have a winning record against the Celtics as they snapped Boston's 48-game Garden winning streak in December behind Magic's 31 points and won the rematch in the Forum, 106-103, as Magic was All-World

About Magic, here preparing for a hook shot against Dennis Johnson, Abdul-Jabbar commented, "He has enough intensity, at times, for the other four guys on the floor."

with 39 points, 17 assists, ten rebounds and a three-quarters-court field goal at the end of the third period that was a *shot*, not a heave. (A year later Magic won a hard-fought contest in the Garden with another three-point runner at the buzzer.) That year Johnson became the clear team leader. Early in 1987 Abdul-Jabbar reportedly told Magic that he was willing to play a supportive role in the offense, and that Johnson should take full leadership of the team on the floor. With the addition of Mychal Thompson, an ideal backup for Kareem who brought experience and muscle to the role, and A. C. Green, who refined the power forward position Kurt Rambis had once occupied, the Lakers strengthened themselves after 1986 in a way the Celtics did not. They also responded to the personal challenge Pat Riley presented them and backed up his "guarantee" before the 1987-88 season that his team would repeat as champions—an unparalleled example of confidence and public team motivation that, among other things, ensured Riley's consideration as one of the game's finest coaches.

With four championship rings to his credit, Riley has arguably been the most successful NBA coach in the eighties. Like Jones, he is an ex-player, a former Kentucky star who played for the Lakers in the seventies. Like Jones, he also knows how to deal with veteran players; he knows the subtle methods of motivation and team leadership. Unlike his predecessor, Paul Westhead, Riley understands that in the NBA it is the players on the floor who make the instant decisions that win games. Riley gives them the context, the motivation and the direction. He trusts his people. Some people have suggested that he has been the beneficiary of great talent and front-office foresight. That is certainly true, but no one can deny that he has made the best of his opportunity, sweating out the down times and finding a new approach when it was needed. Throughout the rivalry with Boston, he has come to respect the Celtics players, and they have come to respect him—quite a move forward from the days a few years ago when he called them "thugs."

Magic Johnson had a personal comeback during those years by breaking Larry Bird's MVP streak in 1987; he completed a distinguished double by winning the championship series MVP as well. The Lakers breezed through the playoffs that postseason, beating Denver, 3-0, Golden State, 4-1, Seattle, 4-0, and Boston, 4-2.

The key game in The Finals was Game 4 in Boston, which L. A. won to take a 3-1 lead. The shot that won the series was a running hook in the lane that Magic hit over the fully extended Robert Parish and Kevin McHale. That shot vindicated his errors of 1984, secured the championship and said, as eloquently as any single shot could, that here was a man who could do it all. That moment was Johnson's apotheosis, even more significant than his leadership in Game 7 of the 1988 Finals, when he led an inspired Lakers performance against the Detroit Pistons, the new kid on the NBA block.

The Pistons had ended the Celtics' domination in the East by beating a tired Boston team twice in the Garden and taking the 1988 Eastern Conference championship, 4-2. The 1987-88 season ended in disharmony and exhaustion as K. C. Jones spent his final moments as coach watching the Celtics lose in the vast and unfriendly confines of the Pontiac Silverdome, so distant from the banners and warmth of the Boston Garden. The regular season had been long and troubling. Bird had his finest season offensively, averaging 29.9 points per game after returning to camp in peak condition, but with McHale injured and Parish suffering problems in his marriage, the team did not find that rhythm they had had the previous two seasons. In Cleveland in January they had a chance to send Jones to the All-Star game as coach, but they lost badly. With Walton remaining injured and Wedman and Sichting gone, the core of the fabled green team of 1986 had disappeared, and the new bench of rookies and free agents couldn't provide K. C. with the relief the starters needed.

The playoffs of 1988 did not compare with those of 1987, which, though long and tiring, had led to The Finals and given fans two intense seven-game series. McHale, who had injured his foot in a game against the Suns on March 11, hobbled gallantly throughout. Walton actually returned in March just as McHale was injured, then returned abruptly to the inactive list until a key game with Indiana in April. In that game, with the best record in the conference on the line, the glories of the previous year were briefly recaptured. The day before the game, Walton, normally jocular in practice, had gone through the workout without a word. After practice Jones faced the press, which bombarded him with questions about Walton's availability. "It's up to Bill," he replied. For the final time the Celtics' Sweet Sixteen team performed its magic, crushing the Pacers and ending a four-game losing streak on the road. Bird (31 points) and Parish (17 rebounds) dominated, and Walton led surges in the second and fourth quarters as the Celtics won, 108-85. Walton would go on to play nearly as many minutes in the playoffs as he had in the regular season, but in Game 2 of the conference semifinals against Milwaukee he fractured the navicular bone in his right foot yet again. "I'm through, damn it, I'm through," he yelled, and though he saw limited action against the Lakers in The Finals he was right.

Boston won the last game of the regular season, against the Hawks, to secure the home-court advantage in the East, then plunged right into the playoffs. The first-round defeat of Chicago was perfunctory but physical, and going into the semifinals against Milwaukee Boston was battered. Don Nelson had put together a new Bucks team, led by Paul Pressey and Terry Cummings, which always played the

"I tell you," Kevin McHale said about the Game 7 duel between Larry Bird and Dominique Wilkins in the 1988 Eastern Conference semifinal, *"there was one four-minute stretch there that was as pure a form of basketball as you're ever going to see."* Here is how the two matched it up from the 5:57 mark in the fourth quarter, Boston leading, 99-97:

5:57—Wilkins hits deep left-corner jumper. 99-99.

5:42—Bird sinks left-handed jumper in lane. 101-99.

5:25—Wilkins puts stutter-step move on McHale and hits jumper from 18. 101-101.

5:06—Bird hits 17-footer from the left. 103-101.

4:38—Wilkins banks one in high from the right. 103-103.

3:34—Bird hits in heavy traffic in the lane. 107-105.

1:43—Bird sticks three-pointer into Wilkins face directly in front of Atlanta bench. 112-105.

1:31—Wilkins hits turnaround in lane. 112-107.

0:26—Bird goes to hoop for lefty one-on-one drive. 114-109.

0:20—Wilkins tries to dunk over pack, misses, gets his own rebound and lays it in. 114-111.

0:01—Wilkins makes first of two free throws. Must miss the second. 118-116.

Bird and Parish execute a pick-and-roll in the semifinal round of the Eastern Conference playoffs, a heroic win for Boston in seven games. Jack McCallum wrote in Sports Illustrated, *"The Celtics obviously had other things going for them: the experience, the mental toughness, the character. Look at Bird's face at the free throw line in clutch situations. Look at Parish suck up the pain and grab 19 rebounds as he did in Game 7. Look at DJ sail headlong into the courtside seats. You're looking at an x factor."*

Celtics tough. They had split the season series, 3-3, as Jack Sikma and John Lucas added speed and height to the club's all-around athleticism. But the Celtics appeared in control as the series began in Boston, winning the first game easily behind Bird's 40 points and squeaking by in Game 2. In the Mecca they gained the coveted split with a thrilling double overtime one-point win in Game 4 that wasn't decided until Bird and McHale swallowed Lucas's transition drive. Free- agent acquisition Darren Daye gave the Celtics an unexpected lift in the game, sparking

hopes that the thin bench might come into its own this postseason. Back in the Garden the Bucks kept their hopes alive by beating Boston, 129-124. Parish scored 30 points and had 17 rebounds, but the play of Sikma, Moncrief and Lucas was outstanding, especially in Game 6, which Milwaukee won by ten to force a seventh game.

Ironically, the series that featured Lucas, a rehabilitated cocaine abuser, was overshadowed for a time by news from Phoenix that Dennis Johnson's name had been mentioned in grand jury testimony regarding possible drug use on the Suns. According to CBS, the aptly named former Sun Johnny High had implicated DJ, a charge repeated, according to *Sports Illustrated*, by Walter Davis. Johnson held a press conference and denied ever having used or purchased drugs, and in subsequent testimony nothing more was said. But the news was upsetting to DJ, and he was afraid to leave his hotel room or answer his phone for the rest of the season.

Don Nelson was also having problems during that series, feuding with the Bucks' ownership and reaching the end of an 11-year coaching reign in Milwaukee. He would have loved to end his time there with a win over Boston, and for much of Game 7 it appeared he might. After Ainge sprained his left knee the Bucks went up by nine, 105-95, with less than six minutes remaining in the season. Celtics fans from coast to coast held their breath while their team rose from the dead: Sichting hit two long jumpers; Bird and McHale scored; Parish blocked a Sikma shot and DJ recovered the ball in a wild scramble. The Celtics held on for a 119-113 victory while the Garden retracted with relief and prepared to watch another Central Division power, the Detroit Pistons, come to Boston. As they had throughout the era, the Celtics were still winning those come-from-behind victories in must-win games.

The seven-game series with the Pistons will be remembered primarily for two things, both of which reflected the ability and maturity of Larry Bird. The first was the steal in Game 5 that saved the game and the series and taught the young Pistons a valuable lesson about celebrating too soon. The second was Bird's response to the famous remarks of Isiah Thomas and Dennis Rodman, his diplomatic and mature way of handling the affair. Against the backdrop of an intense, competitive series, these two incidents added to the legend and stature of Larry Bird and enriched a playoffs that ended in defeat to the Lakers.

The Celtics had only a day to prepare for a Pistons team that had finished a 4-1 demolishing of the Hawks six days earlier. The general feeling in Detroit was that this team, for which experts had been predicting first-rank success since Adrian Dantley's arrival at the beginning of the season, was finally ready for the Celtics. Isiah Thomas, the heart of the club since 1981, remembered well the Celtics' handling of Detroit in the 1985 playoffs, when the Pistons came back from a 2-0 deficit to tie the series, only to see Boston win the next two games. But the 1987 club was stronger and deeper. Dantley gave them an offensive weapon, one of the best in the league, to complement Isiah's explosive ability, and head coach Chuck Daly pointed to the team's 52-30 record and strong finish as evidence that the two men had successfully blended their

In the final quarter of Game 5 of the Eastern Conference finals against Detroit, Robert Parish went down with a severe ankle sprain, the third time he had suffered this injury in the playoffs. When Parish was injured against the Bucks in the previous series, John Lucas paid tribute to his courage. "You could hear Robert groaning all the time. He didn't get the name 'Chief' for nothing."

abilities. Bill Laimbeer and Ricky Mahorn, two of the most prominent anti-heroes in Johnny Most's gallery of rogues, were effective role players, and rookies John Salley and Dennis Rodman had been aggressive from the beginning of the season, willing to challenge more established players for turf underneath. The Pistons also had two excellent off guards, Joe Dumars, a steady, smart player who commanded respect with his composed demeanor and competitive play, and Vinnie ''the Microwave'' Johnson, a streak shooter famous for his havoc-wreaking sprees off the bench. Johnson always seemed to play well against the Celtics, and when he was hot there was nothing DJ or Ainge or anyone else could do to stop him.

The Pistons carried a sinister reputation into the series. Known as the NBA's version of the L. A. Raiders, the Detroit players enjoyed their role as a tough, physical (some would say dirty) team. Mahorn had been brought to Detroit from Washington to give the frontcourt bulk and aggression. Laimbeer was known to mix it up occasionally, and the Celtics, particularly Bird and Parish, never kept their dislike of the Pistons' center a secret. Fans enjoyed Most's colorful play-by-play, which always increased a notch in invective during the playoffs, as the Pistons practiced their high jinks. This series would not disappoint them, especially as Dennis Rodman, who had taken to waving his fist in the air after a big basket, emerged as another object of Most's scorn.

The home-court advantage was also a big factor in this series. The Pistons had not won in the Garden since 1982, and the Celtics had won 94 out of their last 97 games at home. But Boston had played poorly on the road that year, and the Silverdome was the scene of two of their losses. A transformed football field, the Silverdome was not one of Bird's favorite arenas. The eerie lighting and huge space subtly altered depth perception in a way that could disrupt the performance of a perimeter shooter like Bird who did not play the arena regularly. As it happened, the home team won every game of the series, and each win (except for the thrilling Game 5 and the close finale) was convincing.

After winning the first two games easily, the Celtics were confident they would win the set. In Game 2 reserves Fred Roberts and Jerry Sichting had effectively helped the starters, countering a brilliant game by Thomas. Afterwards Bird and McHale chatted confidently in the lockerroom about the Celtics' chances. K. C., however, sensed instinctively that the series would not be as easy as the home games suggested. ''They will be a totally different team in Detroit,'' he said. ''They have the fans behind them, and they believe they can win.'' His words proved true. The Pistons rebounded to even the series, and they did it with intimidating, petulant play. In Game 3 Detroit started a run that seemed to have the Celts down by 20 the entire weekend. Running the break freely, Thomas displayed the form that had scored 20 points in the third quarter of a crucial Hawks game. In a flash fight, Laimbeer had thrown Bird to the floor; Bird fired the ball at Laimbeer's head as Johnny Most took off into courtside polemic. ''The referees let them play that way,'' Bird said. ''The Pistons have a style, and they are promoted that way so the referees have a tendency to allow them to play rough.''

In Game 4 the Pistons scored 145 points, the highest ever against Boston in a postseason game. The series was down to a best of three, and the Celtics' history of easily controlling the Pistons (McHale's 56-point game; the Garden winning streak) was in doubt. Now Detroit had the momentum, and the Celtics were worried. The day before Game 5, Sam Vincent looked at the team before practice and said, "I'm just not not sure what's going to happen." Vincent had led the Celtics in scoring in both Games 3 and 4, a tribute to his effectiveness, but also an indication that the team was not playing its best. McHale was showing the effects of long minutes on his sore foot. Parish's ankle and Ainge's knee

Larry Bird shoots a jumper over Dennis Rodman in a duel during the Eastern Conference final, 1988. After Bird struggled with his shooting in that series, he was counseled in a long meeting with John Havlicek after Game 5. Havlicek told Bird that the best way to shake his shooting slump was to keep moving without the ball.

were also subpar, and there was doubt on and off the floor. Game 5 would be tough.

It was also one of the most dramatic and important games in the franchise's history; certainly it was one of Bird's finest moments. Throughout, Boston tried to use precedent (the Garden) and its main weapon (Bird) to regain control of the series, but the Pistons continued to rebound (Laimbeer), play clutch defense (Rodman and Dumars) and hit the crucial shots (Thomas) as they made good on their promise of self-worth. The game entered the final eight minutes with Detroit on top, 87-86. In those minutes, Bird repeatedly hit difficult, apparently out-of-range shots as he moved to his game-high 36 points (to go with 12 rebounds, nine assists and two blocks). On the bench K. C. was trying to coach with a heavy heart: earlier that day he had heard the news of his mother's death. He would leave after the game, saying, "My mind was never in it. My team and my assistants carried me." Parish had had a tough game: frustrated with Laimbeer's legal and illegal work underneath, he had lashed out at the Detroit center, punching him from behind with a vicious right hand (the punch would earn him a one-game suspension). Then he twisted his ankle twice; after the second injury, with 3:41 left in the game, he fired his mouthpiece at the ground in anger. Detroit was leading, 97-95, and Parish did not return. The Celtics nevertheless gained control, going into the final minute with a 106-103 lead. But that last minute was incredible. Laimbeer hit a jump shot; Bird missed a close jump hook; with 17 seconds left Thomas hit an in-your-face jumper over Sichting. Then came the crunch-time heroics. After a timeout Bird drove along the baseline, muscling in for what the whole Garden hoped would be the game-winner. But Rodman, his young legs propelling him, soared high for a rejection from the weak side. The ball rolled towards the sideline, hit off Jerry Sichting's legs, and went out of bounds. For Celtics fans everywhere it appeared that the fabled Boston Garden mystique was over. The Pistons had the ball with five seconds remaining and a one-point lead. Thomas grabbed the ball and, without calling timeout, threw the ball inbounds.

Larry Bird's awareness, instinct and ability to come through in the clutch saved the game. Flattened after his drive, he rushed in front of Laimbeer to make a clean steal (Rodman was doing a victory dance at the other end of the court, his back to the action). His momentum carrying him out of bounds, Bird stopped precisely at the baseline, pivoted and fed the ball to a streaking DJ, who flipped in a crazy underhand reverse-spin lay-up. In seconds the fortunes of the teams and their individuals had turned. Bird was the hero; Thomas was the goat; Rodman's great rejection was instantly forgotten. In a profession that demands presence under pressure, the Pistons had lost their composure and the game. Later the Detroit players would lose their judgement as well. Games 6 and 7 would follow the home-victory script and move Boston into The Finals, 4-3. But what happened after Game 7 had even bigger repercussions.

Three years earlier Isiah had been a spectator in the Garden, watching his friend Magic Johnson lose to the brash Celtics. Afterwards, Thomas had stayed up all night with his friend, consoling, trying to help. Now it was Isiah's turn. Like Magic, he had been singled out in defeat. After the chartered flight home to Detroit

following Game 5, Thomas climbed in his car and drove around the city all night long. The Pistons, he sensed, had had their chance. He was right. They won Game 6 and then were outplayed in Game 7 (a game highlighted by a three-minute, five-offensive-rebound possession by the Celtics in the fourth quarter, a possession climaxed itself by a clutch three-pointer by Ainge).

The frustration was evident in the Pistons' lockerroom after Game 7, and the media, doing their job, probed the disappointed players. Bird, one reporter com-

Kevin McHale battles Charles Oakley, then of the Chicago Bulls, Game 2, 1987 playoffs. McHale was possibly the best player in the NBA during the 1986-87 season, but a pair of injuries, including a fracture of his right foot, gradually slowed him down. In this game, Oakley sent McHale hurtling into the basket support, causing a back injury. McHale had a great scoring season that year, averaging 26.1 points per game. He earned First Team All-Pro and First Team All-Defense honors.

mented, had had 35, 36 and 37 points in the final three games. What did Dennis Rodman think about that? Bird, Rodman growled, wouldn't even be among the five best players in the league if he were black. Thomas, asked to respond to Rodman's remark, agreed with the rookie. Both statements were made, obviously, in the context of the franchise's most stunning loss. Isiah was particularly crushed, and his words were a perfect illustration of why Georgetown coach John Thompson hates immediate postgame interviews. The press duly reported the statements, which smacked of reverse discrimination, and asked Bird himself to respond. Wisely, Bird said, "This isn't Russia. They can say what they want."

The NBA, like society at large in the late eighties, is acutely aware of the problem of racism (as it is of the problem of drugs). Rodman's remarks could be understood (though not excused) as the bitter reactions of disappointed and immature rookie. Thomas, however, as a veteran known for his community work in Detroit and his status as one of the league's superstars, should have known better than to follow the indiscretions of his teammate, and many members of the press appropriately attacked him for his comments, disregarding his explanation that it was a joke. The issue grew to the point where the league felt Isiah should hold a news conference in Los Angeles, where the Celtics and Lakers were in the middle of The Finals. Bird appeared alongside Isiah at the conference and, in a remarkable display of charm and tact that defused the issue without making it seem unimportant, showed once and for all that the Hick from French Lick had become an adept and intelligent handler of the press. Let's allow the incident to

pass, Bird suggested. "Isiah knows my game is *baaaaad*." The comic touch was timed just right, and the lapse into black slang was a subtle yet forceful reminder that Bird was both aware of the predominance of blacks in the sport and secure in his knowledge that he, a white, was among the best.

Some people argued that Bird let Thomas off the hook, that the Detroit player's comments were racist and should have been treated as such. But perhaps Bird realized that, though the words themselves were unacceptable, the feelings underlying the words were complex. Dennis Rodman was talking in the heat of a loss, but he also saw in his opponents a predominantly white team that received maximum exposure from the press and greater consideration in the marketing opportunities that arise from that exposure. Blacks in the NBA often have to deal with the misperception that their ability is solely natural. "People think blacks are born with major-league ability," Magic Johnson said in an attempt to explain Thomas's comments. "People don't understand the days and nights and more days and nights that go into making an NBA star." And why, in a game dominated on the court by blacks, have there been so few black coaches, general managers and front office people? Only five of 25 NBA clubs have black head coaches—the exact *reverse* percentage of black players in the league. Without condoning Thomas's words, fans can certainly consider those facts and what they mean about our culture at large, and it will be the NBA's challenge in the 1990s to address that problem and rid itself of racism in *all* directions.

A year later, after a more mature and experienced Pistons team defeated the

After K. C. Jones's final game as coach of the Celtics, Larry Bird said, "It was a lot of fun playing under K. C., a lot of fun. He directed us, but he was a player's coach, too. He allowed us input into decisions, but we knew he was the head coach, the boss. He's a great human being. Hopefully, he's made me a better person."

Celtics in the 1988 Eastern Conference finals, breaking the Boston Garden spell of the Celtics and marking the end of an era, Isiah Thomas walked into the Celtics' lockerroom and congratulated a sad and tired Larry Bird on a great series. "Thanks buddy," Bird said. "I hope you get yourself a ring." They made arrangements to meet after the season, when Thomas was to play in a benefit game for underprivileged Indiana youth that Bird was organizing. All series long Thomas had been defusing any talk of a rivalry, insisting that the Celtics had to be beaten four times on the court, and that nothing else mattered. "It takes something special to beat Boston," he said. Obviously he

had learned a lesson, one Bird had helped him learn.

But the sadness of that final Celtics loss was deepened by the knowledge of K. C. Jones's retirement. During the first round of the playoffs he had announced he was stepping down at the end of the year and yielding the head coaching duties to the deserving Jimmy Rodgers. His five years as head coach had been consistently excellent, but his announcement couldn't help but be colored by the team's poor showing against Detroit or the accusations from the press (and from within the team) that he had not used his bench enough.

Jones moved into the front office as Rodgers took over courtside. During the summer the Celtics continued the process of rebuilding so forcefully interrupted by Bias's death. In June they drafted Brian Shaw, a DJ-like guard out of the University of California at Santa Barbara. In a move that puzzled people inside and ouside the Celtics organization, Bill Walton traveled to Italy and reportedly negotiated with the Naples team about playing the 1988-89 season there. The Italian League has a 30-game season, much more congenial to a player of Walton's age and physical make-up, but Jan Volk and Red Auerbach were surprised that he did not inform the Celtics of the trip. A week later he returned to the U. S. and had yet another foot operation, and it appeared that Celtics fans would have to make do with the memories of Walton in '86.

The Celtics headed into the '88-89 season still concerned about their bench, the backup center position particularly. Many fans approached the new season nostalgically, as if the good years were over, the championships not to be repeated. But those fans haven't reckoned with Larry Bird. As long as he continues to suit up, as long as he takes the floor and wipes the soles of his sneakers with his hands, the Celtics will still be a threat to go all the way, no matter *who* is on the bench. During the summer Jimmy Rodgers visited Bird in Indiana. "I've always talked about going out there to do some fishing," Rodgers said. "It was a chance to wet a line." But there must have been some talk between the new head coach and his captain about the season ahead, the changes the club had undergone, would undergo. Rodgers learned that Bird's conditioning program, which called for a six-in-the-morning workout of weightlifting, running and exercise five days a week, was actually being practiced by the nine-year All-Star *seven* days a week.

Some things never change.

Jimmy Rodgers, present coach of the Celts, receives a championship ring from Commissioner David Stern of the NBA. Rodgers originally wanted to take the head coach position of the Knicks in 1987, but was prevented from doing so when the Celtics and the Knicks failed to work out agreeable compensation. In a preseason meeting with Jones in September 1987, Rodgers began to feel that K. C. was preparing to coach his final season with the team in 1987-88.

EPILOGUE

Game 1, The Finals, 1981. From his familiar seat in Loge One, Red Auerbach watched the action, arms folded in front of his chest. Courtside, the graying, distinguished head of Bill Russell loomed from his CBS commentator's post. The game was in the late stages and close. The Celtics had rallied and now needed a basket. The ball was in the hands of Larry Joe Bird.

Lining up for a 17-foot shot from the right side, Bird let the ball fly. After only two years on the club, his form was already strikingly familiar: his head slightly tilted, his shooting forearm perpendicular to the ground, his shot released with perfect backspin. This time, however, the shot was not true; flat and off center, it deflected off the side of the rim while Moses Malone and Robert Parish and the rest of the Rockets and Celtics boxed out and moved in for the rebound.

None of them would get it. The instant he sensed its flat trajectory, Bird was sprinting, heading for the spot he knew the ball would land. Anticipating perfectly the flight of the ball, he jumped, catching it midflight as his momentum carried him out of bounds. Intuitively he adjusted. Because a right-handed shot was impossible from that angle, he switched the ball to his left and, still airborne, took an off-balance shot from 12 feet away that swished through the net as the Garden roared.

Russell looked on, stunned. Auerbach stood and applauded, leading the cheers. Bird had taken individual shots with both hands on the same play, the ball never touching the floor. He had hit a game-turning left-hander with the maximum degree of difficulty while *falling out of bounds*. The timing, the court sense, the ability to find the *only* move possible—all in the clutch closing minutes of a cham-

Magic Johnson wrote about playing with Larry Bird for the first time: "He was a man who stood tall, and playing with him was sweet. There was one game in Atlanta where he and I came down on a three-on-two fast break. I was in the middle. Without looking, I flipped the ball over to him and he immediately responded by flipping behind his back for the lay-in. The crowd went nuts. No-look passes back to back; Larry and I were out there tricking them!"

pionship game—were characteristics not seen in the NBA since the day the CBS color commentator had retired.

"It was the one best play I've ever seen a player make," Auerbach said after the game.

"Larry was able to make the play," Russell said, "because he not only knew where the ball was going to land—he knew that he knew."

He had seen the play over and over. He had rehearsed it before, in his mind. And when the mind-move became reality it told the world that here was an athlete with the classic characteristic of grace under pressure. Here was Larry Bird.

The three men in the Boston Garden that day, one performing, two observing, defined a tradition that spanned four decades. They were the key figures, the men without whom the Boston Celtics basketball team, as we know it, would not exist. Yet all three men might just as easily have ended up pursuing separate and far different careers in Washington, D. C., Oakland, California, and French Lick, Indiana. All three came to Boston in a way that suggests the workings of a benign, providential leprechaun.

When Red Auerbach came out of the Navy after World War II there was no National Basketball Association. But the young man who had played basketball at George Washington knew what he wanted to do, and an assistant coach's job at Duke got him on track. But he soon grew disillusioned with an agreement that called for his promotion when the head coach died. He could not wait and returned to his D. C. home in 1950, where he was prepared to take a high school coaching job, teach and watch his family grow.

A continent away, the young William Felton Russell was attending McClymonds High School in Oakland and discovering, as he grew taller and taller, that he had pretty good basketball ability. As he toured the Northwest with a high school All-Star team (a team he was fortunate to make), he talked continually with the star of the team and, over six weeks, perfected his own moves. He returned with college potential, but his father— "Mister Charley," as Russ affectionately called him—felt that, in spite of the possibility of a scholarship at the University of San Francisco, it would be best if his son went down to the steelyards and started lining up for daily work. The young man agreed.

*Bill Russell waving to the crowd on Red Auerbach Night.
K. C. Jones wrote of Russell: "With those of us who played
with him, black and white, Bill was a thoughtful, giving man.
Russ never looked down on the lowliest sub…and I've spent
time in that category. If you were broke, it was Russell who
put some money in your pocket. If it was serious money, and
sometimes it was with some of the guys, he would go and
borrow the money for them. Many times I saw Russ sense
that a player was down in the dumps—it might be a guy he
wasn't really tight with—and there they'd be, out to dinner
with each other. With Russ picking up the tab."*

Two decades later Larry Bird was having his own high school renaissance, growing in height and ability to such an extent that his brother Mark, no slouch on the court himself, couldn't believe it. The young man had 55 points in one game, 38 rebounds in another. He was the original Indiana high school highlight film, carrying the expectations of a basketball-crazy region and attracting the famous Bobby Knight to French Lick. But things did not work out at IU, and soon Bird was back in his home town, working for the city and making no further plans for college.

All three situations turned out to be temporary, of course. Red Auerbach met a man named Walter Brown who recognized the determination in the cocky young man's eyes and told him to run the Boston Celtics basketball team as he saw fit. A University of San Francisco alumnus, Hal DeJulio, set up a rare scholarship fund for black athletes that gave Russ the opportunity to make history at USF, where Auerbach's mentor, Bill Reinhart, saw him play. Get Russell, any way you can, Reinhart told Red, and soon Russell was in Boston. "I can think of no coach other than Red Auerbach," Russell said, "who could have made me feel as comfortable or work as hard as I did." Larry Bird met Indiana State assistant Bill Hodges, without whom, Bob Ryan said, he would have been "the greatest AAU and summer-park player in the history of basketball." Bird starred at Indiana State in the last glittering moments before gambling, drug and recruiting scandals tarnished, forever it seems, college basketball, and with Magic Johnson he raised the game to a level it has enjoyed since. And when Auerbach chose Bird in the 1978 NBA draft the circle of Celtics magic was complete.

Before Bill Russell assumed the position of player-coach in 1966, he observed carefully the methods of his coach and friend. Talking to seldom-used players, always listening, even during the heat of a championship-game timeout, Auerbach managed always to be authoritarian *and* receptive. Player input was as vital to his system as obedience, and his championships proved his effectiveness. When Russell took over, he continued the process, giving his teammates power, allowing them to come up with ways to win as the Celtics moved on to two more titles before Russell's retirement.

Also listening to Auerbach, for eight seasons, was K. C. Jones. Jones remained on the team for a year after Russell's ascension, assisting informally, providing his usual scrap and hustle. When Jones returned to the Celtics in the eighties and matched his friend's two championships, he re-established the player-oriented system and continued the tradition by appointing Bird captain. On a team of high-powered and individual veterans, Bird became even more of a floor leader. This shared decision-making is often misunderstood. When Bird waved away a substitution in his memorable 1988 Game 7 dismantling of the Atlanta Hawks, the *New York Times* and *Sports Illustrated* suggested he had little respect for his coach. But Bird, knowing he was on a roll, was not showing disrespect; he was exercising the authority K. C. had clear-

ly invested in him. Likewise, when David Halberstam criticized the way Bill Russell "deferred" to Red Auerbach during a 1980 game in the Garden, he was missing the point. "Red's a friend," Russell said in 1986. "I'd do anything for him." Mutual respect, when practiced in the informal environment of a sports team, can appear to outsiders as arrogance. The family feeling of the Celtics organization is not easily understood by those not part of it.

The Celtics may be a club securely lodged in the sports realities of the eighties, but it is also an organization with obvious links to the days in the early fifties when Walter Brown and Auerbach ran the team from a two-room office. Red, of course provides the continuity. His success is rooted in his belief in the Celtics as a "way of life"; in his belief that winning imbues life with a purpose; in his commitment to the people of the organization, from Jan Volk to Larry Bird, from Bill Russell to Robert Parish, from K. C. Jones to Jimmy Rodgers. Jerry West, who understands the game and its people as well as anyone, has said, "Red Auerbach is to be respected, not feared." Ask any member of the Celtics' family and he or she will agree.

Beside Larry Bird's home in French Lick is a basketball court, one of the few extravagances this very wealthy man has allowed himself. Its dimensions are official NBA, its backboards fiberglass. Here he practices offseason, getting into the peak condition he forces himself to achieve before training camp. As the Indiana sun beams down and locals honk a greeting as they pass, Bird moves gracefully around the court,

Red Auerbach as coach, 1964. Behind Auerbach sits John Havlicek. Ed Macauley said of Auerbach as coach: "People said he was tough, but I never thought he was, and I don't think the guys who played for him did, either. His public image is a lot different from his private image. People see him as a tyrant. They see him agitating referees. They think his ballplayers are afraid of him. Actually the only time he'd be extraordinarily demanding was when we'd win five or six in a row. He wouldn't want us to get complacent."

shooting jumper after jumper, refining his game as he has in lots and gyms all his life. He could be playing anywhere, but this court has a different meaning. Like the baseball diamond the struggling farmer constructs in W. P. Kinsella's *Shoeless Joe* (the diamond the farmer hopes will attract the baseball star and save his farm), Bird's court seems less a real construct than an appeal to the spirit of the game itself, to his own artistry and dedication.

What does he think of as he practices here. A decade of great games? A handful of high moments? How about his 36 points and 14 rebounds in Game 2 of the Eastern Conference finals? His 53-point night against the Indiana Pacers, a performance that broke Sam Jones's regular-season Garden record and avenged a beating at the hands of the Pacers the night before in Indianapolis (a game Bird's friends had watched and listened to)? Maybe his Game 7 masterpiece against the Knicks in 1984, or his back-to-back sparklers in Games 4 and 5 against the Lakers less than a month later? How about his 47-point shootout against Dominique Wilkins in 1985 or his 48-point game against Portland a month later ("I thought

The Bird Style. At the free throw line: after sinking the game-tying free throws in Game 7 of the 1981 Eastern Conference finals, he said, "If I'd a missed them, I should have been shot." On the court: he keeps his hands dry by wiping them on the bottom of his sneakers. In action: he shoots lefty against the Lakers.

I would miss," he said of the long game-winner he threw in to cap that night, "but suddenly it seemed to curve into the basket!")? How about the whole *series* against Houston in 1986, when he *averaged* a triple double? His 60 points in New Orleans, his steal against Detroit in 1987...?

About that Game 5 steal Kevin McHale said: "I'll tell my son in the future that once upon a time I played on a team that never gave up. That is the important thing to remember. That there were guys here who never gave up, and that it paid off for them on this night." On that court in the middle of the American heartland, Larry Bird is pushing himself for those payoffs. He never gives up.

Three years ago the Boston Celtics raised the number 2 to the rafters of the Garden and paid tribute to the man who started it all. Every championship team was there that night, from the Bird Era through the Havlicek years to the dynasty teams. After his first championship in 1957, Red Auerbach had gone back to his hotel room and cried for joy, alone. Tonight he was not alone, but he cried again as he embraced Bill Russell and Larry Bird and watched the number rise to the rafters in his honor.

As Bird listened to the man who brought him to Boston, as he looked over at his predecessor with the big laugh and proud disposition, did he think about tradition, about pride, about winning? Probably. But just as likely he was thinking of that spangled court in French Lick, or about where he could go to take a few three-pointers. Hell, the man is paid to *work*.

Red Auerbach on his night. "Without you," he said to players from four decades, "I wouldn't be standing up here."

Photo Credits